D1525597

THUNDERBOLT
TO WAR

THUNDERBOLT TO WAR

AN AMERICAN FIGHTER PILOT IN ENGLAND

JOHN N. ANDERSON

WITH CLINT AND STEVE SPERRY

FONTHILL

Front dust jacket: Clint (left) sitting on the wing of his P-47, *Mary Jayne*, with his great friend and fellow 352nd Fighter Squadron pilot Paul Cles.

Rear dust jacket, top: Clint's P-47D, *Mary Jayne*.

Rear dust jacket, bottom: The 352nd Fighter Squadron emblem.

Rear dust jacket, flap: Lt Col. Bailey with 352nd Ground Officers at Raydon.

Fonthill Media Language Policy

Fonthill Media publishes in the international English language market. One language edition is published worldwide. As there are minor differences in spelling and presentation, especially with regard to American English and British English, a policy is necessary to define which form of English to use. The Fonthill Policy is to use the form of English native to the author. However, to complicate matters, the quotations are from both British and American sources, and the author and publishers believe this should be kept as near as feasible to the original written source. In consequence, the material is a mixture of both British and American English.

Fonthill Media Limited
Fonthill Media LLC
www.fonthillmedia.com
office@fonthillmedia.com

First published in the United Kingdom and the United States of America 2015

British Library Cataloguing in Publication Data:
A catalogue record for this book is available from the British Library

Copyright © John Anderson and Steve Sperry 2015

ISBN 978-1-78155-456-2

Typeset in 10pt on 13pt Sabon
Printed and bound in England

Contents

Acknowledgements

Crown Copyright, Royal Air Force Museum
Imperial War Museum, England
Eisenhower Presidential Library and Museum
The Franklin D. Roosevelt Presidential Library and Museum
University of Illinois, Norris L. Brookens Library
US National Archives

Material has been accessed from a number of sources, including the internet, and whilst in some cases it has not been possible to determine copyright ownership, all material has been used in good faith. While the authors have endeavored to follow the path of complete accuracy in all sections of this book, we request to be forgiven if we have strayed into unknown territory, as it has purely arisen from our efforts to seek fact. This is the authors' work and interpretation and we must absolve those who have assisted from any error or omission that may arise.

It has been more than five years since the authors decided to write this story of an American fighter pilot in England during the Second World War. Our research has naturally been enhanced by two factors: firstly, Clinton Holmes Sperry was the father of Steve Sperry, and secondly, John Anderson became a very good friend later in Clint's life. Our motivation therefore came from a desire to seek further knowledge of Clint and to bring to the reader's attention the extraordinary and difficult conditions that the pilots of the United States Army Air Force had to operate under and endure.

We would like to thank those who have assisted us in our endeavors. Dr Graham Cross is a friend and historian of the 353rd Fighter Group. His selfless assistance and kind permission to quote from his remarkable book on the Group, *Jonah's Feet Are Dry*, have been invaluable. We thank him most sincerely.

Without the veterans of the 353rd Fighter Group we would not have been able to write such a complete story. Many thanks must go to the veterans and their families for the photographs and documents that they contributed to the

353rd FG archive currently held by Dr Cross—although most are no longer with us, their foresight in preserving the history of the Group is deeply appreciated. Also, a few of the veterans' memories were recorded at the 1983 reunion, and by courtesy of the Oral History Collection, Archives/Special Collections, Norris L. Brookens Library, University of Illinois at Springfield, some personal anecdotes were added to the history of the group.

We must thank Ashley Gant, who has assisted with Group records, and Michael Anderson, who has given great assistance in photographic improvement and preparation of the book. We also thank Pete West for his excellent illustration of Clint's aircraft and the 352nd Fighter Squadron emblem.

The authors wish to thank their families. Clint's wife, Ellen, and his daughters, Steph and Jen, have been most supportive in assisting Steve with digging out Clint's records, and our gratitude must go to Jen for taking on the task of proofreading. We thank them for giving us the impetus to carry on to complete our work, for without them the book would not have been written. Also, many thanks to Mo for encouraging Steve's creative writing and research. John wishes to thank his wife, Priscilla, for her tolerance when he was appearing to be in a world of literary confusion.

To all those who have contributed we are extremely grateful, and we must remember that the person who contributed the most was Clint himself. We thank him for enhancing all of our lives.

John Anderson and Steve Sperry

Abbreviations

AWPD	Air War Plans Division
Bandits	Identified enemy aircraft
BD	Bomber Division
BG	Bomber Group
Bogies	Unidentified aircraft
Brig.	Brigadier
Capt.	Captain
CO	Commanding Officer
Col.	Colonel
CTL	Control Tower Log
DFC	Distinguished Flying Cross
e/a	Enemy Aircraft
ETO	European Theater of Operations
FG	Fighter Group
Flak	Ground fire from non-friendly guns
F/O	Flight Officer
FS	Fighter Squadron
Gen.	General
gen	Information
gph	Gallons per hour
IFR	Individual Flight Record
KIA	Killed in action
KIFA	Killed in flying accident
Kriegie	*Kriegsgefangen*—Prisoner of War
Lt	Lieutenant
Mag.	Magneto
Maj.	Major
Met	Meteorology
OLC	Oak Leaf Cluster

Ops	Operations
OTU	Operational Training Unit
PFF	Pathfinder Force
POW	Prisoner of War
rpg	Rounds per gun
RV	Rendezvous
SEFTS	Single-Engine Fighter Training School
Tyro	Fighter pilot in training
USA	United States of America
USAAF	United States Army Air Force
USAC	United States Air Corps
USAF	United States Air Force
V1	Vergeltungswaffe 1 Flying Bomb
WASP	Women Airforce Service Pilots
WIA	Wounded in Action

England WW2 MAR. 1943

Foreword

As a pilot member of the original established 353rd Fighter Group formed in the United States, I am honored to attempt an answer to the following question: 'why do American pilots and their crews return to the wartime airfields in England?'

The following is based upon my own experience, input from fellow pilots, and the knowledge that American pilots have, since the end of the air war over Europe, had a keen interest in returning to England and their bases of operation during the war years.

The desire to return seems to be determined largely by two dominant factors. The first is a genuine wish to be received again by a people who gave so freely of their compassion and support while enduring most difficult times of their own. Like thousands of others, I was greeted on arrival in Scotland in June 1943 by warm, cheerful, and gracious people with an incredible sensitivity to the uncertainties we were to face in the days ahead.

Unsurprisingly, the second desire is to revisit a familiar territory that once served as our home-away-from-home, and to rekindle memories of the many dedicated friends with whom we shared the ever-present worries of wartime life. The airfield and base of operations was a community within itself, surrounded by towns and villages that offered friendly and enjoyable diversities.

The 353rd Fighter Group arrived at Raydon Airfield as a seasoned fighter group. I flew my ninety-fourth and last combat mission from this airfield on 1 July 1944. Personally, a return to England offers an opportunity to pay tribute to those 3,812 Americans on the hillside at Madingley who came to Britain but never went home.

Clint Sperry
(Written for his return to England in 1997, when he was a special guest of the Raydon Wings Airshow)

Prologue

Between June 1943 and September 1944 Clint Sperry was a young P-47 fighter pilot based in England. This story is about the pilot and the missions, the time and the place, and the man. John Anderson, like me, was born during those same years, but when John first opened his eyes he was in England. I was in America.

In the early '90s I began to think it would be a great experience for my father and me to visit England, and more specifically the bases that were his home for most of a year and a half. I decided to campaign for an England trip. Our respective homes in Massachusetts were relatively close, our interests similar (sailing and flying), and I liked my dad and enjoyed his company—so the opportunity was quite simple. I believe I was quite diplomatic, keeping the idea of a trip to England fresh without scaring him off. It was not that difficult, and in January of 1994 he asked me when I could get away.

In that year my father was a very trim and agile seventy-four, an attribute that he took full advantage of and great pleasure from. I believe one of the joys of his life was being taken for my brother. When looking young for his age didn't come into play, he was quite happy to take advantage of his age alone. Taking a senior discount when booking our flight made him smile. Meals and beer at a senior rate were satisfying, but the best was when we rented a car in England and the rental company wouldn't allow drivers over seventy. Of course, having an American chauffeur (me) on UK roads was not always relaxing.

We arrived with no real itinerary or definite expectations other than to find and visit the bases Dad had flown from—particularly Raydon. We also had no idea where we'd stay from day to day for the next two weeks. This, as I've found in previous travel adventures, was not a bad thing. It meant that by mid-afternoon we'd have to ask around, and the best place to do that is, of course, a pub. Clint's time here in the '40s converted him to warm English beer and he never turned back, which by itself made seeking our evening accommodation quite pleasant, but the real bonus was conversation with local people. More than geography, it would be our (and particularly Dad's) interaction with the English people that reconnected him with places and experiences during those violent and desperate years.

Raydon was our primary destination, so we headed north-east from London but did not go directly to the village. We first found ourselves in Hadleigh, partly because Dad would ride his bicycle there from Raydon when he wasn't flying and partly because of his chauffeur's initial difficulty with English 'roundabouts'. Here we experienced something that would present itself whenever we were in a place where he had either flown from or frequented regularly. Both our expectations were that there would be familiarity—that Dad would remember landmarks like churches and places like pubs, streets, buildings, or intersections. Though he didn't say much initially, it was clear that he was not finding much, if anything, that was familiar. I believe he was more than a little mystified by this and no less disappointed, particularly considering that English villages don't really change much in their appearance. There were very few definitive 'I remember this well' statements. For the most part, his memories of geography and structures were vague, and though we didn't discuss the reasons for this in depth, we did decide that subtle changes in landscape, use of land, growth in population, and traffic etc. would not match his mental picture of the same village in wartime England. I know this was disconcerting for him and I think he was a little undone by it to start (I'm sure he thought his mind was playing tricks) but, as we got further into our visit, it became a diminishing issue.

In Hadleigh we explored the village once we'd deposited the car and chosen a pub. If the population of a village is greater than fifty then there will be at least one pub, so in Hadleigh, with a population of about 10,000, we had several to choose from. Another thing that presented itself—unexpectedly and quite delightfully— was the reception we had wherever we went. This was especially the case at pubs. The order of events once we'd chosen our establishment was very similar at each place; as we walked through the door, a head or two would turn to see if we were regulars or not (like any bar anywhere). There would be passing interest because we were not; we'd sit at the bar, usually, and the bartender would wait on us. Now we'd be recognized, by the barman and anyone nearby, as Americans or Canadians. Interest would pick up a little, but we were certainly nothing to get excited about. One or two may have noticed a resemblance between us. Possibly father and son (or, as my father looked forward to, brothers). Next, the bartender or a patron next to us would ask the very conversational question, 'Where're you from in the States?' And sooner or later the clincher, 'So what brings you to England?' This became my cue. I would tell whoever asked that Dad had flown fighters here during the war, and that this was his first visit since then. I can't remember a time when those words did not affect the atmosphere within earshot.

Though for Americans the Second World War is a poignant memory, it has become distant over time. For the English, the same spectrum of emotions remains quite close to the surface. The siege of one's homeland has kept something deep and abiding. So, when two or three people learned that here was a veteran fighter pilot, there would be more inquiry and, of course, it was in the best interest of the innkeeper to further the conversation and include an interested patron or two. Before long Clint would become a celebrity of sorts, fielding questions ranging from engaging German pilots over Europe to drinking warm beer. He was right at home during these gatherings, though there were some questions (questions that were always asked) that he managed to avoid direct or explicit answers to. At some point he was always asked if he'd shot down any German aircraft, or how many locomotives he had destroyed, or how many friends he had lost. Thoughts relating to such questions were painful—even after nearly fifty years. Open conversation about such personal events was difficult even with close friends, and in every case that I can remember, queries of this nature were quickly dropped by very respectful and understanding English people.

From Hadleigh we were directed to a delightful B&B suggested by the innkeeper, which we found at the end of a winding drive near the edge of an incredibly yellow field of oilseed rape. We were winding down our first day out of London and we were only a short distance from our major destination.

We were both excited to be on our way into Raydon the following morning, but we had all day and somehow didn't want to rush it—so we went back to Hadleigh for an ample English breakfast, walked around town a bit, and, having eaten and exercised, drove to Raydon. It took us a while to locate remnants of the old base, but it became quite obvious once we figured out what to look for—Quonset huts near a large, productive field with a long, wide, unproductive strip in it. Actually, it all became obvious when we came upon one of these unproductive strips and realized that we were probably driving on or parallel to runway 09/27. Though nature and farmers have taken back much of the land immediately surrounding these concrete runways, the farmers have chosen to leave some of these difficult old strips to nature's slow but unstoppable forces.

Standing and looking southwest along ragged concrete that would have been runway 05/23, the layout of the field as it was in 1944 came, at least roughly, into focus. The control tower had long since been demolished, but scanning round, the T2 hangars stood out stark and neglected before us, together with the tops of some Quonset huts that had probably housed operations. With these landmarks it was easy to skirt around the north side of the base to these buildings. The Quonset huts were being used as barns for farm equipment and hay, and although we were quite sure we wouldn't be escorted off the property at gunpoint, we didn't want to trespass without asking someone. The area was deserted. We could find no one. As I look back on it, it was like the present tenant of this ground had gracefully removed himself so that a former tenant could quietly remember without being disturbed. I was willing to knock on a door or two until we could be directed to an owner but to my surprise, Dad was not all that interested. I believe his interest was being in the same space that he'd been in those fifty years ago. I also believe his thoughts were of friends and comrades that he hadn't seen for all those years and (maybe more) of those who didn't make it home as he did. He was quiet, and although the buildings and runways marked what had been home for just four months, it was the space and the remembering that were important.

We wandered around the base without seeing a soul for the rest of the morning and into the afternoon, until it was definitely time for lunch. We found a pub in Raydon (I think it was the only one in 1994) and the innkeeper was happy to serve his mid-afternoon customers. Our experience here was a little different to that which we'd encountered in Hadleigh. Here we were the first customers of the afternoon, and though conversation progressed with the bartender as it did in Hadleigh, there were no patrons to include. Our innkeeper, being adept at his profession, asked if we would mind if he called a few friends who he knew would like very much to meet an American pilot with the 352nd Fighter Squadron, which had been based less than a mile from this very pub. This was an exciting turn of events for both Dad and I, as well as the group of several local men who arrived very shortly after being called. Most were at least one generation removed from Clint and each one paid tribute to not only my father, but to those young men who I know my father had visited only a few hours before. Of the group who came and talked with us that late afternoon and evening, I can name only two— Graham Cross and John Anderson. If we had returned to London the following day and flown home, our visit could not have been more meaningful.

Steve Sperry

1

Born to Fly

There were missions that were perceived as easy, those where very little action had been encountered, and others where enemy aircraft and flak made the few frantic hours of the mission exciting, frustrating, and downright dangerous.

For the P-47 pilots, their day started with a look at the Flight Board. That was the time when a fighter pilot could see his name on the list for a mission, with the certain knowledge that he was putting his life on the line once more. It was an almost indescribable kick-start of the senses; fear, excitement, anticipation, or a jumbled mess of them. Some guys appeared relatively uninterested, some tense, and others drifted off to carry out their own special routine for surviving the day. But with most, the knowledge that they were on ops triggered that knot in the guts. It was that time again.

Each individual pilot had his own agenda from that moment—the preparation of brain and body to meet demands that the ordinary person couldn't imagine. He had to force-feed the body at mealtime and the brain at briefing—heading for the hut as he had done on countless occasions. He would listen to the senior officers, with adornments of status or specialized knowledge, tell of what the fly-boys were likely to encounter and help rack up the tension. He made short written notes on the back of his hand as a reminder of times, location, etc., and then out into the cold, dark, dank air again to collect his flight gear. Then waiting; interminable waiting, sitting around fiddling with his visor or ferreting in the pockets of his flight suit. Checking that his Mae West, his life-saver, was not damaged if he had to bail out over the Channel. Trying to read the 'Stars and Stripes', to pass away those few minutes before being driven out to the flight line—quiet, tense, or nervously jocular. That was one of the more difficult periods, when time was a hindrance before getting the job done.

In the aircraft, the pilot then became part of the flying machine—checking, re-checking, strapping in, and waiting for the start-up. If the weather was bad, there might be a delay. More tension: 'Let's get on with it or scrub it.' Green flare. Start up and taxi out, checking, watching out for the other guys. Wouldn't pay to run into anyone now. Line up, final check, then throttles open. Still can't get over that surge of power from the big Pratt & Whitney up front—reassuring, smooth, and powerful. Form up and head out east, over the coast of East Anglia, checking wingman is awake before climbing up through the murk. Nothing but the instruments inside and an occasional flame from the exhaust stubs of your colleague's aircraft to guide you. Emerge safely through the overcast that blankets the earth below—knowing the only contact now with solid earth is the radio. But that has to remain silent. Any use would alert the Germans that the Squadron and Group were hell-bent on doing something nasty to them. Caution and respect for the enemy.

Get altitude. 'Geez, it's cold!' At any time of the year the altitude would freeze the flight suit, the warmer gear underneath, and the bones. That blanket of cloud, stretching as far as the eye could see into Germany. Feet are wet, over the Channel, droning on over enemy-occupied territory. Bursts of flak, not very accurate, weave a little, change height a bit, watching, waiting, anticipating that at any second the cry would go out if bandits were spotted. Mustn't get bounced. Hope the wingman sticks if a break is called. Senses heightened. Still nothing. Then activity on the radio. Another Group has made contact with the Luftwaffe and garbled calls and yells heighten the tension. Sweating now, even at altitude, weaving, and heads swiveling and wary—ready to react. But nothing happens. No rendezvous with the bombers; they were picked up by the other Group, who are seeing all the action today. The boss calls for a heading—turn and watch your tails, don't want to get jumped now. Head for the coast and home. Feet wet. Is the engine running rough? It always seems to over that goddamned North Sea. Wouldn't like to ditch there at any time of year, especially in winter. Survival time three to five minutes if immersed, and a little longer if you can scramble into your dinghy real quick. Nearly impossible with all your gear caught up and dragging you down. The dinghy! Sitting on that and the darned parachute is a reminder that the butt's sore. Boy, is it sore! Feet dry, descending through the murk, homed in and coming round to finals. Squadron still together, take your turn, then feel the reassuring thump of that 7-ton lump of incredible machinery as it hits the plate. Down, home, and safe—this time. A three-hour mission and easy ride? Yup, a 'milk run'. Now imagine what it would be like when the action *really* started.

To those of us who have been earthbound and haven't had that exhilaration of the freedom of flight, there were probably fleeting moments when we have yearned to be a fighter pilot. Sure, there were other special airborne folks; bomber pilots and their crews, reconnaissance, ferry, commercial, and even those merely flying for fun. You name it, but the thought of actually flying and fighting in one of the world's best fighting machines has to come mighty near the top of the list with dreamers.

In the war years, a fighter pilot was deemed by many to be very special. He was perceived to be highly trained, sometimes handsome and dashing, and most of all, fearless. In reality, some were good, and some were … Well, let's say not so hot, and they tended not to grow to old age. In war, however, survival depended on an element of luck, and those perceptions turned rapidly to one of chance for all participants. Clint Sperry wasn't a dreamer. He was a fighter pilot with a great deal of talent to offer his country, and he was about to fly and fight in the plane of his choice—the formidable Republic P-47 Thunderbolt.

On the morning of 9 August 1943, his name was one of those listed on the Flight Board for the first offensive operation to be carried out in the Second World War by 352nd Fighter Squadron—one of three in the 353rd Fighter Group attached to the 66th Fighter Wing, a key component within the Eighth Air Force—'The Mighty Eighth.'[1] Those young and eager pilots were looking for the enemy, and Clint Sperry was going to war.

Clinton Holmes Sperry was born in Cranston, Rhode Island, on 10 January 1920. He was the son of proud parents Ernest and Dorothy Sperry, and made an immediate and pleasurable impact on the family home. In his early years, he began doing the things that young kids do; he learned about nature and the interesting little world that embraced him, and in doing so made a distinct and lasting impression on all who knew and loved his maturing character.

Although not outstanding in his early years of education, he enjoyed the freedom of those younger days and was always happiest during the school vacations, when his family was together. Being young and adventurous, Clint was particularly drawn to the coast and all that it offered, and with those pleasures he was certainly influenced by his father. Ernest loved the beaches and waters of the Rhode Island coast, and his great affection for the natural beauty in that very special area carried into his later years.

The family holidays were split into two camps, for Dorothy preferred the mountains of New Hampshire—specifically Randolph Heights, north-east of the White Mountains, as she was an avid climber and hiker; she loved her summer days in that region. The subsequent result, decided democratically, was that the family—Ernest and Dorothy, and kids Barbara, Clint, Jack, Marcia, and friend Lucien—would manage to spend some time in the summer at the beach, but most was spent north, in the mountains so loved by Dorothy.

Nevertheless, it was the sea that had drawn Clint in his early summer years, and he would eventually be employed as a launch boy at the Edgewood (RI) Yacht Club. He loved the ocean, the beach, and the sun (it is on family record that he was never without a tan, winter or summer), and he remained passionate about all three for his entire life. Running a launch at the yacht club gave him good boat-handling experience and would open the door to further opportunity on larger boats, particularly sailboats. Sailing—here was the perfect platform on which to engage not only his passions, but also a desire for adventure and challenge.

In January of 1938, when Clint turned eighteen, he was looking forward to June and the end of a less-than-exemplary tenure as a high school student. Not

Ernest and Dorothy Sperry *c*. 1918. Note Ernest proudly showing pilot wings on his uniform. (*Sperry*)

Clint with his brother and sisters, enjoying the beach on a fine, sunny day. Clint's tan is evident! *Left to right*: Clint, Marcia, Jack, and Barbara. (*Sperry*)

BOY LEADERS' CORPS

Fourth Row: Marx.
Third Row: Broadbent, Oliver, Adams.
Second Row: Rogers, C. Sperry.
Front Row: Welch, Hervey, Spinella, Razza, Salisbury, Place, Hogan, J. Sperry, Amore, Westcott, Lewis, Stubbs.

Clint the gymnast, second row, right, supporting student doing headstand. Brother Jack is below him. (*Sperry*)

Clint (sitting on the floor) and company at the famous Crag Camp in the White Mountains, New Hampshire. (*Sperry*)

THE CRANSTONIAN

CLINTON HOLMES SPERRY

While with us, Clint has proved that he is a true Cranstonite. His year as President of the Leaders' Corps was especially fine and he is bound to continue his performance after graduation.
Leaders' Corps 2, 3, 4; *Pres.* 4; *H. R. V. Pres.* 4; *H. R. Pres.* 4; *Hi-Y* 4.

Clint as a senior twelfth-grade student, pictured in his high school yearbook, the Cranstonian. He was President of the Leaders Corps prior to graduation. (*Sperry*)

Above left: Clint in the late '30s in Oaklawn, RI. The car in the background is a 1928 Model A Ford, purchased new by Ernest. Clint drove it for several years in the '30s, and then Steve for four years after he got his license in 1960. A stalwart auto! (*Sperry*)

Above right: A 1939 sketch of nude. Clint's ability as an artist was beginning to emerge. (Sperry) that he hadn't enjoyed his school years, for he was an accomplished gymnast and a good tennis player, he participated in his class activities, and he was quite social. However, with the exception of art, he was not a great student. So, as with most high school seniors, he always looked forward to summer, his imagined release to the world and the bittersweet (certainly more sweet than bitter for Clint) milestone of graduation.

By that time, Clint had begun courting Mary Harlacker, a pretty young lady who would eventually become his wife. Her father was a successful business man of Dutch descent who moved his family to Rhode Island from Pennsylvania in the 1920s, and her mother was from Connecticut and of Irish descent. Meeting Mary somewhat enhanced Clint's desire to remain in Rhode Island as opposed to following the call of the mountains; in fact, there's some indication that he remained in Rhode Island to work for his future father-in-law in Providence.

In the fall of 1938 Clint became a first-year college student at Rhode Island School of Design in Providence. He was well-suited for RISD; his talent for drawing was quite remarkable, and together with his training at this progressive school, his illustrative skills would mature and serve him well throughout his life.

Later, while serving in England, he was called upon for 'nose art' on many of the fighters in his squadron, and he was responsible for the Group's 'Slybird' insignia.[2] He also produced a number of pencil drawings of typical English scenes, portraying the beautiful Suffolk countryside around the Group's air bases during his tour of operations. In fact, after he retired from commercial flying, much of his later life was spent in the advertising field, and apart from his work and personal illustrations, he was also notorious for his humorous cards for a variety of occasions.

It is difficult to know exactly when Clint caught the flying bug, but during adolescent years it was almost certain that he, like many other young kids of his age, would have read about the exploits of the famous Lafayette Escadrille. The Lafayette was a squadron of volunteer American aviators who fought for France before the United States entered the First World War, and it was those fearless young men—together with fighter pilots from Great Britain, the Commonwealth, and France—who fought the war-to-end-all-wars. Maybe, in a reflective moment, he even had a sneaky admiration for the German pilots in their multi-colored biplanes, who roamed the skies hunting down their Allied adversaries.

Ernest had been a fighter pilot back then, flying and training in de Havilland DH4 biplanes in France, but he was too late to be actively involved in the terrible conflict. It's fair to say that, had the war continued longer, battle attrition would have seen him in combat, and it was by no means certain that he would have survived in the skies above France.

Although Ernest didn't pursue flying either privately or commercially after the war, he remained interested, and Clint would have received his full endorsement toward anything related to aviation. It was surely the support of his parents and

Ernest airborne in the DH4. This is a rare photograph, indicating how the pilots were exposed to the elements. (*Sperry*)

The De Havilland DH4; this is the plane that Ernest flew at the end of the First World War. (*Sperry*)

Above left: Ernest posing in flying gear. (Sperry)

Above right: Ernest and Dorothy in later years. (*Sperry*)

the excitement of aviation that beckoned Clint to fly. Together with the love of his family and sailing, it became his work, his passion, and his pleasure throughout most of his life. He would have to be well-prepared for that challenge.

As a country slowly emerging from the depths of the Great Depression, America was always going to offer a wealth of opportunity to young students fresh out of college. Sure, times had been tough (especially for their parents), but new ideas and initiatives were emerging, and those young men would be the first to grasp those opportunities. Clint Sperry was one such young man, just like his aviator father before him.

Background to War

The First World War had destabilized nations and left Germans with bitter resentment for the burdens placed upon them by the Allies. It was in the wake of this aftermath of war that Hitler's infamous rise to power began. With extreme nationalism, anti-communism, and anti-Semitism as the key features of his policies, he began his expansionist program, creating a threat to European liberty and independence.

For temporary convenience, Hitler signed an agreement with his ideological enemy, communist Russia, which enabled German forces to plunder and overrun most of Europe—including France, Belgium, Holland, and the Nordic countries Denmark and Norway. When Poland was invaded, Great Britain and her Commonwealth declared war on Germany in September 1939, sending an Expeditionary Force to France in an endeavor to counter Germany's aggressive blitzkrieg across Europe.[1] The scene was set for the second great conflict to encompass the world.

When Winston Churchill succeeded Neville Chamberlain as Prime Minister in May 1940, the British fighting forces had already lost a great number of combatants and military resources in their failed endeavor to stop the German advance.[2] This led to an ignominious-but-successful evacuation of the Expeditionary Force at Dunkirk in June 1940, leaving the British Army with few serious weapons to fight against an anticipated invasion by Germany. France had fallen.

However, Britain wasn't impotent; she still had a strong Navy and, more significantly, they had the Royal Air Force. Although many fighter aircraft and their valuable pilots were lost, it is well documented that RAF Fighter Command was able to defeat the German Luftwaffe in what is known today as the Battle of Britain.[3, 4] RAF Bomber Command also succeeded in stalling the invasion of Britain by severely damaging fleets of many barges and landing craft moored in French and Belgian ports. Consequently, without total control of the sea and skies, Hitler called off the invasion in September 1940.[5] However, Britain totally lacked the ability to win the war outright; it was isolated, and its existence was precarious.

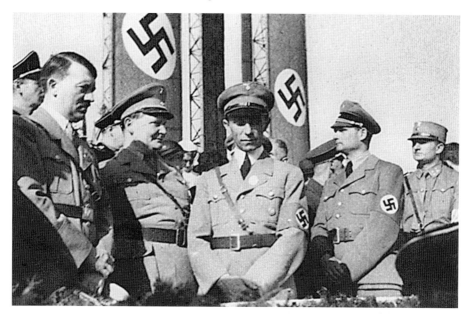

The 'Nazi Hierarchy' attending a rally in Germany. *Left to right*: Hitler, Goering, Goebbels, Hess. (*Franklin D. Roosevelt Library Archives*)

Winston Churchill pointing to a brighter future from the Citadel at the first Quebec Conference, August 1943. Beside him is General 'Hap' Arnold, and on the left is the Countess of Athlone. (*Franklin D. Roosevelt Library Archives*)

In the United States of America, the country was still easing its way out of the Great Depression and President Roosevelt was resisting any direct involvement in the European conflict. It was clear that most Americans did not want to get embroiled in Europe's problems as America had its own troubles, and they desperately wanted to avoid a 'foreign' war.

On the other side of the world, Japan was embarking on a rapid and brutal expansionist program, spreading into China and other vulnerable regions. Although aware for some considerable time that Japan could compromise American interests in the Pacific, US forces were slow in organizing defenses and building up resources to deter a potential assault. As an ominous warning of things to come, Japan joined with Germany and Italy to form the Axis alliance, which was then destabilized in June 1941 by Germany invading Russia—thus breaking their previous agreement. Russia was reeling and the Axis was in its ascendancy.[6] Then came Pearl Harbor.

The simmering conflicts erupted on 7 December 1941, a day never to be forgotten in American history. It was the 'day of infamy' on which Japanese aircraft attacked the mighty US Navy battleships as they lay at anchor in Pearl Harbor, and also attacked aircraft at US Army airfields in the Philippines. Together with the dreadful toll on the ships, aircraft, and military facilities, the loss of 2,400 American lives was a devastating shock for the nation.

US Navy aircraft carriers had fortuitously left their base only hours before the attack and were thus saved from annihilation. They were going to be the only means by which

Airfield damage from the Japanese attack at Pearl Harbor, Hawaii. Ford Island seaplane base is seen, showing USS 'Shaw' exploding in the centre background. (*Franklin D. Roosevelt Library Archives*)

America could take the fight to Japan in the Pacific, while the protecting fleets of ships and aircraft needed in combat zones would have to be built up once more. But it was also catastrophic for the British and their allies in that vast region, as their territories had also been invaded and the initiative was now firmly in Japan's grasp.

It was, indeed, a day of infamy. With Japan being a controversial partner of Germany and Italy, Hitler then declared war on the United States, which resolved President Roosevelt's dilemma of how to get involved in the European conflict. On 11 December 1941 he signed the Declaration of War against the Axis.

The survival and stability of world order was at stake, and America was now the only nation with the potential industrial capability to overcome those who would threaten that survival.

Following the Munich crisis in 1938, President Roosevelt had advocated increased spending on aircraft production and military assets. This accelerated immediately with controlled expansion to meet the demands of war in two major areas of conflict—the Far East and Europe. The United States Army Air Force also needed planes, men to fly them, and the infrastructure to support that vast commitment.

On 31 December 1941 the total number of combat aircraft available to the Army Air Force was 4,475, of which 2,170 were fighters, 1,830 were bombers, and 475 were reconnaissance; there were also 7,820 support aircraft. Of all these types, a significant number were considered obsolete. Personnel, which included officers and other ranks both in America and the rest of the world, totaled 354,161—proof, if it was needed, that the United States of America was unprepared for war.

President Franklin D. Roosevelt.
(*Franklin D. Roosevelt Library Archives*)

Those in command immediately realized that the United States could not engage in total war with full commitment on opposite sides of the world. Having commissioned the originally designated document AWPD-1 (Air War Plans Division-1), President Roosevelt reviewed the requirements recommended for all forces on land, sea, and in the air that, it was calculated, would offer complete ascendancy over the Axis enemy. When the estimate of requirement by the Air Force had been published, the logistics to carry out the policy appeared staggering, with tens of thousands of aircraft and many hundreds of thousands of weapons required to succeed.

The original numbers of aircraft recommended were not allocated to the various services; they consisted of just the types needed to fulfill various roles for all the United States and the Allied forces they were supporting. The predominant doctrine in the Air Force at that time was to get the bombers through to their targets— but they needed fighter protection, and those fighters came at a cost.[7] Training, reconnaissance, and support aircraft were also needed in their specific roles.

It was originally projected that by the end of 1943, the total number of aircraft planned for production would be 139,000. Of that total, 63,000 combat aircraft would be available to the USAAF and the Navy; but the Navy was not happy with their allocation of types, and the initiative stumbled. There had to be synchrony of thinking, and that compromise could only be achieved by reducing those demands when it soon became clear that the number of aircraft recommended was not attainable.

Consequently, on 29 October 1942 President Roosevelt cut the number of aircraft by about one quarter, and the figure for all aircraft finally settled at 107,000. The revised figures in the final document AWPD-42 were those that General of the Air Force 'Hap' Arnold and the USAAF had to work with to carry out the policy of crippling the Nazi war machine.[8]

Furthermore, the planes also required the pilots, aircrews, ground staff, and infrastructure that would enable them to fly. With AWPD-42 projecting the requirement of 2.7 million airmen, the call went out to the youth of America. It was still a tight, almost impossible schedule, but President Roosevelt had spoken. The stakes were high and failure was unthinkable.

Britain also needed the time and resources to rebuild, and it desperately needed American aid with the task. Although difficult to verify from RAF records, by the end of 1941 the air component of the RAF had an estimated 800 fighters and 500 medium and heavy bombers available to join with the USAAF to create the beginning of the massive force that would eventually emerge as the means to destroy German aggression. However, the expansion by both nations would have to occur very quickly and the obstacles were formidable.

With AWPD-42 in place, America and its Allies then established a priority policy to carry out their air battle against Germany. Following many months of discussions, the solution was eventually agreed at the Casablanca Conference in January 1943, when Britain and America concluded that the combined air power of both nations would initially be more advantageous against the continent of Europe than a seaborne war in the Pacific.[9] Consequently, control of those skies was vital if they were to succeed, and their aim was to deprive the Nazi regime of key elements in their armory for waging war against the Allied nations. The elements were listed in the following categories: German aircraft plants; submarine yards; transportation; electric power; oil; aluminum; and rubber.

The original consideration by Churchill and the RAF was that the USAAF would join the RAF in bombing enemy targets by night. However, Major General Ira C. Eaker, Commanding General of the Eighth Air Force, did not agree; he wanted to see the whites of the enemy's eyes. He wanted to bomb by day, and with results of the early bombing raids (albeit short hauls over France) he had won approval. So, it was the Eighth by day and the RAF by night. It would be tough on the Germans— or so they hoped, but absolutely necessary to weaken the enemy and prepare for the eventual invasion of the continent. All it needed were aircraft and the pilots, the crews, and the administrative structure to carry it out on the front line. And that's where Clint would be heading as he followed the ever-growing number of airmen that first trickled over to Britain during 1942. Clint was destined for war.

Looking up one of the assembly lines at Ford's big Willow Run plant, where B-24E (Liberator) bombers are being made in great numbers. (*Franklin D. Roosevelt Library Archives*)

3

Training Begins

Clint started his flying career at age twenty with the government-sponsored Civilian Pilot Training Program (CPTP), which was initiated by the Army Air Corps and the Civil Aeronautical Administration in early 1939.[1]

The CPTP was formed, for obvious reasons, in response to similar programs under way at that time in Germany and Italy. The program preceded what is now the Civil Air Patrol (the CAP was formed in 1941), and in 1939 through to 1944, the CPTP paid for seventy-two hours of ground school followed by thirty-five to fifty hours of flight instruction for thousands of young men across the country. It was invaluable and a great success, with Clint being among the early tyros turned out by the program. He completed his ground-school stint in the fall of 1940 (during his second year at RISD) and progressed to training on Piper J-3 Cubs and Waco-7 biplanes at Hillsgrove Airport in Warwick, Rhode Island. Clint remembered:

> During my first 2 years of college, I qualified for a Government sponsored Civil Pilot Training program (CPT) and completed the full program, which included: Primary Instruction, Aerobatics, Cross Country, and Instrument. Upon completion, I was certified as a U.S. Commercial Pilot, rated for single and multi-engine—course time, about 325 hours. By 1941 I had logged 412:00hrs with my Commercial Pilot Rating before the Air Force flying.

In later years, his son, Steve, remembered that any conversation he had regarding 'CPT' (as Clint called it) was quite positive, with a particularly fond emphasis toward the Waco-7. The Waco was used for the same kind of basic training as the Cub, and it was also used for aerobatic training. However, there were potential and deadly pitfalls, and Clint recalled the following:

> After taking the Waco out solo to practice some positive G aerobatics including rolls, loops, Cuban eights and hammer heads I headed back to the field feeling

pretty cocky about my performance. I made a nice landing which was just another boost to an already inflated ego. I taxied up to the tie downs, shut down the Waco and reached down to undo my seatbelt, which wasn't there. I was sitting on my seatbelt! There had been nothing keeping me in the airplane but positive Gs. A little forward stick at the top of a loop and I'd have been airborne without a Waco!

However, the path to his military career was not smooth, as Steve relates:

Shortly before Dad signed up with the USAAF and their flight training program, he had opted to visit a recruiter for his first choice. The Navy. A reasonable choice considering his marine background, love of the ocean and, I suspect, he was more than a little thrilled at the thought of flying off the deck of an aircraft carrier. With these thoughts in mind he located the Navy's recruiting office in Providence (not far from RISD) and interviewed with the recruiter there. After going through all the preliminary process leading to induction, he was assured that he'd soon be wearing Navy blue. I'm sure he was very pleased at the prospect. The Navy would be in contact with him within 48 hours with the next step. Dad received a call the next day indicating the Navy's regret that he would not be accepted to Navy flight school. He, of course, requested the reason for the denial and was told that he'd checked the box next to hay-fever

Clint looking comfortable in the cockpit during training with the UPF-7 Waco biplane. He especially enjoyed aerobatics in this aircraft. The training would be vital when he progressed on to operations. (*Sperry*)

on the medical form. A blow for a young man bent on being a Navy flier, but instead of whining he located the AAF recruiting office that same day, went to see them and completed basically the same preliminary work with all the same information except for one thing.

As a consequence, the Navy's loss was the Army's gain. Clint was destined to fly for the United States Army Air Force, and it would be far more likely that he would suffer from hay-fever on land than he would at sea!

America had been at war for nearly a year when Clint first presented himself for active duty on 10 November 1942. He was happily married to Mary and living at 83 Wilbur Avenue, Oaklawn, Rhode Island. At that point, potential airman '0793548 Clinton H. Sperry' had already earned a Commercial Pilot rating and was flying for E. W. Wiggins Airways at Hillsgrove. Although not fully appreciated at the time, it would form the vital component of experience that would help him to survive the stresses of the coming conflict. Initially, as an Aviation Cadet, Clint was taught the Army basics such as marching and carrying a rifle before he even got to see a plane. Then on to a course studying codes, aircraft recognition, maps, and other essentials, until finally he made it through pre-flight and on to flight training. But to many, training was no pushover. A large number were washed out at the early stage as being unsuitable or unable to reach the standard set by the Air Force. Fortunately, Clint was not among that number.

Many of the embryo pilots had civilian instructors in the flight-training phase, and if they made it through 'primary'—flying Stearman or Waco biplanes, or monoplanes such as PT19s—a young pilot was then expected to solo with only six hours of flight training under his belt. With a little more practice and when their flight time had totaled sixty hours, the successful ones were given their final flight check.

The next stage after 'primary' was 'basic', on aircraft such as the Vultee BT13, where a further seventy hours were spent honing their new-found skills. By then, nearly 30 per cent of the would-be pilots were already washed out, and more would follow as they progressed to advanced training. Finally, they were let loose on the AT-6 Texan (or Harvard), which was beginning to feel and fly like a fighter.

The flying was intense and exciting, but also pretty darned satisfying—if the young pilots made it through the tough course. Many didn't, and quite a few died trying, although for Clint it had been a further learning experience to add to his already accumulated flying hours. It certainly put him ahead of the majority, and as he progressed it would show in his ability to cope with difficult and potentially dangerous experiences throughout his operational tour. Training certainly wasn't a breeze for anyone, but familiarity with a willful and constantly changing sky gave Clint a tremendous advantage over most of his fellow trainees. As a result of his pre-enlisted flight training in the 'CPT', his services were sought as an instructor before taking the course. Clint commented:

I was accepted for training, US Air Corp at Mitchel Field, Long Island NY 10th November 1942 and was accepted at the same airfield as my father in 1917—who also flew pursuit aircraft out of England in WWI, 1918. Because of pre-enlisted flight time, I was offered an immediate Commission as a 2nd Lt if I'd accept an Instructor position. I declined this offer, and proceeded to full AAC Flight training as a cadet. (I had more flight time than my Primary Instructor— and a lot more fun!)

Clint subsequently recorded on his military Individual Flight Record (IFR) that, apart from initially flying an AT-6A Harvard, he also recorded ten hours of 'pursuit in P-40E Curtiss Warhawk with 382nd S.E.F.T.S'. He had written on his IFR that 'total Hours shown are Military only to date'. That total was sixty hours and thirty-five minutes.[2]

At 5 foot 10 inches, 145 lbs, brown-eyed and blond, he was the epitome of the dashing fighter pilot—except he hadn't made it yet.

In early December 1942, having completed initial training as an Aviation Cadet and now promoted to 2nd Lt, Clint was posted to the 352nd Fighter Squadron, which was one of three in the 353rd Fighter Group. The 352nd FS was now *his* Squadron, and his allegiance to it and to his fellow airmen would be absolute until he ceased to be operational. It was a significant commitment by him to the war effort of his country. It would bring triumph and disaster, but that commitment was total.

His first Group Commanding Officer was Lt Col. Joseph A. Morris. He was perceived by many in the 353rd FG as a tough taskmaster, strict in his interpretation of military discipline. He had, however, considerable background experience as a regular Army Officer and had seen the threat and power of the Japanese air component when based at Wheeler Field during that infamous attack on Pearl Harbor in December '41. Clint's view of him was that 'Col. Morris was fairly aloof (or maybe it was me), for I never got to really know him.'

Apart from the new pilots who joined his Squadron in October 1942, a small number transferred there during early December of that year. Joining the 352nd FS with Clint included Lts Morgan Barton, Leslie Cles (Clint called him by his middle name, Paul), Gordon Burlingame, Clifford Armstrong, and Bill Jordan. All but one of the aforementioned survived the war, although Leslie Cles did find himself a prisoner of war near the end of '44.[3] It appears that Clint's closest friends were from that small entry group, although only a very small number of Squadron relationships would last through to his later years. The war accounted for many of their young lives, sadly lost in training and combat, but he had yet to find that out.

Although originally a cadre formed at Richmond, the group was then temporarily split up by the Air Force. The 350th Fighter Squadron was deployed to Group Headquarters at Baltimore, the 351st FS was posted to Norfolk (the general impression of Norfolk was that it had been a mud-hole!), and 352nd FS proceeded to Langley Field, Virginia, where Clint's IFR shows they stayed until the end of February 1943. There, Clint said:

> I lived with my wife in East Hampton, just 3 miles from Langley. There was a B-18 Bomb Group there, and of course Langley was a major test center (huge wind tunnel) for new aircraft including the P-47. Actually, the P-40 was the first fighter that I flew. Was a lucky one of three in our Advanced Flight Training as a cadet at Selma, Alabama, to switch in the final hours of training in the AT-6 to 10 hours in the P-40. It was a great little fighter with exceptional maneuverability, but much too slow for any challenge to the fighters of Germany.

Following Clint's Advanced Flight Training and his subsequent posting, the 352nd FS under the command of 1st Lt William 'Bill' Bailey was given the important task of testing out P-40s for the 325th Fighter Group due for embarkation on an aircraft carrier to North Africa. There was plenty of flight time for all the Squadron pilots, but it would be a while yet before Clint could get himself into the cockpit of the aircraft that would take him to war. Meanwhile, the new guys first had to learn to be part of the Squadron team, and they would have a very difficult time ahead of them before they were proficient for the battles ahead.

A well-worn P-40 Warhawk of the 350th FS at Dundalk Airfield, near Baltimore. Ground crew, *left to right*: Lisaio, Dossett, and Aron. (*Dossett, via Cross*)

During that period, the onus was very much on the 352nd FS Commanding Officer, Lt Bailey, to bring his squadron up to operational readiness. There was no indication as to where they might end up and what they would fly, but it was Bill Bailey's job to ensure that wherever it would be, they would be prepared. Bailey, as an early graduate of the Civil Aviation Authority training program, was perceived by the young pilots as a regular Army Officer who appeared aloof and paid strict attention to the rule book, only rarely showing his individual style of humor. His character may not have wholly appealed to all the young guys on the Squadron, although it did help to maintain a sensible level of discipline necessary to gain results. There are indications that Clint and a few of the 352nd FS pilots didn't hit it off with their CO, but there is no doubt that as they progressed through training and into combat, any personal views were put aside as they fought for their lives over enemy territory.

The Squadron Commander certainly had them pumped up. Clint recorded his first gunnery practice on 28 December 1942, and there was plenty of firing and night flying to work up the guys to an early form of readiness. They were worked hard.

It was at Langley that Clint and Mary started to make friends as a married couple, and he related that:

> Morgan Barton and his wife were good friends. There were few married officers, and Mary and I enjoyed their company. We corresponded for years following his death. The two girls shared their trials with their respective children.

Tragically, Morgan died in a flying accident in May 1943, and both Clint and Mary were there to support Morgan's widow. With the continuing accidents in the training schedule at that time, the event put the hazards of flight training into harsh perspective. Clint was a married man with family responsibilities, and whatever outward appearances may have been conveyed by that zealous young flyer, it would be an experience that brought home the fragility of life as an aviator during those years of uncertainty.

Accidents continued to happen as training intensified and operations commenced. Clint remembered:

> 'Weep Juntilla' (a respected Officer's Club regular that paid off) was always a good friend. He decided to leave his burning P-40 one night on the way back from Bolling Field. I was not there, but he got out in a hurry and having his dress shoes on, as the chute snapped open, both shoes popped off and he landed in a farmer's cornfield in his stocking feet. It was a sight to see as he arrived at base in a pair of the farmer's slippers hugging a great bundle of chute with squinting eyes and his great smile.

'Weep' would eventually become the leader of the 352nd FS later in the war.

Clint's commitment to his squadron and responsibility to his family were coming into sharp focus. He had become an advocate of accumulating further experience that would continue to expand his knowledge of airmanship. It would be a worthy attribute for a potential survivor of combat, and a caution against any unnecessary and careless actions when eventually flying missions over Europe. For the sake of himself and his family Clint had to do all he could to survive, and that knowledge gained became increasingly valuable.

As Clint and his fellow pilots racked up their training hours, America and Britain waged war on the other side of the Atlantic against Germany and Italy and in the Pacific against the Japanese. The United States had become jittery when German U-boats started targeting ships departing the east coast, loaded with Lend-Lease weapons and materials bound for their allies in Britain. To compound the problem, the appearance of Japanese submarines off the west coast caused a great deal of unease and indicated that the war had come too close for comfort. To prevent any possible attacks by German and Japanese aggressors, all home defense forces were put on alert—even though an invasion would have been unlikely, due to the tremendous distances involved. The 353rd FG was no exception. Whilst still classed as 'Training', the Group were under orders from the Philadelphia Defense Wing. Clint recalls:

We were kept on alert at all times. Night duty (alternating) was the worst because 4 guys had to stay in Operations all night and no place to snooze but in a chair or on a desk. We never actually took off, but had to scramble to the aircraft from time to time to fire up the P-40s taxi out then get called back. OK with me! I was always a little leery of full throttle takeoff with a very cold Allison engine.

The invasion did not materialize, and an uneasy calm gradually descended.

Flying the fastest aircraft that existed enticed many young men into the Air Force—men who said they'd give their right arm to experience the incredible thrill of flying a 400-mph fighting machine. They sought the romance, the excitement, and the respect of most earth-bound souls who thought that all those who flew were just crazy; but they were also very young and disturbingly fallible, as experience would soon show. Following barely sufficient training, many lost their lives—not just through plain bad luck, but also by testing their own perceived immortality beyond the limit. Sadly, they were rapidly projected into a combat situation by a limited and challenging training program that had pushed them through with barely adequate instrument and night-flying ratings. Many would be lost as competency was sacrificed for speed of learning. Apart from an enemy who wanted them dead, the skies over England and Europe would expose those who did not have the essential knowledge of instrument flying.

Clint, however, had a skill that was built on experience, and one that became more critical in the autumn of 1943, when the very bad weather and tough assignments cut short many promising lives. They all had to fly missions (sometimes in almost suicidal conditions), but Clint, with his full instrument rating and greater flying hours, stood a better chance than most of getting home. It is worthy of note that instrument aids were lacking on the ground during his flight training and operations; they were very crude compared to those available today.

His son, Steve, puts the observation in perspective:

It's been mentioned that Clint's father (my grandfather) flew and was a fighter pilot toward the end of WWI. My son and I are also pilots, and of the four generations of airmen, Dad accumulated far more time and was immensely more experienced than any of the rest. I am in the air regularly, and though I'm not instrument rated I am quite comfortable discussing the skill of instrument flying with my feet on the ground. I flew quite often with Clint when I was a boy and there were occasions when we were on instruments. Those times seemed no different than any other except that I would see nothing but white or gray out the windows. I've learned since that special skills were required to do this. Most people interested in flying are capable of developing these skills and, of course, all commercial and many private pilots are instrument rated today and can quite comfortably fly in this opaque shroud of vapor that is cloud. I've had opportunity to fly in abysmal visual conditions with pilots who are simply superb in their ability to manage getting from one airport to another in these conditions and still answer my questions. Some of my favorite flights have been in aircraft with no autopilot where the pilot is required to hold a heading and altitude, communicate with Air Traffic Control, monitor engine health and fuel consumption, ascend, descend or turn while dealing with the above and converse with me! I tell myself that I could do this. That anybody could really do this. Convincing myself is another matter!

4

Intensive Training

Towards the end of the Group and 352nd FS's initial training period, Clint had his own views about the aircraft he would prefer to fly when fighting the enemy. He hoped to fly the P-51 or P-47, commenting, 'It was only a dream at the time and so was the '47, but it was the first.' The Allison engine P-51A was operational during that period, and the few available were predominantly flying with the RAF; however, the vastly improved P-51Bs and Cs (with the famed Merlin engine) were yet to roll off the production line.[1] Still, the P-47s were well into production and fighter groups were beginning to operate them in the USAAF, so Clint didn't have long to wait. The day of his first flight in his dream aircraft was memorable.

He flew a P-47B for one hour on 12 January 1943, and it was the start of his love affair with the famed Republic Thunderbolt. He was ecstatic:

I will never forget the wonderful day that we got the P-47Bs. We had seen one in the Langley test hangar, and of course it looked like a monster compared to the '40. I was literally thrilled to climb into that huge, very solid and awesome aircraft. Nothing was like engaging the energizer and starter to see that big 4-bladed prop smoothly turn until it just as smoothly started firing into an idling engine that you had to see and hear to know it was running. It was just as smooth at full throttle. Nothing, before or since (in 10,400 hours and some 69 varieties of aircraft), has been as solid, as smooth, or as light on the controls as the P-47B, C, D, & N. I was in love with this most forgiving aircraft that brought me home every time.

Costing around $105,000 when first produced in 1942, the Thunderbolt was a big beast with an empty weight of nearly 11,000 lbs and gross weight, with light armaments, of at least 14,000 lbs. In fact, it didn't take long for this to be unofficially stretched to over 20,000 lbs by some over-eager operational units 'experimenting' with different weapon and fuel configurations, and it soon became a 'normal' load when on Thunder-bombing missions. Powered by a Pratt & Whitney R-2800 air-cooled radial engine and armed with six or eight .50-caliber machine guns, the rugged Thunderbolt was special. It needed specialists to fly it and it was a fighter for the big league. Clint, now proficient in flying the P-47, had signed up for the duration; a perfect match to go to war.

The Thunderbolt also impressed others within the 353rd Fighter Group. Recorded at the 353rd FG Reunion in 1983, a conversation between Bill Jordan, pilot in the 352nd FS, and Jim Cope, the 352nd FS Flight Surgeon, went as follows:

Jordan: Richmond we got the P-47s.

Cope: One time we were setting up there at the line, you know, and these hot pilots were talking and here came in one of these new '47s about two feet off the deck. Came down and did a chandelle off the end of the runway and came down and landed, you know. Right out of the plant. Boy, here was this hot pilot and this God damn little ferry pilot that couldn't have been any higher than that, you know.

Jordan: Parachute was dragging on the ground. 'Hello, boys.'

Cope: She was ferrying one of them in.

Jordan: Do you remember that? God, I remember these guys looked at her, never had flown one.

Those monsters were smooth, and very occasionally the pilots were pretty darned cute and capable young WASP ladies—the Women Airforce Service Pilots. The flyboys had to stay mighty cool that day.

At the end of February the 352nd FS moved to Millville, New Jersey, but it was a comedown, as it wasn't a very big base—it was different from Langley and not very plush, as they had to leave behind a very acceptable and essential Officer's Club.

Intensive training commenced, with all forms of combat tactics and maneuvers drilled into the brains of those eager young pilots so that they would become second nature. Their lives depended on their ability to read situations, react rapidly, and (most importantly of all) to obey orders. Clint's recollection of that period is sparse; he said, 'I've forgotten about any special training. It was obviously in preparation for combat with tow target and ground gunnery.... As I recall, we practiced as a Group forming up. Don't really remember.' He was probably just too busy to recall that vital period, loving the flying.

At Millville there were tents on the line, the improvised tower was a truck, the radio truck was at the end of the runway, and married couples lived in town. Just a simple life! Training was relentless but satisfying for Clint and his fellow pilots. To some it came easy, but to others it was tough.

Buzz jobs (where pilots fly as close to the ground as possible) were strictly not the order of the day, but they happened as sure as day follows night. It allowed the young bloods to ease their pain, have some fun, let off steam, and inflate their egos. Clint remembers:

> Buzz Jobs: Yes, we got in trouble from time to time. Particularly while at Millville and Richmond where the land was flat with many huge duck farms. Thousands of ducks for restaurants in New York and far afield. We (the USAC) had to pay for several thousand ducks who in a panic escape attempt piled up against a fence and smothered each other. It was a sad affair, but we (I think I was there) had no idea at the time.

On another escapade the guilty parties had been Bill Streit and Scotty McPherson, and the victims were chickens! The two were ordered to go and apologize to the farmer, who showed them the result of their 'buzz job'. Although they were contrite and willing to pay, the farmer surprised them by offering to share the result of their misplaced exuberance, inviting them to join him in a chicken dinner the following Sunday. Apparently, the poor birds were due for market anyway! Some have it lucky.

Unfortunately, training flights didn't always have a satisfactory conclusion. Accidents can and will happen and in the 352nd FS there were no exceptions, as recorded in an event on 23 April that involved two of Clint's closest friends:

> That morning two ships from the 352nd Squadron were cleared for gun camera mock combat from Millville. The two pilots, 2nd Lt Leslie P Cles and 1st Lt Gordon Burlingame, started their dogfight at 12,000ft with a head-on approach. After making four turns their planes ran together. Lt Cles' aircraft, P-47-C5 (a/c 41-6461), was struck beneath and just ahead of the tail section and he was forced to bail out at 3,000 ft.
>
> Lt Cles reported: After the collision my ship went into a right spin. The spin was violent with oscillating of the nose. Soon it came out of this spin and went into one to the left. When it came out momentarily, I cut the throttle and made an attempt to control the ship but found the stick frozen in the rear position. The plane went into a slow flat spin. I then opened the canopy and unfastened my safety belt. I left on the left side, which was the inside of the spin. I then slowly slid the length of the wing and left clear of the ship.

Lt Cles was unhurt, but as he drifted to earth the tail section of his aircraft came falling past—narrowly missing his opened chute. 1st Lt Gordon S. Burlingame was able to return to Millville and land. It was certainly a very lucky break for both pilots, and Clint's close friendship with them brought home to Clint that the dangers in combat training could, on occasion, be lethal.

Clint saw the month of April out with a temporary move to Richmond, where he '... was assigned to 327th for a couple of weeks, but no flying of record', then back to 352nd FS via Baltimore (Group Headquarters), and to Richmond again until he was shipped overseas.

A good group picture of 352nd FS pilots when stationed at Millville. *Left to right*: Robertson, Fogarty, Sperry, Lepird (KIFA), Burlingame, Vogel (KIA), Cles (POW), Armstrong, Juntilla, Gonnam (POW), and Corrigan. Note P-47 in background. (*Streit via Cross*)

In late spring Clint was designated a Flight Leader, although he was not leading flights until later into his tour. 'My State side advancement to 1st Lt was made within a few months with 353rd Fighter Group, and I was designated Flight Leader from that day until I completed my service in the USAAF.' Dr Graham Cross gives us further guidance through the Squadron structure:

In the Squadrons the base unit of organisation for the pilots was the Flight, a group of approximately seven or eight pilots. This provided an administration unit on the ground headed by a Flight Leader reporting to Squadron Commander and Operations Officer. Although it could be used for scheduling flight positions in the air, conditions very often meant that members of the same Flight did not always fly together, and nor did wing men always have the same leader. Pilots could find themselves flying a variety of positions according to Squadron need. As the numbers of pilots in a Squadron increased, so did the number of Flights. In 1943, Squadrons had three Flights, A, B and C. By the spring of 1944 a D flight had been added to the Squadrons, whilst by the end of hostilities there were additional F and G Flights, although the latter was commonly an OTU Flight attached to the Group organisation.

Both in the air and on the ground the actual Squadron Commander was responsible for ensuring that his unit was an effective combat team, in the same way as the Group Commander provided that curious unquantifiable mixture of aggression and common sense to inspire men to do their jobs.

The result of inspiration is very difficult to measure. However, there is no doubt that Clint was a valuable asset in the 352nd FS, although certain situations that occurred during his active service do indicate that he was slightly frustrated that those skills were not officially recognized as they should have been. Those attributes would come to the fore during the bad autumn and winter weather that the Group had yet to encounter in late '43 and early '44.

The valuable period spent training on his much-loved P-47 didn't go unnoticed or unappreciated by Clint:

> In January '43, we were scheduled to go to Africa with our P-40s, but at the last minute we switched to '47s and spent a few more weeks in the States to master my life saving machine.

It is possible that, as they were checking out the P-40s for the 325th Fighter Group, Clint and his colleagues were initially under the impression that the 353rd FG would be taking them to Africa. But he wryly commented on the proposed move:

> We knew we were not going to Africa when we got '47s and packed away our summer uniforms. It became fairly promising that Europe was the target. Maybe Italy? Packing my bike was a good omen, and certainly England was my hope.

The time had now come for Clint and his colleagues in the 352nd Fighter Squadron to embark with the Group and head for the air war over Europe. He had made it through as an Aviation Cadet, gaining further valuable flight experience and progressing from training aircraft to fighters. Including night flying, he had accumulated well in excess of 300 hours of AAF flight training. Taken together with the hours of flying civilian aircraft before enlisting meant that he had accumulated nearly 800 hours—which was a considerable amount, and far greater than the average pilot in the Group. That training made a big difference to his survival chances in the European Theatre of Operations and, furthermore, he had honed his skills on one of the most modern fighters in the world. However, he would soon find out that combat would be a totally different challenge.

Clint's life was about to change, and with it the security of home and family:

> I said goodbye to a wonderful pregnant wife, which made for a sad trip to the boat, but the excitement of getting underway on the Queen Mary and 11,000 other military personnel made things a lot easier.[2]

Following the journey from Richmond, the men of the 353rd FG collected their baggage, passed muster and embarked on board one of the finest liners in the world. When the ship slipped out of New York harbor in the early morning of 1 June, Clint Sperry and the 353rd Fighter Group were closing, both physically and intellectually, on a new and soul-stirring chapter of their lives.

The P-47 Thunderbolt

You could say that the Republic P-47 didn't just happen as a single innovative design solution; it evolved from a long line of initially civilian and then military aircraft that were designed and produced to fulfill specific military criteria under the genius of Major Alexander de Seversky and his team of creative young designers at the private Seversky Aero Corporation.[1] It is easy to see, during those very tough Depression years, the mix of innovative features that would eventually develop into the aircraft Clint so admired. Progressing under the Republic flag, with de Seversky no longer the driving force, the P-47 became the brainchild of designer Alex Kartveli.[2] Beautiful it was not (unlike the British Spitfire), but it was tough, fast, and uncompromising in its ability to perform the task for which it was originally designed. Looking at the side-on profile, it probably deserved its nickname—'The Jug'—although viewed from head-on (or tail-on), it had a smooth, almost athletic profile. Yet to most of the pilots it was just the 'P-47'—not exactly an endearment, but a type-name to be respected.[3] Putting it simply, it was a high-spirited thoroughbred.

In his 'Flight Journal', test pilot Corwin 'Corky' Meyer had a positive view of the Thunderbolt when he evaluated both Allied and Axis aircraft. To him it was one of the best:

> The P-47's cockpit was roomy and well-suited to 200-hour war-trained pilots. All of the controls, switches and instruments were handily located; its flight stabilities were low enough for fighter tactics but sufficient for hands-off, long-range missions. Its docile normal and accelerated stall characteristics did not interfere with aerial gunnery runs, and with its soft landing-gear shock-struts, three-point landings were smooth and easy. As a tribute to its ability to dish out and take punishment, all 10 of the top European aces survived the war.

Like his peers, Clint soon began to master this heavyweight fighter plane. He guides the reader through the takeoff, handling, and landing procedure when flying the Thunderbolt:

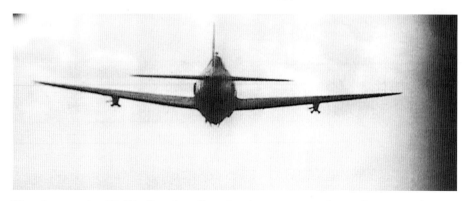

Fine photograph of P-47 tail-end profile, taken by gun camera from Clint's aircraft. Note the connecting shackles for wing tanks. (*Sperry*)

The P-47 can be a complicated aircraft because of the layout of its instrumentation and the placement of controls, but it soon becomes a natural procedure. There are automatic settings for prop control, oil cooler shutters, supercharger waste gates, etc., but one has to understand why, and how to manage them manually when auto is inoperative.

Assuming you have been through the starting procedure and have taxied to a position just off the end of the active runway, there are some checks to be made prior to take-off. First the brakes are set to throttle up to about 2000 rpm to go through the following checks: ammeter indicates acceptable charge, engine magnetos must be checked individually to be sure that both spark plugs in each of the 18 cylinders are performing with a minimum drop in rpm, the prop pitch control in both auto and manual is operating perfectly, the fuel mixture is set at full rich, the fuel booster is full on, the flap hydraulic pressure is in balance, fuel selector is on the main tank, all engine instruments are where they should be, oxygen supply and regulator are in order, radio is operating properly, altimeter is set at field elevation, and the runway is clear for take-off.

You are now cleared to position for take-off—3,000 ft should be plenty. Lock tail wheel in straight ahead position—elevator trim set for takeoff—final check mixture full rich, prop set for full rpm, supercharger engaged if wanted, engine cowl flaps set half open—all engine instruments OK, gyros uncaged, so we slowly open throttle to 2700 rpm and 52 inches Hg. The acceleration will be very evident as the aircraft quickly goes from 0 to 110mph. As the aircraft lifts off the runway, the speed will increase to 120-130 so gear has to come up quickly—Quick scan of instruments, fuel boost off, prop in auto at 2550 rpm and 4" Hg for steady climb at 170 (1,500 ft per min). Except in combat or emergencies, we usually cruised at a conservative 65% power. Level flight about 320-350 mph.

One has to realize that the P-47 is a complex and very powerful machine, with an engine and airframe occupied and controlled by a single person, the figures are impressive (even today).

The engine is an 18 cylinder supercharged giant developing 2000 to 2800 horsepower, turning a four bladed 13-ft diameter propeller. There are no less than 30 individual engine instruments and controls. 8 flight instruments plus a gyroscopic gun sight. Three radio and directional plus navigational instruments. An overall Combat ready weight of 14,000 pounds—on occasion, 21,000 pounds. In spite of the engine size, the Pratt & Whitney R-2800 is notably the smoothest running engine of any fighter aircraft.

In the air, the P-47B was a delight to fly. On the other hand, there were drawbacks, as it had a very poor rate of climb and was not the best combat aircraft at low level. Although it was superior in performance when compared to the Me109 and Fw190 at heights above 20,000 feet, to get there the P-47 was not spectacular. Whilst Clint's first combat aircraft, P-47-D-2-RA, took eleven minutes to reach 20,000 feet, the Me109G took just over five minutes and the Fw190 about seven minutes. It wasn't until water injection and Hamilton paddle blade props were fitted that performance significantly increased, and Clint's new replacement P-47D-22-RE near the end of his tour had those modifications as standard. However, his original SX-E was modified in stages in the early part of 1944. But hell, could the P-47 dive! Once at height it was a dangerous beast to the opponent, and the dive and zoom tactics adopted by the pilots would give it a great advantage in a combat situation.

Clint soon mastered the basic handling requirements. However, as stated, combat was something different. It entailed rapid, uncompromising, and violent movements of all flying surfaces, extremely quick reactions, and immediate and physically draining changes of attitude and altitude as it wholly wrung out the pilot and plane. Clint explains:

First, black out is exactly as it implies and is the result of G-forces experienced in tight turns or dive pullouts usually at high speed. The effects of G-forces may differ between pilots, and that fact may be related to the individual's physical condition at the time, i.e. too many beers the night before—insufficient rest, or possibly not feeling up to par. Actually the main difference is the individual's normal blood pressure range.

Pilots like myself, with a normally low blood pressure will experience Black Out at lower G-factors than one with normally higher blood pressure. Black Out can be fatal if held to the point of loss of consciousness, but normal momentary Black Out in combat is a fairly regular experience.

Without a G-Suit to keep the blood in the brain, here is how it goes. In a tight turn you may be pulling 5-6 even 7 times the weight of gravity and the first sign is a sort of gray-out with still physical control and feel of position—next, everything goes black (like you have no vision), but you're still perfectly conscious - next, the obvious is to let off enough on the G-Forces to bring your vision back. All the above takes place in 4 or 5 seconds—10 at the most or you may run into the guy you were attempting to turn inside of.

To explain the relative commonality of Black Out, in my normal approach for landing (the combat version), I'd cross the threshold of the landing runway at 300 or 350 at about 10 feet off the ground and pull-up hard to the left in a fairly tight climbing circle—chop the throttle right there. In the first 90 degrees, I'd be pulling a lot of G's and would often be in the dark from the 90 degree point to the top of the turn at about 180 degree and 1,000ft a span of maybe 4 seconds. I'd pop the gear down (it would really pop down with the tight turn), by this point vision was back and the aircraft had kept a nice turn with speed down now to 140 and in the descending turn I'd lower the flaps and be soon perfectly lined up for the final touch down at about 110-120—and never have moved the throttle till the end of the landing roll ... my experience says you can get it into 3,000ft if you get on at the threshold.

WHAT'S THE PURPOSE? At mission end we were often low on fuel with the fast approach, if we were to run out of gas you wouldn't need any for safe landing. Actually, if properly executed, you shouldn't have to touch the throttle all the way around...great fun and a challenge to pull wing tip streamers all the way around. It didn't work every time, but humidity in England made great tip streamers. Enough of that.

For experienced pilots like Clint, this method of landing was in practice following many months of training and eventually in combat situations, when

Thunderbolts of the 351st FS peel up prior to landing at Metfield. (*Harris, via Cross*)

tight-formation approach for landings were competitive and considered rather a macho maneuver. Regardless, the State-side training programs were pushing through new pilots with barely sufficient experience to safely handle this powerful aircraft, and to try to copy the 'originals' could prove extremely dangerous. There were several instances when the less-experienced guys would just pull round in a high-G turn in preparation for the landing phase, stall, and auger in. It paid to have a great deal of knowledge of the handling of the P-47 before that kind of maneuver could be attempted. To the unwary it could prove fatal.

> RED-OUT: I don't remember ever reaching that stage. It's just the opposite of Positive G-Forces, and can happen in Negative G's during prolonged inverted flight, but more likely a violent push over or negative turn in combat. Rare in any case … except for the very often blood shot eyes from the night before.

As for altitude change and a more reserved, non-combat approach, Clint had his own solutions, almost certainly carried out with variations by most operational pilots:

> Singing, swallowing, chewing gum, yawning were all helpful exercises to relieve sometime painful situations. Rapid loss of altitude results in a substantial increase in outer pressure on ears, which impairs hearing. Fighters in WWII were not pressurized as they are today.
>
> Landing a P-47 was simpler than landing a Stearman Biplane trainer. There are 14 feet between the landing gear wheels on a P-47, but only 5 feet in a Stearman, and not much more than 6 or 8 feet on a Spitfire. This means that it did not have a tendency to wobble around down the runway. With the tail wheel locked (and it better be) for straight down the runway, when at 110mph the P-47 stopped flying, it placed 14,000 pounds of aircraft very solidly on the ground.
>
> It's not really as simple as that, for every landing depends on many variable circumstances. Traffic, wind direction and speed, visibility, runway conditions etc., etc., so I'll just cover basics. A normal approach is to line up with the landing runway at reduced speed (140–150), at 1000ft to mid runway and break away to the left. Proceed in a gradual turning descent—at the 180-degree point and 130mph lower the landing gear (lots of things to check here—fuel on fullest tank—fuel mixture full rich—flap hydraulics equalized—prop on auto or high RPM—turbo off engine flaps closed—Gear lights indicating DOWN). Now at 270 degrees into turn, flaps down full with speed now at 120-130 for final touchdown at 110-120. Lightly check brakes in early roll to be assured, for the P-47 is heavy and likes to roll on and on. That's the simple procedure.

In his book *The First and the Last*, Adolf Galland, Commander-in-Chief of the German fighter force, had clear views of the introduction of the Thunderbolt into European skies:

As early as January, 1943, the first P-47 Thunderbolt escort fighter with the 8th A.A.F. arrived in England. Two wings were complete at the beginning of April, and a fortnight later the Thunderbolts made their first contact with the Fw190, which was their superior in many aspects. But there was still a long way to go before it could be used in regular operations, and many improvements still had to be made. Its radius of action was not more than 150 miles to start with, and not until May was fitted with additional ejectable fuel tanks. It was autumn before the Thunderbolt escort became fully effective, with an increased active radius of over 300 miles ... With the extension of the range of the American fighter planes the value of our destroyers, well established in the fight against unescorted bomber formations, decreased.

At the end of 1943, when Wilhelmshaven, Kiel, and Ludwigshafen were raided, Galland observed:

These three raids by the 8th A.A.F., outstanding amongst the events of the war year 1943, were all flown with P-47 Thunderbolt escort ... The American fighters learned and readjusted themselves. After January, 1944, they went over to aggressive free-for-all fights in the approach sector.

As a result of this policy, in early 1944 he was devastated to note that his 'brother Wilhelm had fallen; shot down by Thunderbolt escort fighters near the German frontier in the vicinity of St Trond'. It was a personal loss and a grim reminder of the events to come.

Luftwaffe pilot Leutnant Peter Henn, who flew both Me109s and Fw190s in the last two years of the war, certainly had his own view of the Thunderbolt. He stated, 'The terror of the Thunderbolt had spread ... some years before. In Germany we called it the *Trunkenbold*'. Roughly translated as 'drunkard', one can only guess that it was weaving all over the sky and tough to pin down! Although it could be out-maneuvered at lower levels by some enemy fighters, the reassurance of the huge air-cooled Pratt & Whitney up front during ground strafing would be the savior of many USAAF pilots.

For Clint, it would not be long before the tension of air combat would become a harsh reminder that no matter how much practice he had, nothing was like the reality of what he would encounter when he met the enemy. Then, whether fired on from the ground or air, or whether he was alone or scared, one thing was absolutely certain—the enemy were seriously out to kill him and each and every one of his flying friends. Then there was the weather...

The Yanks Are Coming

From the minute that Clint and a few thousand other military personnel hauling their personal gear stepped onto the decks of the camouflage-dulled and war-worn former luxury liner *Queen Mary*, the Germans were out to stop them reaching the other side of the ocean. In June 1943 the Atlantic was a perilous place, and even though the Allies were winning the battle of the Atlantic, U-boats were continuing to consign any luckless ship to the deep. The *Queen Mary*, carrying its valuable cargo, would be a massive prize.

On board, the liner was stark, drab, and vastly overcrowded, showing little outward signs of the superb grandeur of pre-war days of expensive luxury sea travel. Did it make Clint wonder how all that heaving mass of humanity, both male and female, could ever fit into the lifeboats when the ship might be sinking under them? With around 15,000 military and civilian personnel on board and only enough room for 4,500 in lifeboats and rafts, it is certain that if he did, he pushed it to the back of his mind, for the answer wasn't appealing.[1] In fact, the thought was truly alarming. Instead he made the most of the few days that it would take to reach the slightly safer (but still embattled) shores of Britain. Clint remembered with a positive view:

> The trip was fantastic. We had very pleasant weather and could lie in the sun many hours. Nurses were great company. The worst was to see enlisted men (not officers) crowded on deck and in companionways, while I shared with another pilot a class A cabin with 2 large berths, hot showers etc., etc., AND two full course meals in the dining area with linen, silver and service. The best I could do was steal any food left over for the guys eating out of their mess kits. Never was a good officer, which my final military rank will prove.

Obviously he was a good passenger, especially as the crossing was relatively smooth, but for some, even the slightest movement and continuous zigzagging to confuse the U-boats induced sea-sickness, which was probably more acute for those enlisted folk who would class their travelling and bedding-down facilities as far worse than 'steerage'!

Whatever, Clint was still one of the guys and probably a better officer for it, although it did not appear to endear him to those higher up the ladder.

After a fast crossing, the *Queen Mary* safely dropped anchor in the Firth of Clyde, beside the Scottish port of Gourock, at 8 p.m. on 6 June. The next morning, all on board, their gear and their cargo were ferried to the mainland in smaller vessels as the ship was just too big to berth dockside. During the period waiting to disembark, all but those 'in the know' in the 353rd Fighter Group were unaware that their destination airfield would be Station F-345, Goxhill, adjacent to the small village of the same name. It was very close to the Humber Estuary and the major fishing ports of Hull, in the south of the county of Yorkshire, and to Grimsby, on the northeast coast of the county of Lincolnshire.

Quaint and grimy British trains were waiting for the seething mass of military personnel to take them to all their various destinations spread throughout Great Britain in the European Theater of Operations (ETO); the 353rd FG headed south.

As Clint gazed out of the partially blacked-out carriage windows it refreshed his senses; he thought it looked a bit like home. The countryside was a patchwork of small fields separated by trees and hedges, much smaller in comparison to those in the States.[2] In rolling green fields, cattle and sheep were grazing on lush pastures, moist and glistening in the summer sun. It was a scene of tranquility.

The liner *Queen Mary*, offloading troops after safely crossing the Atlantic. She anchored at Gourock, in the Firth of Clyde, on 6 June 1943. (*IWM*)

As the train labored on to their destination they passed sedately through ancient Scottish and English villages and towns, revealing grey stone Scottish homes and then picturesque thatched English cottages. Clint was certainly impressed:

> If you have to be involved in a war, assignment in England was a great relief. There would be no place I'd rather be under the circumstances than obviously at home. The smooth train trip to Goxhill was fascinating. Scenery much like home, and our reception by the villagers of Goxhill was most comforting and greatly appreciated. It had been a long journey with considerable apprehension, but their courtesy and warm hospitality was most heartening. We were also welcomed by Axis Sally through radio broadcast from Germany with a promise of a visit from the Luftwaffe.[3]
>
> We got a first taste of war as the German bombers hit Grimsby and Hull.[4] Also our first air raid alarm as Axis Sally came through with her promise and dropped a small load of anti-personnel bombs on the airfield. No harm done. Anti-aircraft firing was more exciting than the raid.

Apart from the small gift from the Luftwaffe, the bombs dropped around them were meant for those two main shipping ports; it had been a forceful reminder that they had arrived in a war zone. Nothing was sacred to the German bombers as they dropped their lethal loads to force death and destruction on the inhabitants of those two populous areas. The 353rd FG had finally arrived on the front line, and in the coming months life would become even more uncertain as they took the battle to the enemy over Europe.

The fish docks at Grimsby. (*via Cross*)

After America officially joined the Allied cause, new airfields were being constructed all over the East of England to accommodate the aerial armadas yet to be shipped or flown over from the States. Apart from other less respectable names, the region of East Anglia was sometimes referred to as 'Aircraft Carrier Great Britain' or the 'Unsinkable Aircraft Carrier', as airfield after airfield was scraped and leveled out of the virgin landscape. Many virtually bordered on each other as they crammed the region with war machines—and, most significantly, American culture. To the local inhabitants it was an invasion—a pleasant revelation to some, but to a few less-tolerant of their new neighbors, an annoying intrusion on their way of life. It would never be the same again.

Originally built for the RAF in 1941, Goxhill (soon irreverently dubbed 'Goat Hill') was then taken over by the Eighth Air Force as a fighter operational-training and theater-indoctrination base, and that is where the Group soon settled into their sparse-but-adequate quarters. Even though the facilities were acceptable in summer, they gave no indication as to how the new inhabitants would experience a winter on British bases. They would find that out later in the year, as dusty tracks turned to clinging, dark-brown, glutinous mud.

Training could not start immediately for the 353rd FG as their aircraft had yet to arrive. This left them some time to tour round, get a feel for the area, and meet some of those friendly people from the surrounding villages and towns. The airmen went to see the damage inflicted by the Luftwaffe bombers and were shocked and subdued by what they saw—a lesson of what war was really about, heightening their admiration for those who had to endure the punishment. Clint relates:

> Memories of Grimsby and surrounding country, including trips to Hull on the ferry were our first real exposure to English culture … and I loved it. People were friendly and far from the conservative, stoic personality we were led to believe from obviously uneducated Americans.

To Clint, his overriding impression was 'most importantly, the generous and hospitable acceptance of Americans by the local residents'.

It was not long before their aircraft arrived at Goxhill (mainly P-47Cs), and Clint and his fellow pilots finally started to familiarize themselves with their surroundings. Clint remembered those early days after arrival:

> During our pre-combat training at Goxhill, we were involved with getting used to the climate, general topography, the airfield itself and an occasional air raid.

It was time to shake down, to perfect their flying skills and prepare to take on the Luftwaffe in the potentially lethal skies of the ETO. The knowledge gained would give them the edge for survival.

It was also the time when all key senior staff would have been busy working up the Squadrons for action in their new environment on the front line. As in all Groups, there were key guys fulfilling vital operational functions, and in the 353rd FG Col. Morris had key executive officers to back him up. However, Clint would have been much more aware of the workings and responsibilities of the senior officers in the 352nd Fighter Squadron. Although personnel and their ranks sometimes changed during the Squadron's period of operations, some of the key positions are noted to have worked closely with Squadron Commander Bill Bailey during 352nd FS's time in the ETO.[5] Following the move of Lt Stackler to the 359th FG at East Wretham, Capt. Charles Wurtzler became Intelligence Officer. Lt Harry Hammer joined him as his assistant (the Group Intelligence Officer was Major Henry 'Hank' Bjorkman), and together with Operations Officer Capt. Raynor Robertson, who was a pilot and the man responsible for planning missions, their information would be vital to the forthcoming operations over Europe. Flak and enemy fighter types and concentrations could mean the difference between the success and failure of a mission, as would many other important gems of information. Capt. Henry Esperson was 352nd FS Engineering Officer and Lt Eugene Murphy the officer in charge of armaments. Capt. Giles Cook was in the important role of Executive Officer, and at some time Coy Fisher had been the Squadron Adjutant—although Wurtzler had been the first Squadron Adjutant back in the States.

352nd FS Ground Officers at Raydon with Lt Col. Bailey.
Back row, left to right: Lt Hammer (Intelligence), Capt. Cook (Executive Officer), Major Cope (Flight Surgeon 'Doc'), Lt Col. Bailey (352nd Commander), Capt. Esperson (Engineering), Capt. Wurtzler (Intelligence).
Kneeling, left to right: Lt Murphy (Armaments), Lt Lundy (Communications), Lt Spicer (Supply). (*Cross*)

A vital role was the Supplies Officer (Lt Hiram Spicer), as he covered a multitude of wants from ground-crews wanting a tail wheel for a P-47 through to collar studs. Another important function was carried out by the Communications Officer, Lt Irvin Lundy, for in all forms of modern war, excellent communications are absolutely vital both in the air and on the ground. Lack of accurate intelligence, as a result of poor communication, could be catastrophic. The same would apply to the Met Officer, for in the tumultuous skies over England and Europe the weather patterns were unlike those found in the States. Weather reporting was centralized in the Group and provided by Lt Carl Hayes of the 18th Weather Detachment. Wind, fog, and mist were great problems, and to many pilots the cloud and rain would be a hazard to avoid whenever possible—though cloud was sometimes a savior for planes trying to escape enemy fighters. To just a few like Clint, proficient on instruments and confident in their own ability to navigate in those conditions, it caused little problem.

Not least important was the 352nd Flight Surgeon. Captain Jim Cope had graduated from medical school in June 1940 and became a urological surgeon before being drafted to the Army, finally ending up as a Major in the 353rd at the end of the war. Whether or not his specialist subject was used extensively is better not explored, but there was no doubt that he had encountered most ailments and injuries during his time with the 352nd FS. As a person and as a physician, he was ideally suited to the varied role that was required in a fighter squadron, and those young flyers would need him often. His brief was wide, as he had to administer over the terrible crash scenes that regularly occurred and also be there among the pilots and all on the Squadron to check their health through the intensity of battle. His was not a job for the faint-hearted, and he was highly respected in carrying out his specialized duties—unless he sensibly grounded a guy who didn't want to stop flying! With most of the executive background of the Squadron highlighted, a Fighter Group had approximately 1,400 airmen in total to run the whole show. Pilots and other officers aside, the Squadrons had about 250 enlisted men each to perform duties. They were all absolutely essential to the running of the base, and there were many unsung heroes at all levels within the operation.

While on the base, one of the most important relationships that a fighter pilot could have was with his ground crew. Most pilots were attentive and respectful—a few took them as just part of the necessary machinery of a combat aircraft, not fully appreciating the great value, advice, and service they could offer their charge. The crew also loved their aircraft, and many were reduced to tears if their plane and their pilot failed to return. Clint describes his relationship with his own ground crew:

Ground crews were family—close family. I had the same ground crew from the time I arrived till my final mission. Leroy Katterhenry—Crew Chief, was quiet, industrious and dependable, with a superb knowledge of the aircraft.

Jim Cope sitting behind Bill Jordan. Jim learned to fly a Tiger Moth during his time with the 352nd FS. He had an interest in flying, caring deeply about his pilots. (*Nance, via Cross*)

John Kalar, Assistant Crew Chief, was a laid back character who enjoyed erotic British tabloids, enjoyed being the jokester, but always obliging and dependable. Ed Wolinski was armorer, meticulous with never a gun jam—all eight .50 caliber guns fired simultaneously every time without a hitch. His detonation fuse timing for low level bombing was to the second, and I never had a doubt releasing a 500 or 1,000 lb bomb on the deck, for I had 10 seconds to be in the clear.

As an officer, I was often asked to 'chaperone' ground crew parties when local residents were invited. I was considered fairly liberal to their delight. I have a letter, which I cherish, written by Leroy Katterhenry to my wife following my final mission. It's an example of a loyalty and dedication which I very likely owe my life.

Whilst Clint's recall regarding maintenance is based on 'regular' aircraft servicing, it is fair to say that he had several aborts during his operational time with the 353rd FG. However, most could not be attributed to his ground crew as there was an extended period of problems associated with the design and initial use of both belly and wing fuel tanks. The 353rd FG was just one of many Groups who were endeavoring to get increased range from their ships, and all were feeling the effects of the problems. It must be stated that although most instances were random and varied, the greatest difficulty was being experienced with fuel

Clint's Crew Chief, Leo Katterhenry, with his charge, *Mary Jayne*. Leo and his team supported Clint and 'their' Thunderbolt throughout his tour of operations. (Sperry)

feed from the tanks. As a result of poor-quality connections in the initial Group missions, there had been an unacceptable number of aborts on operations where the enemy was engaged, and the reduced number of ships put the mission and the remaining ships in mortal danger. Therefore, whilst the general serviceability continued to be relatively good, the problems with glass and other pipe-feed connections—caused mainly by engine vibration and violent air maneuvers—persisted for many months. Clint experienced those problems, and although SX-E was his favorite aircraft he was occasionally allocated other ships when it was out of commission. Those other ships were of a less-known quality and perceived as less reliable, as time would show.

Accidents unfortunately continued to occur during training, with tragic consequences. With the pilots back on flying status and a hectic schedule being carried out, it was not long before the Group's first 'English' tragedy struck. On 29 June Lt William M. Mathias, assistant Group Operations Officer, crashed and was killed while attempting mock combat maneuvers. An outstanding pilot and an original member of 352nd Squadron, he had been promoted up to Group. His loss was an enormous blow to everyone. Clint was flying a P-47D with him that day:

As a Fighter Group, we had been involved in mock combat training in the US between Squadrons and occasional Navy Fighter pilots from nearby Norfolk Naval airbase. Our skills in handling the P-47 continued by prearranged or spontaneous engagement while flying out of Goxhill. On 29th June, a flight of four led by Bill Mathias climbed into clear air under a layer of broken cumulus clouds with a base of between five and six thousand feet. The normal procedure was to climb to a reasonable altitude and at a proper signal fall into an in-line sort of rat race separating into elements of two for a series of wild maneuvering to avoid being a target with someone on your tail (Radio silence was the rule to keep radio channels clear for combat operational units).

On this day, while still just beneath the broken cloud layer, Bill Mathias, a highly respected pilot, was moving into a position that in actual combat could be deadly. We were just below the cloud base of four to five thousand feet, and because I could not out turn this experienced pilot, my only escape was to pull up with a roll out of the turn and continue the roll while climbing into the clouds. By completing a full roll in the clouds, I broke out on top and was elated to have shaken Bill (as a commercially rated pilot before the US Air Corp, I was a reasonably capable instrument pilot, and with a full attitude Gyro, a roll on instruments with a P-47 was a simple maneuver).

I circled in the clear on top for a break in the clouds to hopefully spot an unsuspecting Bill Mathias or anyone else in a game position. After an unsuccessful search for an engagement, I returned to base. Bill had not returned, but timing of flights was not that precise and he may have tied up with someone else.

I was completely undisturbed until back in operations it was announced that a P-47 had crashed in an open field a few miles from our base. In disbelief, witnesses had identified the aircraft as that flown by Bill Mathias.

I could not imagine what had caused this tragedy and was terribly concerned because I had been with Bill just minutes earlier in an ordinary practice mission. In shock I sat down with others to explain our encounter and attempt to determine what could have happened. I gave all the information that I could including the fact that Bill was on my tail as I rolled into the cloud deck and lost him as I broke out on top.

Dr Cope and others were going to the crash site and I went along. It took only a glance at the scarred earth to realize that Bill had hit the ground at a very high rate of speed at almost level attitude. The aircraft disintegrated into hundreds of pieces with the engine as the only recognizable part nearly 1,000ft from the point of impact. There were tears in my eyes (and there are as I write), as Dr Cope quietly led me away from the scene and they drove me back to base.

In sad reconstruction of the cause, it became apparent that Bill instead of completing his roll behind me, decided to pull through in a split S maneuver (a common tactic of evasion when inverted, you pull through as from the top of a loop). Bill misjudged his altitude and at a very high speed failed to pull the aircraft through before hitting the ground. A P-47 needs at least 9,000ft to safely complete such a maneuver and in a state of competitive edge, it cost

The crash site showing some of the remains of the P-47 flown by Lt Bill Mathias. (*USAF*)

him his very young life. The loss of Bill Mathias and the circumstances made a lasting impression on me through the war and one that has been with me through my life.

There is no doubt that the loss of good friends had a profound effect on Clint, and to be so closely involved in such a tragedy was a brutal and massive blow. Losing friends was bad enough and although certainly not responsible for the loss of Bill Mathias, Clint showed that he was deeply disturbed and extremely sensitive to the outcome of his part in the mock dogfight that led to the crash. However, Doc. Cope probably took it easy with Clint following that terrible incident; it is almost certain that he was keeping an eye open for after-effects, and he would have quietly taken Clint off flying for a break if he had considered it prudent at the time. Clint carried on flying; that was his job.

It was not the end of tragedies for the 353rd FG—in fact, far from it. As the training intensified and the time for operations approached, the need for improvement in combat tactics and maneuvers became more vital for the pilots as they sweated and wrung out themselves and their planes to offer a chance of survival in the coming months. But this came at great risk, and 24 July turned out to be another very bad day. Lts Jack Lepird and Harry McPherson were returning from a 352nd FS high-altitude practice mission when both were killed in unexplained circumstances. They had been up awhile when ground control heard one of them saying, 'Let's go home for lunch.' They never made it. The disaster inevitably led cynics to comment that the 352nd FS was becoming a 'bad luck' outfit. Needless to say, those accidents were certainly depleting the Squadron just at the time when all should have been combat-ready. Clint remembered:

> Both were great guys. I have pictures of both during our escapades to Thorpe Abbotts with female escorts. On the 24th, I was on base bicycling from barracks to Operations when I heard the terrible whine of a runaway prop and witnessed McPherson (not identified then) in a vertical dive that was unrecoverable. At an estimated 300ft, there was (now understood) an unmistakable sonic boom followed by the impact concussion. We hear sonic booms occasionally now, but this was in 1943.

Could that have been the impact sound of Lepird's plane hitting the ground a mile or so away, or was it the result of McPherson losing control when the incredible and almost uncontrollable speed of the P-47 built up in a dive? This was possible as the pilots were beginning to encounter 'compressibility' when the aircraft approached the speed of sound, and the controls stiffened or froze, making it nearly impossible to recover.

As newer and faster fighters were introduced compressibility would become a feature of flying to be avoided, but back then it was a little-known phenomenon that was ready to kill the unwary pilot. The Thunderbolt became renowned for that propensity due to its weight and fast diving speed. Diving was a typical maneuver encountered in combat, and one that could get a guy both into and out of trouble in double-quick time. But in a climb—that was a different matter. As previously observed, the Thunderbolt labored to gain height. Whatever the case, there were no further clues as to why those two were killed. Sad and chastened, the rest carried on and prepared for the move from their operational training base to Metfield, the recently completed operational airfield. Isolated in deepest Suffolk, with facilities capable of housing all the airmen, it would be the base for the 353rd Fighter Group for the tough eight months ahead.

Metfield Missions

A great deal of information was recorded by official and personal documents in England, forming the history of the 353rd Fighter Group's combat tour. It is most fortunate that in later years, and as a result of the efforts of a few key personnel in the Group and also one or two responsible historians, those records have been retained and archived. However, due to the passage of time, information has been difficult to access, and this has resulted in some events not being fully confirmed. As a consequence, when recounting facts relating to a mission or situations involving Clint, there may be a paucity of information surrounding that event or him personally. We therefore offer the most likely scenarios, which may enlighten and offer potential conclusions based on what is known. Nevertheless, it does appear that the records improved as the war progressed, and during the period of the Group's operational tour more detail began to emerge to enlighten and enhance their contribution to the war effort. That contribution commenced on that summer day in the fourth year of the Second World War.

The 353rd Fighter Group Headquarters moved to Metfield (Station F-366) on 4 August 1943, even though it was far from complete and still under construction.[1] Originally designed as a bomber base, there was accommodation for just under 3,000 airmen, but work was needed to bring the base up to operational status as soon as possible. However, the Group were soon to commence operations, and the Squadrons were allocated call signs following their move. The 350th FS was given 'Pipeful', the 351st FS was 'Roughman', and Clint's Squadron, the 352nd FS, was 'Wakeford'. These would be used on all missions until the move to Raydon in April 1944. Whilst the 350th FS and 351st FS moved in on 4 and 5 August respectively, the 350th FS were then sent on to Halesworth to work up with the already operational 56th Fighter Group, and the 351st FS were sent to Debden and the 4th Fighter Group. However, Clint and the 352nd FS flew direct from Goxhill to Duxford to work up with the experienced 78th Fighter Group. His memory of the move may have been somewhat hazy, for he sparingly recollected: 'All I remember is a short flight to Metfield'. Nevertheless, one thing

Clint's personal P-47, SX-E *Mary Jayne*, on a damp hard standing at Metfield. (*Sperry*)

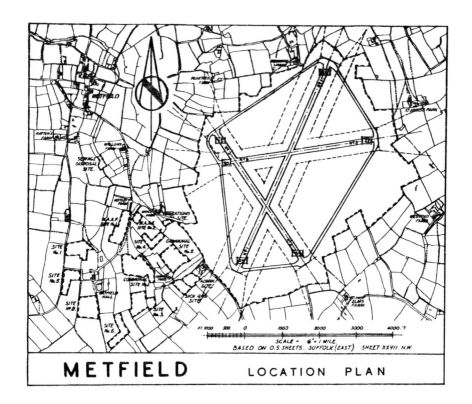

Metfield location plan. (*Crown Copyright, Royal Air Force Museum*)

was certain—Clint and the pilots in his Squadron were very much aware of the commitment they were about to make to the war effort. As volunteers, they had signed up to fly for the 352nd Fighter Squadron for the duration, and if they survived they would have to rack up at least 200 hours on operations in the ETO before they could head for home.[2] It would then be their choice as to whether they came back for a further tour or not. Throughout that time most would be fully aware of the total hours they had flown and also the number of missions, although it was the operational time in combat situations that determined their period on the front line. It mattered a great deal because it determined the time when they could return to their homes and families; that's what they were fighting for.

At that stage in the air war, the prime task of the fighters was to provide escort for the big guys. Eighth Bomber Command had still been building up its strength with front-line bombers and also the airfields to accommodate them. Their two main 'heavies' were the Boeing B-17 Flying Fortress and the Consolidated B-24 Liberator.[3, 4] Although different in performance and appearance, the aircrews that flew them had their preference, and most swore by whatever they were allocated to fly. Also available (in limited numbers in mid-1943), the Martin B-26 Marauder medium bomber suffered heavy losses by Luftwaffe fighters during unescorted early missions, but it also came with a 'killer' reputation.[5] Its advanced flight systems and high landing speed took the lives of many unsuspecting crews, although once mastered and transferred to the Ninth Air Force it performed with distinction.[6] However, it was the Fortress and Liberator that took the worst of the punishment by enemy fighters and flak in those early days, and it was those ships that the fighters had to protect. They just had to stop the Me109s, Me110s and Fw190s from attacking their 'Big Friends'.

The time had come for the first operation; although the 352nd FS continued putting in the hours, the initial training for war was finished. They carried out their first mission from Duxford on 9 August 1943, accompanying the 78th FG. During a day when the planned operation was on, postponed, and then reinstated, Clint and the 352nd were to make their first tentative steps over the North Sea to get the attention of the Luftwaffe. Life had an increasingly deadly edge from that day, as it was now the real deal and time for the Squadron to show its spurs.

It can only be imagined what the pilots were thinking as they entered the Duxford briefing room for that first operation; it was then delayed for a few hours, and they had to kick their heels and wait awhile for their first taste of combat. The Group had by then converted to the improved P-47D-2s, and as the day wore on they must have been in a strung-out state, riddled with anticipation and perhaps a little fear, sweating it out and hoping that their new Thunderbolts wouldn't let them down. Then they were finally being called to readiness and heading for their planes—getting that massive prop rotating and lifting off as a Squadron. It must have both looked and felt impressive—indestructible. Nerves

Lined up at Metfield and ready to go. Fully fuelled wing tanks, with extra gallons, for a long mission. (*Sperry*)

began to disappear, training kicked in, and their concentration became absolute for the task in hand.

To give the 353rd FG a taste of what it was like to intrude over enemy territory, Colonel Hubert 'Hub' Zemke (Group Commander of the 56th FG; fast becoming a legend in the Eighth Air Force and later with his feared 'Wolfpack') initiated the 350th FS of the 353rd FG on a sweep over Holland. Meanwhile, Major Christian led the 351st FS together with the 4th FG as they swept Le Touquet and Dunkirk. The 352nd FS were led that day by the young and aggressive Major Glenn Duncan, who hailed from Bering, Texas, and they were flying with the 78th FG. They were airborne for one hour and fifty minutes as they also carried out a sweep, this time over Abbeville. A total of 139 P-47s went to war.

As it happened, the Squadron didn't make contact with the enemy. Of course, they were full of nervous anticipation, alert, and even hoping that something would break the tension. With head swiveling and eyes alert, Clint was flying with Lts Johnson and Durlin, with Armstrong at the tail-end. For the 352nd FS, their sweep to Abbeville produced nothing; the 'Yellow-Nose Abbeville Kids' didn't come up to play.[7] Clint had a candid view:

> I flew on the first mission with 78th Group (fighter sweep) ... and was probably pleased that there was no conflict at the time. Like every *honest* pilot, a little apprehensive but grateful to be with a group with experience.

Clint was not operational again until 15 August, when his name was on the Flight Board for two missions. Going through briefing and pre-flight, he experienced the same feelings as before; there was the knot in the stomach, the anticipation, and then the surge of adrenaline as the 352nd FS, together with the 78th FG, lifted off from Duxford to rendezvous with several other Groups to carry out a diversion sweep around the region of Gravelines and Knokke. In spite of the flak around key defended areas there was no trade or loss, and Col. Morris led the Group home to land safely and prepare for the next mission later that evening. As ground crews rapidly checked over the aircraft, the pilots reflected on the previous hour or so over enemy territory and hoped that the missions would all be as easy as that morning. Although some were keen for action, others were just relieved that the mission had been 'a piece of cake'. However, as the action began to intensify and the 353rd FG began flying deeper into Germany, there would be very few easy operations. All the same, they had made a good start, and their discipline in the air had been encouraging for the operations that were to follow. Reflecting on that discipline and his flight position in formation during operations, Clint observed:

> The Squadron was normally composed of 4 flights of 4 aircraft each. There were designated Flight Leaders (usually senior pilots). From Langley to England, I usually led a flight with often the same wingman as a two aircraft team. Positions obviously advance as time passes. I occasionally flew wing position for Col. Duncan, and sometimes led his 2nd element.

It was early evening as the Squadron lifted off again from Duxford for the second mission of the day. Clint was leading one of the Flights from the 352nd FS in a joint operation with several other Groups scheduled to provide high cover escort for bombers coming back out from Calais. However, it was an abortive mission as the fighters didn't make contact, and after one hour and thirty minutes in the air the Squadrons landed back at their respective bases. Although there was no contact with the enemy, there was a tragic reminder of the possibility of random accidents befalling the unfortunate; one of their fellow pilots from the 78th FG crashed and was killed while landing back at Duxford. It was a sobering representation of what was yet to come.

The light was fading as the 352nd FS took off for their home base to be fitted with long-range belly tanks and get ready for action the following day.[8] Clint was not to join them as he was picked for another task—carrying out two flights on a vitally important sortie. As he recalled, it was 'the ice cream run!'

Clint had entered these two flights on the 16th as 'Met' (probably training); being recognized as one of the smoothest flyers in the Squadron, he not only carried out his weather duty but was trusted to bring the valuable supply safely back to home base.[9] Naturally, the higher he flew the cooler it kept the cargo, and it can only be guessed that he was looking forward to a privileged portion as befitting the courier on completion! Naturally, in the height of summer, it was a vital 'menial' task!

For those who were chosen for the bomber-escort operation that day, the outcome was far from favorable as they got split and tangled up with some

Clint fully geared up and about to enter the cockpit of *Mary Jayne*. His seat parachute and dinghy pack look mighty uncomfortable! (*Sperry*)

352nd Fighter Squadron P-47s in loose formation over France. SX-R, and although difficult to decipher, probably SX-Y. (*Sperry*)

Focke-Wulf 190s. Tragically, they lost their Group Commander, Col. Morris, who was leading the 352nd FS on that mission. Although against his own clear order of staying with the bombers, he was seen to break away and chase and damage a Fw190. Constantly harried by enemy aircraft, he followed yet another down in the mêlée, but was not seen again. Whatever his young pilots thought of his actions, Col. Morris was a brave man with a purpose and he went down fighting.

For the remainder of the Group there were mixed results as they broke off the fight, returned to base, and licked their wounds. They claimed two Fw190s damaged for two of their own. After Col. Morris's loss, the rest of the Squadron landed back at Duxford to prepare for the mission the following day. The Group had been blooded, in more ways than one. The ice cream had a sour taste that night.

In giving an insight to the kind of tasks the 'ordinary' pilot would have to carry out for his Squadron, first and foremost it must be understood that they did not fly all missions—in fact, it is on record that at least half their flights would be predominantly training and non-operational flying. No matter how good the pilot, no matter whether or not he wanted to go on operations, he would be rotated to provide Squadron support and training for missions, together with other menial tasks to assist the running of the Squadron. Amongst those that involved flying were: filling in as a spare, in case anyone dropped out of a mission; cross-country familiarization flights to get used to British flying conditions and locations; and instrument practice, particularly for bad weather and night flying. There was gunnery and, later in the year, bombing practice on the coastal ranges. Also, as if that wasn't enough, there were Met missions checking out weather for Bomber Command (a specialist task that was often allocated to Clint in the coming months), and 'slow-timing' to check out new or repaired ships.

It was also necessary to take up new Squadron pilots and introduce them to the area, and to have mock dogfights for combat training to give them a chance against the predators waiting for them over the other side. The Luftwaffe had to be respected as they were a very formidable force, and still very much in control of the skies over Central and Eastern Europe. For that reason alone, no 'rookie' pilot could be expected to be thrown in at the deep end, and, if time allowed, he would be given an 'easy' introduction to operations—probably ending up as a wing-man to an experienced pilot. In the RAF, a new pilot deemed 'fit' to start operations in the early days of the war would probably have been put as 'weaver' or 'tail end Charlie'—more irreverently known as 'Suicide Corner'. In the USAAF it was known as 'Purple Heart Charlie'. Whatever name it was given, that position was usually a baptism of fire and could mean an early death until the 'finger four' flight formation provided greater visual protection to that small group of ships. From the start of their operations in England, the USAAF generally operated that formation, shaped like the fingertips (no thumb) on an outstretched hand to enable each pilot to cover the sky and each other's 'six' (their butts!).

'A' Flight of 352nd Fighter Squadron, taken in the summer of 1943. Middle top is Durlin, then clockwise: Cles, Dansky, Armstrong, Sperry, Johnson, Vogel, and Geurtz. (*Sperry*)

After the aforementioned tasks had been carried out, there may just have been time to kick the starter and get airborne, hone their own combat skills, and improve their chance to survive the tour of duty on the front line. If they did, it was because they had been through the grinder, and most came out better for it. They may not have been great leaders of men, maybe not even wanted to be, but they were the very best that the Air Force could produce in the time available. Most were good enough and just a handful were exceptional, but virtually every one of them put his life on the line and had to fight for others—often.

Following the loss of Col. Morris in the scrap with Fw190s on 16 August, the experienced Lt Col. Loren G. McCollom, from the seasoned 56th FG, was an immediate and excellent choice as a replacement. He would soon be appreciated as a good tactician by the Group, and was very capable when carrying out his duties. This was seen on 17 August, which will forever remain a day to remember in the annals of the Mighty Eighth Bomber Command; it was a day of miscalculation, fortitude, bravery, sacrifice, and death.

The scientists and statisticians were constantly seeking ways of shortening the war by finding the panacea—the quick knockout, a body blow to bring a

B-17G named *Big Yank*,
with plenty of missions
painted on the nose,
and what appears to be
a picture of President
Roosevelt. (*Franklin
D. Roosevelt Library
Archives*)

rapid end to the conflict. They had determined a need to attack Schweinfurt, in Germany, as it was the center for the manufacture of ball bearings. To those in authority it seemed like a good idea and quite logical, as virtually all modern machinery—including aircraft, motorized vehicles, and production equipment—required the use of these insignificant but vital spherical components. But could it be successfully carried out? The Eighth was thrown the curve-ball.

On that fateful day, B-17 Flying Fortresses from nine Bomb Groups assembled at their respective air bases with the aim of attacking Schweinfurt. At a further seven air bases yet more B-17s gathered to prepare to attack Regensburg, with its Messerschmitt production factory and oil refineries—a grand total of 376 aircraft, laden with the means to destroy. To defend them, 240 P-47s were dispatched to escort them partway to and from the targets, and the mission for the 353rd FG was to protect the 146 bombers bound for Regensburg on the initial stage to the target. Although there had been very little opposition in the shape of the Luftwaffe, Lt Col. McCollom was leading the 353rd FG and managed to close onto and destroy a Messerschmitt 109G—the Group's first kill.[10]

However, the opposition knew the range of the P-47s, and they were just standing off until the fighters turned for home. When this occurred, Col. 'Hub' Zemke's 56th FG took over the escort duty, and because they had a 'straight-liner' to catch the B-17s, they were in a better fuel state, managing to go further into Germany and engage the German fighters with some success. The 353rd FG were naturally somewhat cut up because their excessive use of fuel—as they swung and fussed around the slower bombers on their way into the target—made it easy for the 56th FG to get into the enemy with a direct rendezvous. It was they who were tasked to protect the bomber streams further to their destinations; but it was not far enough, for the B-17s still remained unprotected by their 'Little Friends' for hours as they gallantly fought their way to and from their respective targets, and the carnage heaped upon the vulnerable and rapidly depleting force of Flying Fortresses was terrible as they struggled to keep decimated formations together. The German pilots were out to annihilate the bombers they called '*Viermots*' or '*Dicke Autos*', although in the final analysis they didn't quite succeed.[11]

Clint was leading a Flight on that first mission, although he did not participate in the second, again led by Lt Col. McCollom later in the day. As they escorted the straggling bombers home, it was evident that they had been very badly mauled, and the 'Little Friends' were a welcome sight—but for those bomber crews who survived the day, it was just too little too late. The P-47's lack of range prompted some severe and protracted debate and anger amongst the Bomber Groups, who had lost sixty aircraft and nearly ten times that number of young crewmen. It was an appalling day for the Mighty Eighth, and the fighter pilots could only feel intensely frustrated that they were unable to provide the cover so desperately needed for their 'Big Friends'. The airmen still retained a fighting spirit, but it was a bad day and their morale was low, and morale was a vital part of their combat psyche. Clint's own frustration was evident:

Eighth Air Force bombing raid over a German city. Bombs falling from the B-17 where this picture was taken have smashed off part of the tail-plane of the war-beaten Fortress below. Did the next bomb hit, or did the wounded ship make it home? (*Franklin D. Roosevelt Library Archives*)

Our mission was to protect the bombers, and in early days, it not only served to dissuade enemy fighters, it was a morale booster among the bomber crews. However, experience at war has proven that a mission accomplished more if the enemy fighter threat was pursued and destroyed. The protection tactic was also admitted as a mistake by the Luftwaffe in their earlier bomber escort missions as expressed by the Commander of German Fighter Forces, Adolf Galland, in his writing *The First and the Last*: 'The relay system worked well when the progress of the bombers was on schedule, but if they were late, the first fighter group would have to leave earlier than planned and there were often dangerous gaps without fighter cover. When bomber formations got spread out, our coverage got equally spread out, leaving areas open to alert fighter attack'.

The controversy over the close-escort tactics eventually came to a head and led to the ultimate replacement of General Hunter, the head of Fighter Command who was sitting in the hot seat during that period. If there were disagreements, it is likely that his advocacy of continuing with fighter sweeps was not Fighter Command policy during that period. With close support being given by the 'Little Friends', the bombers were still taking a pounding and were overwhelmed by enemy fighters, and that was apart from the serious numbers being lost to flak. With the limited range of the P-47s and P-38s at that time, there is no doubt that fighter pilots would feel that they had let down their 'Big Friends' and left them to their fate as they had to turn and head for home. The pilots wanted to get to the enemy before they approached the bombers, and they were aggressively agitating for this—yet they just didn't have the range to achieve it. The fighter pilots were all too aware that for many of the crews manning the bombers, it would be their final journey as they forged further into the Reich. It would be hard to take; Clint, for one, was clearly frustrated and distressed, and it showed during conversations with him in later years.

In spite of those emotions, the longer missions were just beginning for the Squadron, as the Group had been cutting their teeth on short escort missions and sweeps to gain experience. They had now begun to fly further into Europe to try to provide the protection so desperately needed by the bombers. As soon as they fitted drop tanks, and even though they were unreliable in operation, they eventually started to get that increased range. However, the Luftwaffe, sensing a weakness, had been a mean opponent, as they intercepted the escorts earlier to make them jettison their valuable lifeblood. The Group would have to persevere and take many more casualties until a conclusive answer to long-range bomber protection would emerge.[12] As for the targets on 17 August 1943, the bombers would have to return later to finish the job. And the fighter boys? They remained totally frustrated.

Met Flights

Bad weather then stalled more bombing raids, although there was one advantage that Clint had gained in the recent few days of action. He had gotten to know the new leader of the 353rd FG, and his view was that 'Col. McCollom was a great leader and real gentleman. Easy to be with and easy to talk to'. Regardless of his general opinion on authority, it is evident that Clint could and would occasionally connect with certain types of senior officer. He was obviously impressed with those who showed respect to their charges, and there is no doubt that Clint reciprocated and felt more comfortable in their presence.

As a further insight into his character and attitude at that time, Clint did confide that he just wasn't the kind of person to suck up to authority, be round the bar with them, or be noticed. Perhaps he could be viewed as a bit of a loner, being more reflective, aware of his family responsibilities, and even philosophic. On the ground, although he had good friends, he was more inclined to be away from those with whom he did not connect, and he enjoyed a life away from the base that did not encompass authority. It was there to be respected, though not necessarily fully embraced.

By now the pilots were getting well used to their P-47Ds, and as they were usually allocated the same aircraft on operations, they began to personalize them in the time-honored fashion. Having seen Clint adorn his aircraft with the name of his wife, Mary Jayne, the Squadron pilots turned to him for artistic inspiration, as recorded at the 353rd Reunion (352nd FS cadre) in 1983:

Waggoner: ... I've been trying to figure... my first nacelle that was painted was done by either Morrison or Sperry, I think. Who would it have been, up at Metfield there that was painting...?

Wurtzler: Sperry, Sperry. Sperry was an artist. I know that for sure. You've seen the picture of our Ops room that's in the Mustang book? Shows the thing above our place? Sperry did that with an air brush. Sperry was an artist. And

Lt Col. Loren McCollom was seconded from the 56th FG when Col. Morris was lost. He became a well-respected leader of the 353rd and a good tactician. He was brought down by flak to become a prisoner of war on 25 November 1943, and ended up at the same Stalag as his old boss at the 56th FG, Col. Zemke. (*Cross*)

I'll never forget one weekend he and I went to … I don't know where it was …. Colchester, Ipswich. And, of course, he liked nice things and we went in this stationery store and all he could talk about was the fine grade of paper, and of the stationery, you know. Of course, that was his….

Reinhardt: He's still in the business.

It certainly was a flair that Clint carried through life, and the authors were the recipients of several sketches as Clint visually expanded a story or two for them. These were greatly appreciated, proving that he had a fine artistic touch and a creative temperament that were very evident to his family all through his life. Clint would obviously have been carrying out those tasks in his free time; however, there were other distractions for a pilot with a little time on his hands or on leave:

I often slept late if not required in operations. It was more for the purpose of catch-up, for I spent many wonderful evenings at the local pubs. 'Time Gentlemen Please!' was a very familiar call in those days. If a bunch of us had a day off together, we often got on our bikes and toured the countryside.

Great, but there were rules relating to the use of bikes. For example, when Clint wanted to take a bike off base for a casual ride in the country, he would have to heed the missive circulated a few days earlier:

The picture when on the ship is actually about 34 or 35 inches high - The "mini" Mary about 10" high - Do the whole thing look fairly nice - Thats supposed to be a picture of you darling - Does it look like you?

Clint's sketch of the nose art for *Mary Jayne*, which he had sent to Mary for approval. (*Sperry*)

352nd Fighter Squadron artwork. This has probably been painted by Clint. (*Johnson, via Cross*)

Effective Monday 16th August, 1943, no bicycle issued to or used by members of this command will be allowed off limits of this station without proper lights. Bicycles will be equipped with both front and rear lights. The Provost Marshal will enforce this by checking the bicycles of both officers and enlisted men as they leave the limits of this station.

However, it is not known what penalties would be incurred if anyone were to perpetrate such a heinous crime!

In fact, there were rules relating to many things that an officer and enlisted man could or could not do. For example, a list was regularly updated as to which pubs were out of bounds. Sometimes the reason was segregation, other times dubious health issues—although one could probably state that in one form or another, the rules were for the discipline of the airmen! In actuality, poor drinking water and a lack of sanitation were the problems with those pubs, and there was a danger of catching something dire like trench mouth—or, of much greater concern, bovine tuberculosis, caused by milk not being pasteurized. So if Clint wanted to remain in good health and not be in trouble, it paid to be a regular reader of the Group 'Daily Bulletin' to keep up with the latest regulations.

Meanwhile, those at the highest level had more serious problems, far removed from the difficulties of individual communication and control at the lower levels of operation.

Relaxation for Clint in the peace and quiet of an English country lane. (*Sperry*)

Clint was back on the flight roster on the morning of 27 August, and although his Flight Record shows it was 'Training', he had over-written the entry as 'Met'. His navigational and flying experience had encouraged those in authority to recommend him for training for that vital meteorological task, and Clint was often sent up alone or occasionally with others to gain further knowledge and awareness of what was required during those flights. On that day, records show that he was flying as one of eleven Squadron ships instructed to locate to Predannack, near Mullion, on Cornwall's Lizard Peninsula. They started out from Metfield mid-morning and returned in mid-afternoon.

The Eighth AF was taking advantage of improving weather, and Clint, having returned from Cornwall, was on the Flight Board and with the Squadron for a late mission to provide close-escort support to B-17s coming out from a raid on Watten, in France. It would be the first Eighth Air Force attack on still-secret V-weapon rocket sites; the launch ramps and support facilities were being built for Hitler's new wonder weapons yet to strike fear into the lives of those in the east of England. Together with other Fighter Groups totaling 173 P-47s, McCollom was leading the Group and Bailey the 352nd FS as they patrolled north of the St Omer area, shepherding the bombers home. Second Lt Vogel of the 352nd FS was temporarily reported 'Missing in Action' (MIA), but he had been forced to land at another small base with no communications, and after a delay was eventually counted home. Records show an item of 'friendly fire' was noted, as one of the escorting fighters of the 56th FG was attacked and damaged when RAF Spitfires bounced the flight. One can only guess that it did not enthuse the Thunderbolt pilots, who occasionally were mistaken for Fw190s! The Group were in the air for about two hours; no gains, no losses, and another mission under the belt for Clint.

With 'friendly fire' always a distinct possibility in the whirling confusion of battle, it was understandable if pilots got a bit twitchy or superstitious about flying a mission. It was bad enough to have the enemy out to kill you, but with 'friendly fire' in the air, together with flak (both German and 'friendly'), mechanical failure, weather, fear, pilot error, and 'gremlins', the situation could get to a pilot. Clint, being pretty laid back, was philosophical about it:

I have my own inhibitions, but really no superstitions that I am conscious about. When the mission area was known or anticipated as being over France, I'd always wear my best flying clothes, including a well-polished pair of GI shoes and used to publicly show them off in operations and joke about it.

It was relaxing to consider the possibility of bailing out over Southern France and hiding out with some lovely French gal. If that was superstition it was a very pleasant thought.

Although at times he would be sorely tested, Clint appears to have had a pretty clear view of how he was going to get through the conflict. His confidence in his own flying ability was apparent from the outset. The only thing that could interfere and upset the situation was the lack of experience of others, mechanical failures, the Luftwaffe, flak, and a 'lovely French gal'! Of the latter, he would have to keep dreaming; he would encounter the others frequently. However, there were further problems that had to be considered.

With the increasing numbers of Allied aircrew finding themselves down in enemy territory, it became necessary to consider giving them aids to assist their evasion from the Germans. Therefore, apart from escape kits issued to all USAAF and RAF crews, they were also issued an identity picture showing them in 'civilian' clothes. However, an astute German intelligence officer would soon spot that the shirts, ties, and jackets often appeared to be (and were) identical. When the photographs were taken, they only had limited amounts of non-military clothing on base, and that meant guys from the same squadron or group would tend to have repeating attire—a small but vital error, as civilian clothes were not readily available in vast numbers during the war. However, if luck was on their side, the identity picture on a counterfeit document provided by the Resistance usually passed muster, and it was always best to try to get assistance from the Underground and wear 'original' local clothing and footwear.

The following day Clint logged an 'Ipswich–Met' flight, which appeared to be another training sortie, and he landed back at Metfield at 6.50 a.m. According to the 'CTL' (Control Tower Log), the weather then clamped down for the rest of the day and there were no further operations.[1]

The Met flights were not confirmed as such in some of Clint's earlier operational reports or in Squadron records, but by September '43 they ceased

This is the standard head-and-shoulders photo taken of Clint in case he was unfortunate enough to have to bail out or crash-land and attempt to evade. (*Cross*)

to be training and were occasionally entered in his Individual Flight Recoᵣ 'Other Operational'. However, he did confirm that he made quite a few of them during his combat period and intimated that they weren't all an easy ride. Bad weather, flak, and enemy aircraft were a constant danger to a single aircraft, and it would have to be an experienced pilot, confident flying on instruments, who would brave those great dangers to report on conditions suitable for Eighth Air Force operations. That may have contributed to a slightly lower mission rate for Clint in the difficult months both leading up to and beyond the winter of 1943–44, although his contribution to missions would have been no less vital. In fact, to return to base with valuable data on weather and enemy activity over the continent would be of paramount importance to the lives of many young fighting men. However, it does seem strange that those important flights didn't warrant mission credits. Steve observes:

When the Generals wanted intelligence that would do the greatest damage to the German war machine, he and his group and squadron commanders wanted the best information possible that could in any way benefit the men and aircraft to be put in harm's way. Reconnaissance flights to gather weather data over the Channel and the continent and ground movement when possible were high on that list of information.

Clint was good at this. He had his commercial and instrument rating before he joined and was comfortable boring up through overcast, heading over the Channel in dismal conditions to breakout over Holland or France or Germany. Knowing where he was at any given moment was critical both for himself, for bomber command (to whom the report would go) and, of course, the bomber crews who would use the information gained. What he'd bring back was directly dependent on what he could see so a heavy overcast that reached many miles east over the continent didn't allow for much ground observation unless he descended through the cloud to get a close look. This could be tricky since an altimeter reading based on barometric pressure could vary a great deal depending on what side of a front you were on. Your altimeter might be telling you that you were 500'~ higher than what was true and you couldn't ask German ATC for a local barometer reading. Most weather flights were just that and the info retrieved was to do with cloud cover and precipitation. How far did it reach, how thick, what altitude were the tops and what was the icing situation? Many of Clint's missions (plus several unrecorded missions) were reconnaissance of this nature.

So what was the routine for a Met flight? The first stage is to understand the meteorological problems. Weather patterns varied from England over into Europe on a constantly changing basis. Of course, it was (and still is) also appreciated that certain conditions would be localized in many areas, and those shifting weather patterns did disrupt planning for the many different types of sorties over enemy territory. The seasons naturally had an influence on daily weather conditions, but depending on the time of year there were many situations that caused potentially serious trouble for aircraft trying to fulfill missions. In the months leading up to and beyond winter there would be fog, snow, sleet, heavy cloud, and rain, compounded by freezing conditions at all levels. Furthermore, during the warmer months around summer there would be thunderstorms, early mist, rain, and cloud—although it remained intensely cold at height all year round. Also, in certain conditions there would be haze that formed even on the brightest of days, making it difficult for bombers to spot their targets and fighters to spot enemy aircraft. However, one element caused problems on many occasions throughout the year, day and night—wind. A ground wind of anything over 20 mph could make a cross-wind landing tricky, although it was not unknown for some aircraft to take off and land in strong gales. In doing so, they would have to try and carry them out against the prevailing blast, which was not always possible.

Of even greater danger was the unknown phenomenon now called the jet stream, which caused the most serious problems for aircraft during the war years. It puzzled the meteorologists, who could not accurately predict wind directions, and caused many Met officers to give a flawed forecast that could seriously compromise a mission over enemy territory. An anticipated wind speed could be given at a certain height, but when the height was exceeded wind could double in strength and even change direction, reaching speeds in excess of 150 mph. Thus, many times throughout the war, aircraft flying on estimated times in cloud by 'dead reckoning' could be seriously mistaken when trying to locate their position. Many aircraft had either overshot their home base or, conversely, thought they were over England and had not even left the coast of France! In that way it could be a killer, and it was on many occasions. It had therefore become regular practice to send out experienced pilots before any mission to report on conditions as they found them, on the routes to be predominantly flown by bombers and fighter-bombers—but it wasn't a perfect science.

On the morning of a planned bombing mission, Clint would have been warned in advance, probably by his Commanding Officer, Bill Bailey, that Bomber Command were requiring weather and reconnaissance reports for the route they were planning to follow. Most times he would be on his own. There was no Squadron briefing for him, no wingman to assist if he hit trouble, and probably breakfast on his own if he was lucky. He would carry out the same routine to prepare by getting his gear together, drawing a parachute (don't come back without it!), paying a visit to the latrines, stuffing his evasion kit in one of the many pockets of his flying suit, and stumbling across in his polished boots to see the Squadron Briefing and Intelligence Officers to discuss the route and requirements of the flight. Clint would also touch base with Lt Poindexter (a fellow 352nd FS pilot) in Operations to discuss any particular items that would be relevant to the flight.

There was much information to absorb apart from weather conditions, such as areas of flak to avoid (or confirm if unlucky), making notes of aircraft disposition on enemy aerodromes, troop concentrations, and many other requested observations. It was advisable to have a discussion with the Met Officer, taking notes on his knee-pad, maps about expected weather patterns, and being told what to look out for and observe. Clint would then make a quick visit to the control tower and finally hack watches for a take-off time.

Having cleared all the information through his memory bank, he would hitch a ride in a jeep over to his P-47 and check out with his ground crew that all was in order for his flight ahead. Someone had already told them how much gas to put in, and Clint would then know that fuel, ammunition, and the aircraft were prepared for flight. It was time to go.

In later years, Clint recounted that he favored flying alone on that type of mission:

I discovered that my 94 credited missions did not include 13 weather reconnaissance flights made for Bomber Command. I held an advanced instrument rating and a knowledge of Meteorology, which put me on the roster for such flights.

I thoroughly enjoyed these flights. They offered the challenge of weather flying (lots of instrument time), but most enjoyable was to be in the clear to view and study the continent without the normal distractions. On occasion I'd draw a few bursts of flak, but I'm sure for the most part to simply prove they knew I was there. Some of the returns to base were far more exciting but I'll save those stories for another time.

Checking over the information for the next mission in the 352nd FS Ready Room at Metfield. (*Cross*)

Activity in the Metfield 352nd FS Ready Room taken from another angle. (*Cross*)

Apart from the high likelihood of poor weather conditions on return, Clint's last comment may have referred to the constant problem that most fighters encountered when flying over the English Channel and coastal areas of England—the British Royal Navy always fired first and asked questions later! Also, the defense batteries along the English coast were especially prone to mistake the Thunderbolts for Fw190s, and the Spitfires (and eventually Mustangs) for Me109s. This was most annoying for a guy sweating it out to return to base! Fortunately, their shooting wasn't too good at the fast moving targets, though several did become victims of so-called 'friendly' ground fire.

So for the guy picked to do the weather sortie, it wasn't just getting up there, looking around, and reporting that the sun was shining or it was raining; it was considerably more important and involved. If it was for Bomber Command, and most of his Met flights appeared to be, it was necessary to give clear reports on cloud formations at various heights, barometric pressure, wind speeds, temperature, condensation and icing levels, and also to note any enemy dispositions that may have changed or altered from information previously gained. It was a very important and challenging job, one that could cost lives and result in the success or failure of a mission. It was a great responsibility and it was Clint's job on several occasions throughout his tour.

Grim Finale to Summer

On 30 August Clint flew locally on a couple of occasions, one flight being recorded as 'Local–Cine Gun'. In all probability, that was shooting at sleeve targets or carrying out mock dog-fights with RAF fighters and bombers, as shown in some gun camera footage Clint had been allowed to retain for himself. However, it is also possible that he was carrying out some firing practice over the coastal ranges.

Apart from cine-gun practice, Squadron tasks and duff weather, conditions on the ground around the airfield were still far from ideal, and the Duty Officer recorded in the 'CTL': 'Inspected airfield—obstructions & ditches still scattered all over field. Extreme danger for all A/C not staying on perimeter track...' That was yet another problem the pilots were faced with before they could fly and fight—a partially finished air base. All but the permanent RAF bases, established well before the war, were suffering from similar problems, but to a slightly lesser extent.[1] The necessity of timescale had not allowed the overstretched but somewhat-labored workforce to complete the many bases set up for the USAAF when they joined their allies in 1941; some would never be completely finished, even at the end of hostilities. Ironically, many were then decommissioned and returned back to their original state for agriculture.

Clint was again requested to do a short Met sortie on the 31st, *en route* to Thorney Island, and following that flight joined 160 P-47s, including the 353rd FG with other Fighter Groups, in a close-escort mission to B-17s destined for targets around Amiens, in France. It was, however, a bad day for the Group, and particularly tragic for two pilots of Clint's flight:

On 31 August, 353rd Fighter Group led by Col McCollom was to escort a B-17 Bomber Group over southern France. I was leading the 2nd section flight of 4 on top of a solid overcast. As our fighter group attempted to sight the bomber group, we were executing a shallow left turn. As in any group turn the outside flights slowly slide under the flight or flights above in order to hold position at turn completion with minimum power change. The maneuver is a normal procedure

Col. McCollom briefing a small number of pilots from all three Squadrons.
Front row, left to right: Lorance, Odom, Newhart, Pidduck, Dinse (all 350th).
Second row, left to right: Angelo (350th) Treitz, Maguire, Field, Albert (351st).
Third row, left to right: Juntilla, Newman, Sperry, Fogarty, Jordan (all 352nd).
At the back, with spotted scarf, is Fred Lefebre. (*Sperry*)

and applies to a four aircraft flight as well as with a Group. In this case, my wing man was on my right and as I signaled for a left turn, he automatically slid slowly to the left under me while Dansky (leading my 2nd element) slowly slid to the right and his wing man would normally (simultaneously) move to the right under Dansky to the outside as we turned. If properly executed, at mid turn all four aircraft would be stacked vertically and at turn completion would be in normal flight configuration but with the 2nd element now on the right. Both Dansky and Murden were below and behind me out of sight at mid turn when they collided. I witnessed out of the corner of my eye one of the two spin off to the right but was not in a position to know what had happened, and had to hold my course to avoid further trouble. A split second with a tragic result. It was later learned that the bombers we were supposed to escort aborted the mission because of weather and two of them collided over the channel during their return. A very sad day.

Sadly, Lt Lester L. Dansky was killed as a result of the collision, but Lt Robert T. Murden was captured to become a prisoner of war for the duration.

Following the tragic accident, and checking Clint's records, it appears that he was returning to Thorney Island when he experienced a magneto problem. He states on his Flight Record: 'R.O.N. [Remained Over-Night] Thorney Island Engine trouble'.

It is apparent from Clint's earlier recollection relating to this occurrence that he may have initially confused the Isle of Wight as a base instead of Thorney Island. He recalled:

I experienced a minor power drop a few minutes out of Isle of Wight, a base we often used for more range into Southern France, and discovered that only 1 magneto was working.

Before the outbreak of war there were several airfields on the Isle of Wight, but when the specter of a German invasion loomed during 1939–41, the landing areas were obstructed to prevent their use by invasion forces. Only one strip remained open, although it was far too small for P-47s and certainly not a base for refueling. Therefore it appears that Clint's later recall is more precise:

Missions from Thorney Island and Ford were of course to be closer to western France. It would be hard to distinguish between the two. I do remember most hospitable treatment and the great teatime refreshments in old, but handsome quarters. RAF crews at Ford (an airfield from which my father flew with the US Army Air Corps in November, 1918) were unaccustomed to the huge R-2800 engine in the P-47.

I had lost my right magneto following a mission return to Thorney Island and had to delay my return to Metfield hoping to get it fixed. Finally gave up and flew home on one mag (one plug firing per cylinder instead of two).

In a handwritten note in his Flight Record for the next day (1 September), Clint reports that after accepting the hospitality offered by the RAF they were unable to repair the problem, so he carried out a fifty-minute flight from Thorney Island to Station F-366 (Metfield) with only a single engine magneto operating.[2] On arrival at Metfield he was subsequently 'disciplined' for that misdemeanor as it was considered a serious risk to fly with only one mag. serviceable. After he landed he then carried out a one-hour flight, probably to check on his repaired magneto— no doubt still smarting from the kick in the butt from the boss!

It is possible during the one-hour flight that Clint just might have been in the same bit of sky as some pilots in his Squadron, as they were also shown the dog-house. At 3.45 p.m. the 'CTL' records:

Combat operations filed complaint against pilots of 352 for alleged low flying over Lowestoft, Coltishall, & Yarmouth. Want written report from squadron as to actions taken in the matter. Time approx 15-00. Referred matter to 352 operations (Lt Poindexter) with instructions to comply.

It was probably a big dog-house that night, but for Clint, with the previous days' mission and tragedy still on his mind, it was a sobering time. Perhaps that infraction of the rules helped to detoxify the events just a little?

August had been a month of many varying incidents for Clint and the Squadron, and during that period he flew six missions and recorded over ten hours of operational time. It was an interesting and difficult start to his tour, but he had a long way to go before he could even start to think of going home.

The missions slowly began to rack up, and even though the weather was not complying, September operations commenced with a close escort to bombers over the Brussels area on the 2nd. In fact, during the coming month, out of a total of just over thirty-three hours flown, Clint recorded in excess of twenty-five hours of 'training', with flights to various airfields around the south of England. Other pilots would have been similarly assigned, as the Squadron gained more experience from that type of training for the intensive operations anticipated in the months ahead.

Whilst the pilots put in the hours, the guys on the ground were constantly on alert for any sign of the enemy, and exercises were frequent to keep them on their toes in the event of an emergency—or at least that was the intention. There were gas alerts, air raid warnings, and reminders to watch out for saboteurs and strangers on the base, although it didn't stop an embarrassing situation that was laid on 352nd FS on the 5th. The 'CTL' recorded:

Two ships SX-K and SX-P took off from this field. We put in a call through to 352 ops for information concerning them and they were unable to furnish it. Lt Reggis called from Halesworth saying two pilots, Lt Barnum and Lt Godfrey, had taken these ships without anyone knowing and flew them there as part of an escape exercise. Called 352 ops and notified them of this. Called Group ops and notified them of same.

That was a very painful example of the lax security on the base, and it was extremely embarrassing for all concerned. Someone would have been hauled over the coals for that audacious episode; nevertheless, it would probably be a very good guess that 352nd FS pilots would have had a sneaky admiration for those two rustlers from Halesworth! One wonders if anyone reminded them that cattle thieves used to be hung out West.

The search for the vital answer to extend the range of fighters continued. Many aircraft manufacturers, scientists, and maintenance outfits were experimenting with different options of size and application for belly tanks to increase the performance, reliability, and endurance of the fighters. Some were fabricated out of resinated paper or papier-mâché originally designed for ferrying aircraft, while others were being fashioned from aluminum. They had all created a tough challenge for the technical experts; with the paper configuration, for example, if fuel was left in the tanks too long then the seals perished and the tank would leak. Fuel connections were also a problem that continued for many months and became a serious threat to a pilot deep in enemy territory. The design, application, and operation had not yet become a precise science, and the innovators were in the middle of a learning curve.

During the previous weeks the Group had been testing a variety of drop tanks to extend their penetration and provide bomber protection further into enemy territory. At that time it was observed that the most reliable tank, and the one most likely to increase the P-47's range in the second half of 1943, was the 75-gallon 'teardrop' tank. Slung under the fuselage of the Thunderbolts, they enabled the aircraft to increase their theoretical range to 340 miles. Unfortunately, there were problems of quality and performance. An example of the frustration suffered by P-47 Groups was a mission flown by the 56th FG on 6 September, when there had been a substantial failure that resulted in an incredible nineteen aborts. It was these kind of incidents that were dangerously unacceptable.

As the bombers extended the range of their operations, so the fighters tasked to protect them continued to experiment with ever-increasing tank capacity, and eventually both belly and then wing tanks became vital for the majority of missions. As soon as enemy aircraft were sighted, the tanks would be dropped (if they had time or remembered), as it would be most unwise to mix it with them attached. Clint had his own view:

Belly tanks or wing tanks posed few problems. Their attachment to the fuel system was a glass elbow which would break off the tank(s), but at times, if not carefully aligned, would break during take-off or exceptionally rough air. Obviously, release prior to impending combat allowed more maneuverability (even if empty). We wanted to keep them as long as possible until empty. Occasionally, at release time, there would be a hang up of either a wing tank or belly tank causing excessive drag which could cause a trim problem when a wing tank. Fortunately the problem was rare.

Two fuelled-up P-47s just about to lift off from Metfield. Although difficult to discern, there are two P-47s ahead that had just taken off. (*Sperry*)

This was a retrospective view by Clint given many years after the event, and probably did not fully reflect the difficulties that were experienced during his combat tour. However, it is relevant to the current period that 'tanks' in general were becoming more vital for the fighters to carry out their task of protecting bombers as they fought ever deeper into Germany. From the pilots' point of view, the sooner they got rid of them the better. They were a hindrance in combat and a hell of a fire hazard if punctured by flak, machine-gun fire, or cannon fire.

Major Bailey again chose Clint for a lone operation in marginal conditions on 9 September; he was tasked with carrying out a weather reconnaissance flight for Bomber Command. Clint was in the air for an hour and his findings were reported back to Bomber Command Headquarters. The 352nd FS and the rest of the Group took off in the late afternoon, their aim being to escort B-17s from the 3rd Task Force. The weather had unfortunately rapidly deteriorated and, after encountering dense cloud at 17,000 feet, it was decided to abort the mission and head back for base.

Although it was not a successful outcome to the mission, Clint's observations would have been carefully noted. It did not necessarily follow that his report came with a recommendation, but it would provide a good indication of what conditions were like over the Continent. It was left to those in higher places to make that decision. The pressures on Bomber Command were such that they flew many times in very marginal weather, and there would be other elements in their final decision that indicated a go or no-go for a mission. Whatever the case, the Met flights were a vital part of the decision-making process, and the result of Clint's mission that day was an indication of things to come.

Appalling weather then closed in, covering East Anglia with a thick and impenetrable blanket of fog that forced all operations to cease. Apart from very

A very relaxed Major Bailey sitting on the bonnet of a jeep in the sun, with binoculars at the ready to spot aircraft in the circuit. (*Sperry*)

local air tests or 'slow timing' aircraft that had new or repaired engines, there were no other air movements. It was just too perilous.

When requested to explain an event that occurred during the inactivity of that period, Clint replied, '14th Sept? Must have been two flights but I don't recall the problem. Can't remember ever being confined to base except day before D-Day. Sometimes wonder where I was?' Well, it is here that we must take up this small 'problem' with the young fighter pilot. 'Squadron Order Number 36' reported:

> Under the provisions of Article of War 104, the following named Officers are hereby restricted to the limits AAF Station F-366 for a period of one (1) week effective this date and will forfeit their forthcoming days off privileges.

Amongst the eight names is a certain '1st Lt Sperry, Clinton H. 0793548'. Apparently, their misdemeanors relating to the incident were covered in the War Department Technical Manual, Article 104, and represented 'minor infractions of the rules'. It appears that his single mag. problem and the low-flying fun the Squadron had on 1 September came home to roost! Whatever those 'privileges' were, the guys would have to suffer without them for a week, as a lost visit to the local pub would do them no harm.

Clint was also fortunate that his pay wasn't docked for that 'infraction'. As a 1st Lieutenant he would have an annual salary of $2,000, with a small extra for service time. There were also bonuses. He would get a further allowance of 10 per cent of base pay for overseas service, and if he put in a minimum required number of flying hours (most did!), he was entitled to a further 50 per cent of base pay. Putting it mildly, in those austere times, Clint was wealthy! With not a great deal to spend it on in the locality, he would send a sizable sum to Mary at regular intervals. She would have found his provision of support for their expanding family extremely welcome, and if they were able to save their dollars, it would assist in setting them up for the future—whatever that might be.

Being confined to base would have concentrated further thoughts regarding discipline. It was during this period that the 'Daily Bulletin' was giving all sorts of guidance and instructions on many things pertaining to the running of the base and the guidance of all who worked therein. There were furlough rules, security and behavioral discipline, German bomb recognition lessons, rules to do with observation of military courtesy on and off the station, rules on blackout violations, rules on limitations of telephone calls and restricted use of flashlights, rules on security of arms, and rules regarding the shooting of game on farmers' land. In fact it seems that there were rules for simply everything! Whatever 'minor infractions' had occurred, there was a war on, and rules had to be obeyed. Most of them were, but many were bent more than a little!

On the 22nd Clint was with the Squadron when the Group carried out a late-morning Rodeo fighter sweep in the region of Rotterdam and Utrecht. They were

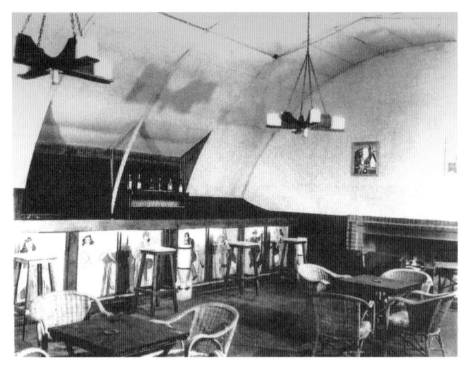

If the English pubs were out of bounds, it was necessary to 'rough it' in the Group's own Auger Inn. They did have a little luxury at Metfield! (*Cross*)

Lt Col. McCollom exchanges salutes as Metfield is officially handed over to the 353rd Fighter Group on 20 September 1943. (*Byers, via Cross*)

Two P-47s, SX-I (Bill Geurtz's aircraft), nearest the camera, and SX-Y (Bill Streit's aircraft) take off from Metfield; both are hitched up with teardrop belly tanks. (*Sperry*)

bounced by Me109s over Schoonhoven but were able to turn the tables on them, with Capt. Hoey (Group Headquarters) and Lt Gonnam of the 352nd claiming one apiece in the action; however, for Clint the mission had been unusually uneventful. Late in the day, the Squadron hitched up belly tanks and flew down to Ford with the Group in preparation for the operation on the 23rd, although it appears that Clint had problems; a note logged at 11.50 a.m. in the 'CTL' states: 'Ops B controller called and said that SX-E was having trouble with his radio...'

Clint's regular ship was SX-E, as many of the established pilots had their own allocated aircraft. As an interesting footnote to his troubles, the authors of this book are each proud keepers of a model P-47D that was handcrafted in wood by Clint to show his regular aircraft. He had painstakingly carved two pristine models from the ancient broken timber cover from the old Sperry family well, and then painted them both with the markings SX-E. They were extremely precise in detail and most superbly made by Clint the craftsman. Although the coincidence is not proven, it is quite probable that it was Clint who reported 'that SX-E was having trouble with his radio' and was unable to participate in the operation that day.

Clint was again in the air on the 25th with a flight to his old fighter operational training base at Goxhill, where he carried out a short local hop and then returned to Metfield. He recorded no more flights until 4 October as special orders were cut, giving him a few days' leave:

If I had a 3-day pass, I'd either head for Wales on the train to visit with friends whom I met during a leave in London. I don't remember RAF pilots visiting with us at Goxhill, but I do remember meeting with them at Hornchurch after we got aircraft. During the summer's double daylight War Time, on occasion I'd fly my P-47 to Hornchurch and go into London on the tube with RAF friends I met during a short stay there. A wonderful (wild) bunch, who would treat me to

Taken at Metfield, this picture shows Clint
looking a real cool dude in his Zoot hat. The
smiling face behind the window is Lt Leslie Cles.
(*Burlingame, via Cross*)

the Embassy Club, which meant staying over to fly home next day. Readers of
this stuff are going to wonder what WAR was.

Maybe Clint just came up on the roster, or did Jim Cope suggest it? The 352nd
Squadron Flight Surgeon, Capt. James Cope, was a very well-respected and astute
reader of the stress and strain that followed the fighter jocks. The majority were
young, devil-may-care guys who thought that they could carry out their duty, day
after day, without any effect upon their persona—but it soon transpired that the
majority couldn't. Jim Cope would mostly spot the signs, both physical and mental,
before the pilot did himself and others harm. He would quietly take him to one side
and check him out, and if the problem was likely to manifest into something more
serious, he would recommend a few days away to let the pilot clear the problem.
Maybe the guy just didn't realize he was jaded; maybe he didn't want to be labeled
as such and be taken off operations. Others, more aware of their varying ailments,
would confide in him, probably before the ailments became obvious to others.
However, the vast majority needed those breaks to cut the throttle and just chill out.
    Whatever the case, it is fair to say that all Flight Surgeons had a tremendous
responsibility and generally handled their charges with great care. The guys
couldn't be wrapped in cotton wool, for their role was to knock down and
destroy the enemy. They had to be tough to do it, but it was the Doc who was
usually consulted when the time came to slow down a spent jockey. However, if
Clint did head for Wales, it is unlikely that it would be at Jim's behest. Maybe he
had other plans? Whatever they were, he would note that he was operationally
involved in five more missions, totaling nearly seven hours, in September. It could
be perceived as a slow start, but it counted.

10

The Fog of Autumn

It was often perceived by non-flyers that life in the Air Force was glamorous, but that was far from the truth. In every Squadron, in every Fighter Group, jobs were performed that were onerous, boring, annoying, and sometimes downright frightening; in fact, there was always something to complain about. Every time a mission took place, many tasks were fulfilled on the ground to enable it to happen; unless those tasks were completed by airmen at the front and rear, according to orders, the mission couldn't possibly succeed. It would take a book in itself to paint the full picture, but a short chain of events offers a clue.

On the day of a mission it was likely that those on duty would begin in the pitch blackness, especially as winter was approaching. Not such a bad thing in summer, but in winter there would be some poor guy who would make his way through mud-splattered walkways, slipping and sliding on wet or frozen duck boards, to find the relevant Quonset hut (known in England as the Nissen) and give the wake-up call to those least likely to want it.[1] Those low-slung, corrugated-iron huts where the pilots hunkered down were no luxury hotels, and warmth was an old pot heater that the Limeys swore by and at, throwing out just enough heat to warm the butt of a fly if it pan-caked on it. It needed fuel, and there were coke-covered guys who hauled it. Those apologies for heaters were basic and totally inadequate, and, as winter approached, men in their bunks were hidden under layers of clothes and blankets to stop from freezing. They were delighted to get the wake-up call and hear the news that there was a mission later that morning; the caller was roundly cussed for his trouble.

They had to eat. To wake up cold and hungry, accompanied by grumbling stomachs (and occasionally hungover), they had to rely on the delectable cuisine prepared by the cooks. Those culinary guys sometimes got it right, but wartime food, with British produce thrown in, could be barely tolerable— putting it mildly. Even though the cooks were up at the crack of dawn to prepare the chow, appreciation for them was limited; on the other hand, they were vital if only to serve that absolutely necessary first steaming hot coffee of the day. For the pilots, theirs was the best fare—ham and real eggs if they were lucky—but the ground-pounders had a tough time waiting to be fed, as they had to hang on in there until the planes had departed. It was rarely real eggs for them—just the powdered variety. There was muted conversation, silence, or the odd question like 'Who was that dog you were walking last night?' Then, having completed chow (if their guts could take it), there was the statutory visit to the latrines to say, 'Hi,' or 'Tough shit,' to the poor airman who'd been put on a charge the previous day, and for his sins had drawn the short straw for keeping them clean. Someone had to do it. Others broke out into the cold, damp air and squelched their way to do whatever job they had drawn for the coming day—admin, engineering, armaments, intelligence, or one of the hundreds of other tasks that made the mission happen and the base tick.

While this was going on, the crew chiefs, armorers, and all guys who made the ships fly were attending to the tasks around the P-47s to prepare for the mission. Some were probably up all night repairing airframes and engines that had got in the way of a Jerry shell or two. Trouble with some vital part of the aircraft could cause it to abort or crash if they missed something essential—they dare not miss anything. With extremities frozen and wet, they were more often than not out on the flight line before daylight, ensuring that 'their' pilot, flying 'their' plane, had no cause for complaint over the next few hours—'their' pilot, who they would most likely shed a tear or cuss for if he failed to return.

So what of the pilots' preparation following breakfast? They gathered in the smoke-filled briefing hut to await the Group Commander, who greeted them on entering and introduced the other key guys. It was just part of the formality, as the jocks already knew them well. He succinctly informed them of their task for the coming mission as the target map was exposed to the occasional and irreverent comments of those gathered. He proceeded to inform them of the courses to be flown, who they were to escort, and where to rendezvous with the 'heavies'—or, as the months progressed, it could be a mission for a bombing or ground strafing job. Now, that screwed them up and they'd complain. They were told when to press starters, the time for take-off, what altitudes to fly, codes for communications, and all other incidentals vital to the mission. More often than not, the whole exercise was short and to the point, with only an occasional moment of light relief—usually reserved for the Met Officer, who had an uncanny knack of raising their doubts or being over-optimistic as to what kind of weather they were about to encounter. If there were no further questions, the jocks (now laden with their flying gear) then stumbled out to the jeeps to be taken to their ships, or first to pay a rapid visit to the latrines to satisfy nervous tension and squeeze enough to last them back to the barn a few hours later—no way did they want to use that goddamned relief tube. Mounting up, they taxied out and took-off in a pre-arranged sequence, all planned to occur in the shortest possible time as time was fuel, and fuel was the valuable commodity that enabled their mission to help the 'Big Friends'.

Then there were those flyers not on missions, who were briefed for 'other duties', or those on furlough or sick leave. These pilots had to do the 'other' jobs, such as air tests and practice flights, for it wasn't their shift to shoot down the enemy, blow up locomotives, or to be shot down and (if lucky) spend the rest of the war in one of Adolf's Stalags. For the earth-bound airmen, it was just another day of grind to keep those guys in the air and to keep Jerry guessing. Without them there was no squadron, no flyers, and no war to win. Those guys were the backbone of the Air Force, and it was they who felt the pain as they counted the ships back in and someone was missing.

On 8 October the air was again thick with tension at the morning briefings on many USAAF bomber and fighter bases throughout East Anglia. A force of B-17s of the 1st and 3rd Bomb Division were ordered to attack shipyards and industrial areas around the City of Bremen, while B-24s of the 2nd Bomb Division targeted the U-boat yards at Vegesack, a few miles from Bremen on the Weser River. Together with other Fighter Groups, the Squadron and 353rd FG prepared for the anticipated battle ahead. Clint and his fellow pilots were, as usual, screwed up with anticipation and eager to wrap their defense formation around the 'Big Friends'. On this occasion they would be flying high cover, escorting the bombers into their target. It was a tense and exhausting day for the Group, and it was the start of what was soon to be known as the infamous 'Black Week'.

All three Group Squadrons made contact with the enemy as Me109s, Me110s and Fw190s fought to get up close to the bombers, with one fighter just getting too close in his pass and ramming into a B-17, ripping it apart. It was mayhem, and the 352nd FG were actively engaged chasing off attacking German fighters that were desperate to get at the 'Viermots'. Apart from one 'kill', several enemy aircraft (e/a) were damaged, but there was no loss to the Group. Out of nearly 400 bombers dispatched to both targets, thirty were lost and a staggering 236 were damaged. Clint observed:

> The frustrations were heart breaking as we watched relatively helpless bomber after bomber go down. Having to leave or risk losing our own aircraft made it much worse. The Luftwaffe was desperate and showed real guts in their attacks—straight on from behind and underneath. We would try to intercept them before the attack, but they were well aware of our range and waited for the advantage.

It was a vicious and bloody battle, and while many fighters saw action, many others of the 274 P-47s dispatched from six Groups saw very little; only twelve e/a were claimed destroyed, although the gunners on the bombers claimed an astounding 167. This was surely a case of over-claiming in the heat of the battle, but such were the inconsistencies of air combat. There was no doubt that McCollom and Duncan, together with the pilots, were terribly cut up when they couldn't escort the bombers all the way to their targets and back. The sight of so many of their 'Big Friends' going down in the costly battles had been frustrating, and must have given the impetus to Duncan to consider other possibilities for their protection. The fitting of belly tanks had been a start, but they were operating inconsistently and causing problems. What they needed was a more aggressive policy to tackle the Luftwaffe; one that would hit where it hurt and get them before they got to the bombers. It would come soon, but not soon enough for Bomber Command.

It was probably on this mission that Clint encountered compressibility. His son, Steve, recalls the occasion when Clint told him that it was encountered south of Bremen, following a Fw190 attack:

> Dad often spoke of the possibility of breaking the sound barrier in a Thunderbolt. The occasion … focused on a dive away from a '190 where he felt his airplane approached (or exceeded) 580 knots out of 30,000 feet. Certainly a '47 could dive faster than most if not all WWII fighters and was probably rugged enough to handle the stress but whether a pilot could recover is a definite question.

He recovered.

Bad visibility initially closed the field on 10 October, but the weather eventually improved later in the morning, and it was Mission 34 for the Squadron (and sixteen for Clint—excluding Met flights) as they gathered to hear the Briefing Officer give them the gen for the afternoon operation. They were ordered to escort Flying Fortresses out of Münster, where they were to bomb railways, the rail workers' homes, and canals—that is, tasked to destroy the enemy transport infrastructure. The pilots heaved their gear and themselves into trucks, and were driven to their planes; after pre-flight checks, all three Group Squadrons were recorded airborne at 2.04 p.m. They were soon busy. Just after rendezvous with the battered bombers, many of the Group became embroiled in a running fight with the Luftwaffe. Led by Major Bailey, the 352nd FS had a short engagement with a Me110 as they returned from their escort duties; however, although it was damaged it managed to escape a more decisive consequence. All ships in the Group made it home without loss, accounting for five of the enemy. It was a good day at the expense of the Luftwaffe but a bad day for the bombers, who lost thirty of their number—in particular the 100BG, which was virtually wiped out and thereafter labeled 'The Bloody 100th'.

Following the mission to Schweinfurt and Regensburg on 17 August, lessons were learned by both Fighter and Bomber Command. They were hoping for better results on 14 October, as the Eighth headed once more to Schweinfurt. Clint was not on this mission as the 353rd FG lifted off to provide penetration support for 149 B-17s of the 1st Bomber Division. Cloud conditions over Europe were difficult, but the Group were 'sitting on the perch', waiting to pounce on

On returning from a mission, Clint is debriefed by Capt. Wurtzler, the Intelligence Officer of the 352nd Fighter Squadron. (*Cross*)

their prey; they were soon involved in hectic dogfights as they endeavored to protect the bombers. In frenetic exchanges with Luftwaffe fighters, the Group were able to claim eleven e/a destroyed, but they lost two pilots from the 350th FS. Lt Dwight Fry was able to bail out and evaded capture. Lt Robert Peters nearly made it home but fatally crashed near Brentwood, in Essex—heartbreakingly, just a few minutes from home.

Whatever lessons had been learnt during the earlier mission, the Luftwaffe and flak had been able to inflict very severe losses yet again on the bombers, as sixty were lost to all causes. It was a significant watershed, and the Eighth didn't carry out further deep-penetration raids into Germany for several months. The ability to provide limited escort support to the 'Big Friends' on extended missions was just too costly, so the strategy changed and bomber missions were only carried out where escort could be provided by P-47s and P-38s all the way to the target. That would change as drop tank sizes increased range, but also when the Mustangs with their long legs were able to penetrate deeper into the Reich.

Apart from occasional and limited breaks during this period, heavy fog blanketing the airfield had been the big problem for Metfield and the rest of the region, and Clint's Flight Record gives the strongest indication that most ships were earth-bound for that period; the fog was typical of the English weather at that time of year. It was just a grey, damp, undesirable blanket of vapor!

This picture of a flak-damaged SX-E was taken on 14 October 1943, following the raid on Schweinfurt. As Clint was not flying that day, 2nd Lt Joseph Schillinger was the pilot. Note many small strikes below cockpit. (*Cross*)

Taken from the other side of SX-E, damage behind the cockpit hood and antenna is quite clear. Also, although not in colour, the picture confirms the red roundel around the star. (*Cross*)

An empty Metfield Ready Room, probably the result of the bad weather period. 'Intelligence and Operations' for the 352nd FS, showing Major Bailey's desk on the left of the picture, with Charlie Wurtzler's (with 'bomb' ashtray) at right angles to it. (*Cross*)

The time suspended again gave those around the base time to catch up on several personal chores, base regulations, and other tasks vital to the smooth running of the Squadrons. There was time to re-check combat film and also put in some hours on the Link trainer, the rather crude but effective flight simulator used extensively during the war.[2] There were regular gas alerts and almost every day there had been air raid warnings to keep the guys on edge. The gunners could sharpen up on base defense, together with aircraft recognition to ensure that they were firing at hostile (not friendly) aircraft through the fog—if they could see them, that is! In what little spare time the men were able to grab, they could buy basics at the commissary or watch a dated film from Hollywood to take them away on a trip of nostalgia or humor. Then there were notes in the 'Daily Bulletin' for airmen to assist the local folk in the area; for example, searching for a lost (or stolen!) dog that wasn't allowed on base. And there was skeet shooting that all pilots would practice to aid their air-to-air deflection marksmanship. There was plenty to fill their time, and there is no doubt that Clint participated in many of those activities—however, there's no record that he'd kept a dog.

That darned fog persisted for several more days, and the base was socked in and missions scrubbed. There were odd times when the occasional movement occurred, and two are noted in the 'CTL' on 17 October—the first at 10.07 a.m., when the writer states: 'SX-W Maj. Duncan up on local weather check, SX-I Lt Sperry up on local slow time'. This was followed at 10.40 p.m. by the entry:

Obviously dogs were allowed on site. The B-24 is B-24D-75-CO, 'Satan's Angels', 42-40604 of the 328BS, 93BG, coded GO-I. A Ploesti veteran, she landed at Metfield on the afternoon of 11 September 1943. She subsequently, crash landed on 11 November 1943 at Lympne, Kent (nose wheel collapsed), and was salvaged 13–15 November 1943. (Sperry)

'Lt Sperry landed from slow time'. It was just one of those jobs that had to be carried out by all pilots from time to time, and Clint was no exception in having to prepare a repaired or new ship for operations.

There was another duty that suddenly would have called a pilot into action. On many occasions the 'CTL' recorded 'RED ALERT' when unidentified aircraft jumped up on radar screens around the coast of East Anglia, and although not always recorded in the Log, someone from the Group may have been ordered to check them out. For all Allied aircraft it was yet another hazard of taking off from or approaching their home base. The Luftwaffe often sent over lone raiders at dusk or during inclement weather to catch out aircraft lifting off with full loads, tired pilots returning with a damaged ship or zero fuel, or even pilots locally slow-timing. Although the intruders were mainly targeting bombers and their crews, it paid for everyone to always be alert, for anything could happen during that period of lousy weather.

There had been an abortive mission on the following day, when all Group aircraft failed to make the rendezvous with the 'Big Friends' as a result of bad weather. The bombers were recalled over the North Sea and one B-17 crashed into those cold and forbidding waters: ten young crewmen were missing as a consequence. Lives risked and lost, resources wasted, sack-time missed, and mission scrubbed! It happened.

The Ju88 was the prime candidate for long-range night interceptions for the Luftwaffe. The photograph shows a captured Ju88 (flown by the Fighter Development Unit at Farnborough) making a low pass over Raydon Airfield. (*Sperry*)

Clint carried out two flights on the 20th. The first, taking thirty-five minutes, is marked down in his Flight Record as 'Other Operational' and was probably a local Met or flight check, because at 1.28 p.m. he took off with the Squadron to escort B-17s out from bombing Düren. The Squadron encountered a few bandits, and it was reported that:

Capt. Hoey took over when Major Bailey was forced to return. Near the R/V point Capt. Hoey encountered 4 Me109s and claimed 2 damaged but was only awarded one.

1st Lt Edward Fogarty, flying spare that day, moved into Red #4 position when Lt Sperry was forced to abort. Lt Armstrong moved from Red #4 to #3. Further aborts eventually left himself and Armstrong as members of White Flight. When his a/c started to have engine trouble he returned early with Armstrong as escort. Spotting a Me109 they made a dive onto its tail and fired. Fogarty was awarded the Me109 as probable. His escort Armstrong also fired at the 109 but made no claim.

Clint's next movement that day is recorded in 'CTL' as 'SX-D Lt Sperry down from mission'. It was a chastened Squadron that eventually straggled back to Metfield, but at least all hit the plate safely by 3.44 p.m. As Clint previously explained, if attacked by e/a and there was a problem with dropping tanks, it could place the pilot in a very dangerous situation. With several aborts that day, it is very likely that Clint and others had tank problems of some sort. The pilots must have been getting mighty concerned about early returns and serviceability, and there was no denying that the effect on the structure of the Squadron would have been compromised.

The situation regarding 'aborts' or short missions needs to be explained further at this stage in the narrative, as it became a very misleading and emotive subject in relation to fighter aircraft (and their pilots) during the approaching winter period of the air war. There had been no doubt that the pilots flying the escort missions in Fighter Groups at that time were struggling to protect the bombers all the way to their targets. It was for that reason that external gas tanks were fitted to provide the longer range necessary to improve the situation, but, as previously explained, there were problems, and the abort rate increased dramatically. Clint encountered those problems and had a few caused by broken glass elbow feeds and other faulty connections. But that was not all—there were many other misfortunes that could stall a flight, sometimes over enemy territory and sometimes closer to home. Many thousands of component parts came together to build the P-47, and those components failed or wore out at critical times during operations.

For the aforementioned reasons the authors have not listed all the problems that affected both Clint and his fellow Squadron and Group pilots, but have rather documented some examples that Clint experienced during his tour of operations. With one or two aborts, he was still given a mission credit as it occurred well into the operation. It should be noted that serviceability was an issue not to be treated lightly, and together with the fuel tank problems and the prevailing winter conditions, early returns were widespread throughout all the Fighter Groups in the tough months during that period.

The pressure of combat and poor serviceability could get to the pilots, as Clint recalled:

I'm certain there were superstitions that many pilots had that they kept to themselves. Fighter pilots would rarely admit concerns whether fear or superstition. I always (probably falsely) suspected that the gung-ho, let's go get 'em guys had more worries than the pilots who just accepted their role with a sort of controlled concern and apprehension about particularly tough missions. I truthfully don't remember any specific cases. There were one or two very intense guys who seemed by their stubbornness to be within themselves and probably had many very uncomfortable superstitions. Sadly, I fear, it got the best of them and both were eventually lost.

Winter Bites

With winter approaching, the weather continued to deteriorate further. The good days for flying were reducing and the operation on 22 October was no exception. It was another mission doomed from the start when the 353rd FG, together with seven other Groups, were ordered to fly escort to 9th Air Force B-26 Marauders that failed to show. The fighters took off in fearful weather, and very soon the 350th lost two aircraft and their pilots when they became detached, peeled away, and went down into the grey and forbidding murk. Was it lack of instrument training that caused their disorientation? Maybe, but neither were seen again. Tragically, in panic, one had left his transmit button pressed, and his dying screams were heard by the entire Group as he plummeted out of control. It was horrific, and that mental image became etched into the memories of those who were there for the rest of their lives. The pilot's terror had been incredibly disturbing to all who heard, but it happened quite often. In that kind of situation the pilots (and sometimes their Ground Controllers) were forced to listen, but they had to try to put it to the back of their minds. There, by the grace of God…

When recounting the mission, Wayne Blickenstaff, flying with the 350th FS that day, said:

> …the mission was a complete fiasco, botched from the word go. The weather prediction was wrong. The mission should never have been scheduled to start with. The B-26s aborted early but the word never got to Jonah [the Group's call sign was still 'Slybird' at that time]. About a third of the 353rd pilots were smart enough to turn around when they realized that they'd never find the bombers.

In foul weather, and although having confidence in his own ability to handle difficult conditions, Clint would have been very grateful that his instrument flying experience had saved him that day. For those who flew the desks it would be a salutary lesson that mistakes cost lives. Sending out their boys in conditions like that was a sure-fire recipe for disaster—that day, it certainly was.

Did those Generals care? One has to appreciate their dilemma as they carried on turning the screw on the Nazi war machine, even though the conditions were marginal. Subsequently, they and their staff fouled up many times, as reading weather conditions was not a refined art. Quoting a classic example, it is recorded that the British Prime Minister visited an RAF bomber base during the middle of the war, was introduced to the Met Officer, and asked him how often his weather predictions were correct. Rather taken aback, but confident in his reply, he faced the steely eyed PM, shrouded in cigar smoke, and answered the great man by telling him it was correct on 50 per cent of occasions—to which Churchill sharply retorted, 'So you were wrong half the time!'

As noted, those at the top had a most difficult job to determine who might live and who might die, but war had no bounds when fighting the Nazi regime. It was total war, and there were always going to be casualties—and that included the Air Force.

Two days later, the Group headed out to support 9th Air Force B-26 Marauders over the Saint André area. They hit really lousy weather and it was time on instruments yet again. Fortunately, no losses or accidents were reported.

Following his return, Clint recorded no further flying time for several days as the Eighth AF virtually abandoned operations. Nothing moved; the weather had really clamped down. The time had come when the deteriorating weather would govern the lives of many young airmen stretched throughout the United Kingdom. It had caused the loss of life for some, and allowed others to carry on fighting a very capable enemy. The flying, fighting, and dying would take a break for a few days—a respite that was very welcome. We are unaware if Clint was off base or confined to Metfield, but he probably would have found time to put in some artistic work around the base, painting personalized nose-art on his buddies' Thunderbolts; some were quite simple, some complex, and one or two were rather descriptive!

It was also a time when the ground crews were putting in many hours bringing their respective aircraft up to the mark, trying to improve the abort problem, and being ready for action when the weather broke—or at least when those 'at the top' deemed it necessary to carry on with operations. Nevertheless, Clint flew on eight missions in October, and his butt sat through over seventeen hours of operational time. He still had a long way to go.

After ten days of kicking their heels, with the odd false alarm for a mission, the Group was active once more on 3 November. It would be a very good day for 352nd FS as they took off to provide high-cover escort for B-17s returning from bombing the port area in Wilhelmshaven. The Squadron took the honors when about ten Me110s and Me210s endeavored to attack a rear box of Fortresses. In very quick time, five of their number were dispatched with no loss. It was a bad day for the 'Zerstörers', as 1st Lts Juntilla, Newman, and Poindexter (2), and 2nd Lt Morrison all claimed air kills. The total for the 352nd FS and the Group was a great morale boost, having waited for so long to give the Luftwaffe a bloody nose. Clint had been on the operation, although it appears that he escorted Major Bailey back to base as the Squadron Leader was forced to hand over to Lt Juntilla when experiencing trouble with his radio. Regardless, it had been a good day for a change.

During the period of limited missions, some of the Squadron were given authority to carry out bombing practice over the Humber Estuary, and later The Wash area over the north Norfolk coast. There was a message built into that activity, as there were plans to carry out different types of operations in the coming months.

Glenn Duncan was a quiet, intelligent, and impatient guy. Not being satisfied with the daily grind of escorting bombers to their increasingly distant targets, he wanted more aggression. He was seriously considering the suitability and extension of the P-47 as an air weapon during those long escort missions. There were occasions when nothing was seen of the enemy, and although the 'Little Friends' were doing the job for which they were designed, he thought that the opportunity to inflict further damage on the German Air Force was being wasted. In effect, if the 'Big Friends' could drop bombs, then why not the fighters? The more they could add to the carnage, the greater the pressure on the enemy. Although the loads would be small in comparison with the bombers, it also served the purpose of agitating the Luftwaffe at their bases to come on up and do battle. The P-47 was more than capable of carrying further ordnance, so why not? [1]

So, the Group experimented. Duncan organized shackles to be fixed to the underbelly of the ships and tasked the pilots to 'go try out dropping bombs' over the East Anglia coast. However, there were potential problems that would need to be considered and overcome. Theories were discussed at gatherings around the planes and their shackles, and in meetings and informal chats around the bar. His enthusiasm was infectious, and the guys were beginning to see good reason and sense with the possibility of seizing the initiative. Dangerous, yes, but heck, so was escorting at times. There was no doubt that the German bases would be ringed with flak and that was the greatest danger, as the method initially favored would be dive-bombing for accuracy as opposed to a straight and level drop at altitude.

Many theories were expounded and investigated. One key question had been raised as to whether there would be a problem for belly-mounted bombs to clear the props on release. Clint had his own view:

Practice dive-bombing did take place over the Humber ... my stated analogy was that there should be no problem. They were comparing German dive-bombing with the Stuka, which had a design figuration that allowed the bomb to clear the prop in any case, but the Stuka used dive brakes in the dive thus decelerating the platform so they needed the clearance. With the P-47, we would be accelerating and the bomb would fall behind the prop for me—at least one of my theories. The second was that a split-S entry into the vertical supplied sufficient centrifugal forces away from the aircraft for a clean and amazingly accurate result.

The Squadrons practiced and methods were tried, with considerable concern about the steep angles of attack that would be adopted for accuracy. The P-47 would certainly build up a dangerous speed in the dive, and pulling out would be tough on the pilot—it was therefore considered sensible to roll over to the target at about 15,000 feet and release ideally at 10,000 feet, but absolutely no later than 7,000 feet. This would also give the German anti-aircraft defenses less chance of a lucky strike, or so they hoped! However, the time soon came for them to put their new skills to the test.

To compound the difficulties of operating in bad weather, on 25 November the Group was hit hard when they lost Col. McCollom on that first 353rd FG dive-bombing mission. The new, aggressive policy introduced by Major Duncan had not gone well. Clint was not on the mission that day as all three Squadrons took to the air at 10.24 a.m. to attack the airfield at St Omer/Ft Rouge in France. It was planned that sixteen aircraft of the 351st FS would each carry a 500-lb bomb, with the other two Squadrons acting as cover. McCollom dropped his bomb and was pulling out when his P-47 was badly hit, and although he was severely burned, he managed to bail out and be taken prisoner. The Colonel eventually ended up in Stalag Luft I, where, nearly a year later, he met up with his former 56th FG Commander, 'Hub' Zemke, who went down at the end of October 1944 when his aircraft disintegrated in bad weather. There they became involved in intelligence gathering and anything that would make life difficult for their German captors.

The attack was not a great success and bombs were wayward, but lessons were learned and it was to be the precursor of the new bombing initiative soon to be adopted permanently by the Group. Although Col. McCollom would be sorely missed, it would be the start of the aggressive and outstanding leadership of Glenn Duncan, who was promoted to Colonel a few days later.

Quiet and laconic on the ground but fiercely aggressive in the air, Glenn Duncan was a good choice for McCollom's replacement; Clint respected him, but at a distance. Clint's personal view was that:

Glenn Duncan was not aloof. He pushed hard to impress the Generals and was inclined to have his favorites (which did not include me). He was a capable pilot and a compassionate man following tragedies. We never shared a close relationship, but he did respect my flying ability, and trusted me. I was not one of the regular Officers Club boys.

Glenn Duncan was astute and eventually the longest-serving leader of the 353rd FG. It would have been apparent to him that Clint's experience would be suited to the type of assignments that he carried out during his combat tour—tasks that confirmed the trust that Duncan and Bailey had in his flying ability.

On 30 November Clint was scheduled to carry out another Met flight; it lasted two hours and was entered in his IFR. It was apparently carried out in poor weather, and he reported a very narrow escape. He later noted: 'Bad weather return from weather flight in instrument let down—hit Barrage Balloon cable'. His son, Steve, relates:

> This story as I recall concerns ... returning from a mission and letting down over England on instruments. As he let down through overcast he felt a distinct impact. Like maybe a bird (he was too high for terrain) but birds don't fly in cloud. When he broke out (I don't remember him saying he was not where he thought he was) I'm guessing he was further inland than he thought. When he landed he and his ground crew found cable marks in the aluminum near the hub of the propeller. From that they figured that he'd luckily hit a barrage balloon cable square in the middle and the prop had broken the wire.

Clint needed every bit of luck that came his way, and the gods were on his side—there was no way he was going to 'buy the farm' and not make it home that day.[2] The number of those flights continued to grow as the persistent bad weather became more unpredictable, and bases for returning aircraft got socked in. When completing operations, aircraft continually had to seek refuge wherever they could after the weather clamped down while they were airborne. On one day late in November, the 'CTL' noted some ships had landed at Bodney, others at Thorpe Abbotts, and even received confused messages like: 'Lt Streit and Lt Jordan are down at some field in East Anglia'. Having received that information regarding the two 352nd FS guys, the writer then recorded:

> Capt. Beckham called and said the pilots requested Coltishall to inform us. I checked with them and found this to be true. In my estimation this is a piss poor situation.

It sure was, and it would happen time and again as the aircraft spread across the local counties trying to find a place to land.[3]

For Clint and the 352nd FS it had been another difficult month, and excluding Met flights he was only able to add three more missions and three hours and thirty minutes to his operational time. At that rate he would be in England forever!

The Squadron and Clint were on operations on 4 December, when the Group conducted another dive-bombing sortie supported by the 56th FG. This type of mission had now become officially designated as 'Thunder-bombing', and

Bombing up. The bomb is pumped up into place to be fixed to the wing shackles. (National Archives)

the unlucky target for the day was Gilze-Rijen Airfield. With Major Rimerman heading the 351st FS and the 353rd FG, the 350th and 352nd FSs acted as top cover with the 56th FG while the 351st FS picked the short straw. The attack commenced. This was certainly a different ball-game to fighter escort operations, as the 'bombers' pulled over and dived down to the target, accelerating at speeds up to 350 mph. The pilots then released their 500-lb bombs and pulled out, just being able to discern (through G-force grey-out) the explosions, fires, smoke, debris, and other forms of mayhem around buildings and dispersals as they climbed back up, regrouped, and headed home. The flak had not been very accurate as the ships left the scene, which was a great relief as it would have been deadly had it caught them in the dive. The mission was a success. Thunder-bombing was 'go'!

As a postscript to the mission, at around 2.45 p.m. RAF Typhoons shot down eleven out of fourteen Do217s that had apparently left that same airfield at Gilze-Rijen just prior to the bombing. Their initial relief must soon have turned to sheer panic as the British fighters descended on them. So be it.

Following an uneventful Group bomber escort mission in the Paris area on the 5th, the airfield was then all but closed for the next five days except for local and slow-time flights. Apart from the weather, it was a constant battle to keep the station operational. Since moving to Metfield an inspection was carried out every day by the Duty Officer, who would tour the base checking on the state of all facilities and recommending and obtaining permission from higher authority to act on any vital work that needed to be carried out. This would include checking runways, perimeter tracks, and hardstands, and initiating any action to provide repair. It was the civilian work gangs who had to struggle in the worsening winter weather. There was a constant need for them to avoid vehicle and aircraft movements while still carrying out repairs on those areas beginning to suffer from constant use by the big planes—which, fully loaded, could weigh well over 7 tons. Not only had civilian laborers assisted the military in the construction and infrastructure of the airfield from virgin land, they were also doing their bit in keeping it open for action. However, there had been delays that were compounded somewhat when the laborers infuriated their American allies by taking the statutory and frequent tea breaks. As the song of the day said, 'Everything stops for tea!'

The weather broke to allow another extended mission of over three hours for Clint and the Squadron as they provided high-cover escort to protect B-24s and B-17s targeting the port areas of Bremen on the 20th. In total, the aerial armada consisted of 546 bombers and 491 fighters, and it must surely have made an awesome sight as it rumbled its way inexorably towards Germany. Forming up in the skies over East Anglia, those watching below could be forgiven for thinking that there was no way that the Allies could lose the war. However true that might have been, millions of lives had yet to be sacrificed before that day would come. Nevertheless, it was a good day for Col. Duncan leading the 352nd FS. The Squadron had been covering B-17 stragglers when a couple of Fw190s started attacking one of the vulnerable bombers; Duncan led down a few of the Squadron and latched on to the unequal battle below. Trying to evade the attack, a Fw190 soon fell to Duncan's guns and spiraled down out of control. This was his fifth confirmed kill, and officially designated him as an 'ace'. His wingman, 2nd Lt Edison Stiff, dealt with the other Fw190—it was credited to him as a 'probable'. The wounded bomber forged on, and the guys hoped that the 'Big Friend' would make it home. Low on gas, they re-formed and headed back to base.

The missions continued to rack up for the Group as two days later they pressed starters and commenced their take-off at 12.30 p.m. Orders were cut for them to provide target and withdrawal support to more than 570 bombers heading to Osnabrück, where the 'Big Friends' were out to destroy communication centers. There was a solid cloud overcast and a strong west wind that disrupted both bomber formations and fighter positioning. German fighters appeared just as the bombers reached their targets, and the 352nd FS, led by Capt. Robertson, had a mission of claim and then despair. Following the mission and the Squadron claim, Clint put in his report:

Col. Duncan reporting in to Group Intelligence Officer Major Hank Bjorkman, demonstrating, as only fighter pilots know how, his recent air battle. (*Cross*)

I was flying at approximately 31,000 ft when one 109 went nearly head on to us. He then made a steep rolling turn to the right. This e/a had no wing or fuselage markings. I rolled over and followed his roll taking a short burst from about 500 yds. He had much more speed than I so I followed him for about 1,500 ft then broke away to join my flight. I left him going straight down. On the way back to the flight, I glanced back to be sure he was leaving, and he was nearly out of sight going straight down, I would say about 15,000 ft below. I then joined the flight and we continued out. I make no claim pending the assessment of the film.

Regarding the incident, Group historian Dr Graham Cross writes:

The Squadron were flying over the bombers at about 30,000 ft as they turned over the target area. Three mottled-brown Me109s made a diving attack from 5,000 ft above and Lt Clinton H. Sperry, flying Blue 3, fired a burst at one of the attacking a/c. Although he made no claim, after assessment of his gun-camera film he was awarded a probably destroyed.

The tragic downside of the mission occurred when 1st Lt Leroy W. Ista of 352nd FS was lost when heading for home; apparently, he went down in the North Sea. An RAF Squadron of Spitfires and a Beaufighter, together with an amphibious

Walrus and motor launches, searched for many hours without luck after an accurate fix 10 miles from the coast was reported. He was not seen again.

Even to an experienced fighter pilot like Clint, the North Sea was a cold and forbidding place; to an inexperienced young fighter pilot, the water always threatened to suck his ship down and swallow him into its depths—even from a great height. Many complained that whenever they headed out over those treacherous waters, something didn't sound right with the engine, or some unusual noise would start up to then fade away as they reached land. It was mostly imagination, but to those who succumbed to its fatal attraction, be it by bailing out or crashing, the sea didn't give them up easily. The rescued would be forever grateful when a boat or string-bag-type flying boat from the dark ages pulled up alongside and hauled them to safety, but for those never to emerge the legend persisted with all those left behind. Too many were lost in its murky depths, especially the less experienced and the plain unlucky. That day it was young Lt Leroy W. Ista; he had joined the Squadron a mere seventeen days before he lost his life.

The 22 December mission ended 1943 for Clint. The year 1944 would have to be better, and judging by the number of missions that he had yet to fly, it would be a progressively frenetic period of intense and bloody action.

For those who would enjoy the festive season so far away from their homes, it was a case of making the best of it. Excerpts from the Unit History show that

Clint flying low over the North Sea. Not the place to visit, especially when it looks this angry. (*Sperry*)

they certainly made the effort. The season commenced with a candlelight service on the evening of 19 December, when the newly formed station choir performed Christmas carols. On the following day there was a party for English children, which was much enjoyed by both the station staff and all the kids. Those guys loved the kids, and the kids loved the 'Yanks'! Those of the Jewish faith celebrated Hanukkah on the days following the 21st, and the Red Cross sponsored a party at the Aeroclub on the 23rd. The new Officers Club was also opened with great relish on the same day, when, no doubt, a small amount of liquor was consumed! A midnight mass was held for those of the Catholic faith on Christmas Eve, and there was a general service for all on Christmas Day.

By the time the New Year was about to be ushered in, a 'Beer Bash' to celebrate the coming of 1944 had to be postponed for a day due to a temporary shortage of beer—but this was surely made up for the following day.

It is guessed that the majority enjoyed themselves over the festive period away from home. Those who organized the prayers and celebrations certainly understood the mood of the men—the loneliness of being away from loved ones, having to celebrate without them, and perhaps thinking of all that had happened in the past year and what life (or death) might hold as the New Year beckoned. For all of them, for those who may have chosen to take a furlough or those left on base, it would probably be a festive season they would never forget. It's a pretty sure thing that Clint exchanged Christmas greetings with everyone at home, and they certainly reciprocated and exchanged gifts, but he was surely hurting and full of emotion from being away from Mary, his new son, Steve, and the family. However, he would have found that the season offered some blessings and perhaps even some guarded hope for the future.

Clint had also managed to complete a further six missions and over fourteen hours of operational flying during December to complete the tally for 1943. It would be busier for him in the coming year, so it's hoped that he made the most of his seasonal break!

The New Year

The New Year dawned, and with it the growing awareness that the Allies had to intensify their efforts to break the Luftwaffe in the air and on the ground—the vital prerequisite for preparation of the largest military airborne and seaborne invasion in modern times. Their ultimate aim was freedom for the oppressed people of Western Europe and the final battle for the destruction of the Axis powers.

The landmass so tenaciously guarded by Hitler's forces could not be overwhelmed without control of the skies, and a great deal more effort was needed before guarded confidence could prevail. The question had to be asked: what had been achieved in the previous year to give any comfort to those in command to carry out that immense and highly dangerous attack on the enemy stronghold? Although destruction had been increasing on the German industrial infrastructure and the Luftwaffe was being hurt, at the beginning of 1944 the task still appeared awesome. German manufacturing capability was still formidable, their armies strong, and their control of the people vicious and unrelenting. Their air force, although slightly weakened by loss of experienced airmen, was by no means spent—in fact, new and dangerous weapons were soon to appear that would put all the Allied plans at great risk. It would be a battle to the death, and in the air the bombers, fighters, and the guys who flew in them were the ones who constantly bore that massive burden. German aircraft and the industries that supported them had to be destroyed, and any hint of complacency was not an option.

Although Clint returned from his Christmas break on 1 January, it wasn't until the 4th that he flew his first mission in 1944. Led by Major Bailey, the Squadron took off at 9.30 a.m. to provide high-cover escort support for the rear Combat Wing of B-17s from the 3rd BD, who were assigned to target Münster City. The 353rd FG was listed to fly with eight other Groups as part of a combined force of 430 Thunderbolts. The 'CTL' offered one entry of an incident during take-off from their base. It recorded:

Under new procedure Flag man fired Green flare from end of runway this morning. Flag man fired Green before last A/C on 27 was clear. Aircraft taking off on 33 just missed single A/C on 27. Flag should have waited till A/C on 33 was absolutely clear.

One can only assume that the 'Flag' man was just not concentrating on the vital role he was playing, and it could so easily have resulted in a catastrophic crash. It was yet another way for someone to get killed.

Two of the bombers were seen by the fighters to collide *en route*, but no other losses were reported. A couple of Me109s were called out on two separate occasions, and after rapid pursuit and a brief engagement, a 'damaged' was awarded to Col. Duncan. The Squadron landed back at Metfield after just over three hours in the air, minus two ships that landed safely away from base.

During any break in flying, Clint would be attending to all his personal chores. Life became almost normal. An extract from a letter Clint sent to Mary at around this time certainly highlighted the extremes of life as a fighter pilot. He wrote:

Our laundry comes back so messed that I have started quite a business, ironing the boys shirts for six pence (about 10 cents) a shirt. Tonite I ironed seven shirts—three of which were my own. Our flat iron has sure come in handy over here.... Before they send any stuff home to the paper (if they do) I have decided to tell you that I shot down a German fighter (Me109) the other day. I made no claim on him, cause I wasn't sure—well, Eighth Fighter Command gave me a probably destroyed whether I wanted it or not. Hope the little Bastard bailed out, but no chute was seen.

Obviously Clint had little respect for the German pilot, but didn't wish to see him lose his life. Many would feel the same.

When a new Group came into the combat zone, the Eighth adopted the policy of linking the new guys with an established Fighter Group. Just as this situation had occurred with the 353rd FG after they arrived at Metfield and were 'parented' by the more experienced 56th FG, it also happened on 4 January, when the 353rd became the 'parent' to the 361st FG. As previously with the 353rd and the 56th, ultimately the two Groups worked well together by imparting knowledge of combat; by sharing and learning about equipment and general operations, they were able to ease into the fight against the common enemy. From this operational relationship grew occasional friendships, although the Group already knew Major Wallace Hopkins as he had been a former CO of the 350th FS, being transferred out in the spring of 1943. Clint was involved in the sharing process, for on his next mission he would be flying a P-47 from the 361st FG. He would sure miss his regular steed, SX-E, when the flak started flying.

Clint did not fly again until the 11th, when he recorded two flights marked up as 'Other Operational' on his IFR. Although there is no record for his second flight of one and a half hours, the first flight was an extended one of three hours with forty-five minutes on instruments, which was pretty taxing even for an experienced pilot. It was a radio relay mission along the Belgian coast for the Group as they headed for Germany. Relay missions became necessary because of poor reception on radios as operations extended progressively further away from base. The importance of two-way contact was a vital component for the reporting network within the Air Force, but of greater necessity was keeping those back at base in communication with the pilots. The result of a relay flight for a mission would be some poor guy circling at altitude, sometimes for hours, just off the coast of enemy-occupied territory, listening out for chatter. He would either be as bored as hell if nothing was doing or spitting blood if they were encountering e/a on their combat mission. As the New Year progressed and the Group pressed deeper into enemy territory this became a necessary but lonely task for the guy stuck out over the Channel or along the enemy coastline.

Clint later recalled his flight on 11 January:

> I loved these flights for two reasons. I could usually get plenty of instrument time in a P-47, which was a beautifully handling instrument aircraft. I also got half a mission credit in an unmolested sight-seeing tour over enemy territory. They'd certainly not send anything up to 30,000 for a single fighter, except an occasional round or two of flak.

The Mission Report recorded that Clint had been flying a 'relay' in 'E9-D' [a 361st FG aircraft] and had been awarded a 'single credit'. The report further stated:

> Our Squadron [352nd FS] furnished a relay who flew over enemy coast from Noordwijkerhoutto, Ostend. He drew meager, heavy, accurate flak all along his route over enemy coast.

As to the type of flak encountered, 'meager' indicated not very much, 'heavy' alluded to the caliber of guns, and 'accurate' points out that what was there happened to be too darned close!

There was a note on 13 January from the 'CTL':

> Col Rimerman landed in good order—when he reached end of runway his tank and bombs fell off. Went out immediately—removed tank—Called Sqn—they removed bombs.

Accidents will happen, but that one would have set some pulses racing.

After a break of three days, with Clint leading a flight and back flying SX-E, the 352nd FS, led by Capt. Robertson, were involved in an area patrol with the Group on the 14th. As a result of the weather being marginal over Germany, there was a big turnout by bombers and fighters targeting secret V1 flying bomb launch sites in the Pas de Calais area.[1] The aircrew were not aware of the vital importance of their targets at that time, as those in high authority did not wish to spread panic throughout the country. The pulse-jet flying bombs that had been developed by Germany had yet to be launched on England, and it was the bombers' task to delay or eliminate their launch-sites at the earliest opportunity. There could be no complacency, as success by those fiery carriers of death would critically endanger the Allied plans for the invasion in the spring. The sites had to be destroyed—easier said than done.

Therefore, on that day a grand total of 552 bombers set out with the sole aim of destroying Hitler's ability to launch the new 'terror weapons' on England. Altogether twenty sites were hit, but the results understandably varied—as both Allied air forces found, to their cost, over a period of several months. The 'Crossbow' or 'No-Ball' targets, as they were called, consisted of a small, narrow ramp and extremely well-hidden and camouflaged launch facilities. To compound the difficulties for the bombers, they also had a deadly ring of flak around the sites for protection. To get a direct hit was rare, and even if sites had been badly damaged or destroyed then more would spring up at different locations—and the numbers were growing daily.

To support their 'Big Friends', a massive complement of 645 fighters (consisting of P-38s, P-47s, and a growing number of P-51s) was dispatched from twelve different Groups. Their task was to sweep the area of Pas de Calais to give the bombers a clear run to their targets. Very little trade was found and all 353rd Squadrons landed back at base after three hours in the air.

The Group didn't fly another mission until the 21st, which meant one full week without operations. On the 20th, thick fog again made visibility appalling at Metfield when a B-24 from the 94th BG endeavored to land while carrying out a training mission. Capt. Emory (Duty Pilot) of the 351st FS tried to guide it down with flares; however, despite a normal landing, braking problems were encountered and the ship over-ran, crashing with the loss of one life. Death came in many guises.

January 21st ushered in a different but deadly ball game for waging war. As previously recorded, apart from the zealous Glenn Duncan there were a few fighter leaders (one being Zemke, of the 56th FG) who had been very unhappy with the policy of continuous close-escort-to-bomber formations during missions. Much has been written previously about their viewpoint, but in simple terms they strongly advocated the freedom to take the initiative and attack the enemy before they got to the 'Big Friends'—not just to defend the bombers in the proximity of the bomber stream. In their view, it was better to sweep ahead of the bombers to stop the e/a taking off, or, failing that, to disrupt and destroy enemy fighter *Grüppen* before they had a chance to reach the bomber formations, as Clint made reference to earlier. Yes, they were Thunder-bombing, but that tended to be a localized 'area' strike and the results tended to be rather random. What was needed was a more specific and accurate attack on airfields and aircraft. They needed to stop the e/a way ahead of the bombers, and also hit them at their bases by strafing them on the ground. There would naturally still be close protection

Trying to land in thick fog at Metfield on 20 January 1943, this B-24 nearly made it safely down, but failure of the brakes caused it to overshoot, ending up in a ditch. Sadly, one member of the crew was killed. (*Cross*)

for the bombers, but the number of fighters available to carry out a new initiative had been growing daily. In recent months East Anglia was nearly submerged with aircraft as the expansion of the Air Force continued apace; between them, by day and by night, USAAF and RAF bombers were slowly becoming a competent and unstoppable force in the sky over Europe. It now needed increased aggression from the fighters, and Glenn Duncan was one of the guys to provide it.

The situation definitely required fresh thinking, and consequently higher authority was requested to consider sanctioning limited missions to initiate that new policy. However, prior to 21 January no 'official' raid had been carried out, and several weeks would pass before it became an accepted method of operation. Action by the 353rd FG on that day would herald that change.

A massive force of 795 bombers was again assigned to hit 'No-Ball' ('V' weapon) targets in the Pas de Calais and Cherbourg regions of France. Covering them had been another large force of 628 fighters, the majority gathering in the Pas de Calais area—including the 353rd FG, whose pilots were destined to be in the air for three hours and thirty-five minutes. As the aerial armada of destruction gathered momentum, the sky began to get mighty crowded as over 1,400 aircraft assembled to carry out their mission.

Col. Duncan was leading the 352nd FS, carrying out their specified protective duty near Amiens, when a sighting was made of a couple of e/a. Diving down to intercept, he soon lost the bandits in cloud, but then spied the airfield near Albert (Dreux Vernouillet) below, with an enemy aircraft in an exposed position—ripe for attack.[2] Acting on impulse, he dove down to strafe the field, swiftly followed by Lt Johnson and Clint.

Clint explains what happened next:

We were in an ideal position to investigate the field. Col. Duncan went down through the hole and fired on an aircraft parked in a revetment. I could see a cloud of dust and smoke and many flashes from strikes, but could not identify the aircraft from my position. Lt Johnson followed Col Duncan on to the same target and again there was a spray of debris and a belch of flame for a second. In order to avoid possible gun fire from the airdrome and prop wash from the other two ships I went down onto the taxi ramp, which was a long straight one. I guess I was about five feet off the ground because I could see people running on my right out of the corner of my eye. With a quick look around the field, I could see no other target; so pulled up and pushed my nose down enough to fire into what was left of the aircraft Col Duncan and Lt Johnson had fired on. There was still so much smoke, dust and debris around that I could not possibly recognize the aircraft ... The third man had to be careful. I was on the deck before reaching the runway end at a speed of 400+mph. There was a mad scramble on the ground and I hit the Do217 and other equipment in the line of fire. No big deal, but a great surprise to them.

Col. Duncan subsequently reported:

My #2 and #3, Lt Johnson and Lt Sperry managed to get in some very nice shooting on the same twin engine airplane and with their description of the combined shooting I claim a destroyed twin engine airplane to be shared by the three of us.

Hidden by the smoke created by Duncan, Johnson, and Sperry is the destruction of the Dornier. The enemy aircraft was well-covered by the joint strafing efforts of the three attackers. (*Sperry*)

The kill was granted. The 351st were also able to claim three air kills, with Major Beckham again being the victor of two Me109s, and 1st Lt William Thistlethwaite downing another. The combined Fighter Groups carried out their allotted tasks and hacked down eight e/a for the loss of one of their own. Only six bombers were lost that day; it had been a critically significant mission, and one that would set the scene for ground attacks during the coming spring.

Clint did, however, have one observation to make regarding the use of guns during flight:

> I discovered why on occasion ammunition belts would jam. The clips forming the belt of 50 cal. bullets rolled through without a hitch until you fired while on your back or with extended periods of negative G's. At that point the open ends of the clips would catch and cause a jam. It took little time firing while inverted over the North Sea to discover the problem.

Once again, the guys were working out their problems with armaments by flying tests out over the coast. It was a form of 'learning on the job', but it was extremely vital that any glitches in the operation of weapons be sorted as soon as possible. Waiting until combat to find that guns wouldn't fire and bombs wouldn't drop wasn't an option—it could be a deadly mistake.

The 'CTL' reported that it must have been a rough night on 24–25 January, as it noted that the Group 'liaison' Tiger Moth hack had 'turned over in last night's gale'. The conclusion was that it hadn't been tied down sufficiently. This aircraft had been named *El Pistoffo Jnr* by the 350th FS Flight Surgeon, Capt. Joe Canipelli, and would soon be flying again.

It is recorded on the 29th that the Group had problems getting together enough planes and pilots to carry out the briefed mission, as they were to begin converting to the P-47D-15. A vital modification on the recently delivered aircraft, and a big step forward for the 353rd FG, was the introduction of the new and effective paddle-blade prop. Operating in conjunction with the water-injection system fitted to the '15s', a greater rate of climb provided a much-desired improvement in performance. Also added at this stage were valuable extra fuel capacity and standard fitted wing pylons. As the older D-2s were not suited to aggressive dog-fighting (especially at low altitude), the modified Thunderbolt provided a great tactical benefit, and the change subsequently became a major factor in improving the morale of the pilots. It would unfortunately take many weeks for that process to be completed, but Clint would have immediately recognized those potential benefits. However, from later discussions it appears that he didn't seem in a particular hurry to upgrade to the '15' even though his current *Mary Jayne* was becoming the oldest P-47 in the Squadron. It appeared to be a matter of pride for his crew chief, Leo Katterhenry, that he and his crew had kept the aircraft in top condition.

Clint fooling around, apparently making it seem that he was the pilot who caused the Tiger Moth's demise. (*Burlingame, via Cross*)

Gordon Burlingame also fooling around to make it look as if he crashed the plane. Both Clint and 'Gordo' were having their bit of fun at the expense of the de Havilland DH82 Tiger Moth blown over in the gale on the previous night of 24–25 January 1944. (*Burlingame, via Cross*)

Eventually, as the months progressed and the missions increased in intensity, all the pilots would be grateful for that added advantage—but when the aircraft later went through modification stages, the perception of some pilots tended to vary according to personal preference. For example, one of Clint's colleagues in the 352nd, Horace Waggoner, had his own view. At the 1983 353rd Reunion, he remarked, 'The P-47B and Cs through to the D-16s were more maneuverable, less sluggish and better at altitude than the D-25 with the bubble canopy.'[3] However, they had yet to find that out.

With the dawning of 30 January came the last mission of the month for Clint and the Squadron. It also turned out to be a good day for the Group. A three-hour-plus mission saw them lifting off at 11.15 a.m. to provide escort to nearly 800 'Big Friends' from the 1st, 2nd, and 3rd BDs attempting to bomb Brunswick. To protect them, fighters from thirteen Groups once more provided the escort. However, there was such a concentration of smoke and contrails from the activity over the target area that some bombers diverted to Hannover to drop their weapons on targets of opportunity.[4]

The 350th FS took the honors, although Major Beckham of the 351st FS (having taken over the Group from Major Rimerman) chased down several Me109s that had dived through the bomber stream and, concentrating on one, inflicted severe damage on it before it spiraled down with no chance of recovery. The next fell to Lt 'Wild Bill' Tanner, who suckered his wingman into following him home, but had in fact spotted a couple of Fw190s. He dispatched one before 2nd Lt Chauncy Rowan, his wingman, realized what was happening—however, he lost the other as it dived away. 'Wild Bill' was no slouch—he wanted both and wasn't about to share them! Lt Walsh, in the 350th FS, was able to claim a Me110 destroyed, while Lts Jordan and Newman of the 352nd FS shared a Ju88 (renowned as a tough nut to shoot down), and Lt Streit winged another. With further claims of two 'probables', the Group turned for home.

Yet again, it was a difficult mission for the Eighth Air Force bombers. Twenty were lost in the aftermath from that vast armada, but at least High Command would be encouraged by the loss of forty-five enemy fighters by the 'Little Friends'. Clint, flying again as flight leader in SX-E, had recorded three hours and ten minutes of flying time. Was he looking forward to getting his hands on the new, upgraded P-47-D15? The improved performance for the Thunderbolt would soon give the Luftwaffe something fearful to contemplate, but he would have to wait a while yet to discover that for himself.

January had been a mixed bag for the 353rd FG, but with fifteen e/a destroyed for the loss of one valuable pilot, the outcome could only be considered as favorable, and the attrition by Fighter Command was hitting the enemy where it hurt. As for Clint personally, he was able to record seven more missions and nearly nineteen hours of flying time as the hours began to stack up. However, as February commenced, the situation wouldn't be quite so favorable for the 353rd 'Slybird' Group.

13

Tough Times

Clint missed out on the early missions at the start of the month, although weather continued to be a serious problem and curtailed operations for the whole Eighth Air Force.

During an especially tough mission for the Group on February 3rd, they lost three pilots when covering 1st BD Fortresses returning from bombing Wilhelmshaven. It was a sober reminder that the Luftwaffe posed a continuing threat to all Allied aircraft penetrating into Germany. For those forced to bail out and who managed to survive the fall, their problems were only just starting. Shocked and disorientated, they would have to gather their shattered nerves and bodies and attempt to evade capture. There were quite a few who made it, and those who managed a 'home run' to tell their tale gave very helpful advice on how to evade capture. The Unit History recorded:

> Lt Dwight L. Fry of the 350th Fighter Squadron returned to the Group. He was reported missing on the 14th October, 1943, when the Group participated in the famous Schweinfurt raid. He successfully escaped from enemy occupied territory and was able to make his way to Spain where he turned himself in to the British Consul and was then returned to this country. He gave a talk to the pilots and intelligence officers on escape and then gave a second talk for the ground officers on his experiences. The enlisted men heard the tale at the theater and it can truthfully be said that his talks were a great inspiration to all who heard him and were a great morale builder. It gave us all courage to have one of our boys escape from the enemy.

At one time during his memorable escape journey, and accompanied by a British airman, he was taken to the apartment of Anne Brusselmans in Brussels, Belgium.[1] There, at great risk to herself and her family, she hid the two evaders from the Gestapo. Just before Christmas 1943, the two airmen were sent on their way to Paris and eventually home via Spain.

Clint was not flying that day. It was most likely that he attended when Lt Fry told his remarkable story. It is hoped that he learnt fast and cottoned on to the fact that with his 'best flying clothes' and 'well-polished pair of GI shoes' he would be a standout certainty for capture by the Germans! It was imperative that any shot-down pilot would have to rapidly take on the appearance of the locals and blend into their way of life in the area where he landed. Clint would need to find that 'lovely French gal' pretty darned quick!

That night, the 'CTL' reported:

> Received a gale warning from Weather Officer, notified alert crew and all Sqds. Alert crew said they were afraid to try and move Proctor [hack plane] to hangar, it may be blown over taxiing to hangar.

To compound the problem, the Weather Officer also reported that there was 'the possibility of frost or light snow during the night'. Winter was beginning to bite harder.

The weather was continuing to play havoc with operations as Clint checked that he was on the Flight Board for the 10 February mission. He would be flying SX-H as his usual mount, SX-E, was due for an overhaul. The pilots trudged to their hut for the briefing at 10 a.m., as the wind was rising and the cold morning air seeped through their leather flight jackets, causing shivers of chill and anticipation. The Squadrons had been briefed to cover the bombers as they departed from their target of Brunswick. Lt Frank Emory of the 351st FS reported:

Clint in a relaxed pose for the camera. Note the emergency whistle on the front of his flying jacket. (*Sperry*)

Clint's sketch of an overhaul of *Mary Jayne*. This appears to be a very thorough check of all key components, for taking off a wing, the tail, and stripping down the engine were no small tasks. It may have been the time when the retro-fitting exercises of new props, vents, and plumbing hard-points on wings were carried out, although Steve considers that SX-E was in for repair after having been shot up when flown by another pilot. (*Sperry*)

> Metfield base was overcast at 500ft with frequent snow showers and sleet. After briefing we went out to our planes and had to wait until the sleet and snow died down enough to see our way clear for taxiing. Take off was accomplished between squalls.

Having crossed the North Sea and well into Europe, flight positions changed as a result of several aircraft having problems. After their aerial reshuffle, the Group were able to pick up the bombers as they left their targets brewed up and burning around the industrial areas of Brunswick. Lt Emory latched on to a lone Fw190, and after twisting and turning while following at high speed, he was able to get a bead on it and manage several gun-strikes to send it on its way to the ground. Also seen by Emory was a Me110 that apparently was playing stooge for a group of bandits that bounced 352nd out of the sun. The twin-engine Messerschmitt was attacked by Lt William 'Bill' Jordan, who was awarded a 'probable'; however, they were then bounced by the mix of around fifteen Me109s and Fw190s, and in successfully extricating themselves Lt Cliff Armstrong was given credit for a Me109 destroyed.

Reporting to the Intelligence Officer back at Metfield, the pilots were pleased with the results in spite of the earlier setbacks. Clint was one of those who reported a problem but was given full credit for the mission. It had been a day of high activity for the Group, and the 351st and 352nd FSs recorded two destroyed, one probable, and one damaged. However, the evidence was clear that the Luftwaffe was still extremely determined to protect the Fatherland and that the battles ahead would be increasingly intense.

On the 13th the workmen were still laying tar on parts of the perimeter track as the Squadrons lifted off to escort 469 B-17s and B-24s that were targeting 'No-Ball' sites around the Pas de Calais region. It was planned to take the Group in at 22,000 feet over Gravelines and proceed to Albert, where they were to be vectored around that area at the discretion of the controller. However, there were slim pickings for the 353rd FG, although Major Beckham (leading the 351st FS) managed to damage an Fw190. The 352nd FS, led by Capt. Hoey, also called out several Me109s and Fw190s, but for whatever reason they were not engaged. With three hours and ten minutes in the air flying SX-B, Clint was pleased to complete the sortie by not tempting providence again with 'H', which had given him problems on the previous mission.

Although he flew several times after the 13th, Clint was not on another operation until the 20th. Snow, ice, and clouded skies were prevalent for the period leading up to a significant day of reckoning. It was absolutely vital that weather conditions should improve at the soonest possible date, as the Eighth Air Force had a major plan to carry out. Apart from bad weather, absolutely nothing had to interfere with that plan, but it didn't look good. 'Big Week' was in jeopardy.

By 20 February the charismatic and aggressive Major General James 'Jimmy' Doolittle had replaced Major General Ira C. Eaker as commander of the Eighth.[2]

A still from Clint's gun-camera footage as he makes practice passes at B-24 Liberators over England. (*Sperry*)

Pressure began to be exerted on the Air Force to gain control of the air to meet the anticipated date in May 1944 for the invasion of Europe—D-Day. They were slipping behind schedule, and the result was that there would be a planned all-out assault on aircraft and aircraft industries in Germany that commenced on 20 February 1943—if the weather allowed! All bombing raids prior to that date were but an arduous and bloody prelude to what was about to happen.

The bad weather on the previous day broke just as the Cal Tech teacher-turned-meteorologist Irving P. Krick had predicted. His method was distinctive but unconventional, as he based his forecasting on the theory that weather patterns over the years had tended to repeat themselves. The key men who had to make that momentous and critical decision were Major Generals Spaatz, Anderson, Kepner, and Doolittle; they agreed, and 'Operation Argument', commonly known as 'Big Week', was 'go'.

The bomber bases exploded into an overture of sound that morning, as East Anglia reverberated with the thunderous roar of over 4,000 Wright Cyclone and Pratt & Whitney engines. They created an intoxicating aroma of burning aviation gas that spread in a growing shroud across the countryside as the 'Big Friends' formed up, ready for battle. The main objectives for two-thirds of the force would be the airfields and aircraft industries in Leipzig and surrounding areas, while the balance of the force would be unleashed on the airfields and targets of opportunity at Tutow and Rostock, known also as the 'eastern industrial complex'. Although cloud precluded some aircraft from bombing their primary targets, the damage wreaked upon the Nazi industrial infrastructure on that first day of 'Big Week' was indeed substantial.

A total of fifteen fighter Groups provided cover for that deadly aerial armada as it droned inexorably towards the centers of the industrial power that were key birthplaces for aircraft of the Luftwaffe. German Fighter Commander Lieutenant General Beppo Schmid had to marshal his defenses against that onslaught; it had seemed a formidable task as he listened to the early warnings emanating from the German Freya radar. Initially it was indicating that the bomber force had been heading for Berlin, but Schmid had been advised wisely to hold his fighters until it was determined that Leipzig would be the main target that day.

There were many stories of heroism on both sides during those frenetic hours of fighting, but for the Americans it was vital that they should succeed. Immense damage was inflicted both in the air and on the ground. The gunners on the bombers claimed a staggering sixty-five e/a destroyed, while losing twenty-one of their own. The fighters claimed a further sixty-one destroyed, losing only four from all Groups as the Luftwaffe threw all of its available resources at the aerial invasion. As the bombers staggered home and the fighters from both sides landed back at their bases, the evaluation of success, damage, and resources began.

First, the heavies had done their job well, and their losses, whilst bitter to take, were comparably minimal. The Fighter Groups also had a very productive day. Lt

General Schmid, however, although relatively pleased that some of the bombing formations were broken up and forced to bomb targets of opportunity, was a worried man. He had lost many good and experienced pilots and planes. The planes he could replace, but the same could not be said of the pilots in the scale of time allowed, for he knew that the American Air Force would return soon.

For the 353rd FG, the 20th would be an easier day than most. The Group had provided valuable support when most needed, and although they had sight of the bombers flying to their targets, they had not tangled with the Luftwaffe. It must have been a terrific boost for Clint (flying SX-U) and his fighting colleagues in the Squadron to experience the Mighty Eighth at work. However, for the American Generals, the day was arguably the zenith of success for Operation Argument, as they would soon discover.

On the day before the start of Big Week, Krick had indicated that there would probably be three days where the conditions would be suitable for the bombers to carry out their task. Thus it was on the 21st that preparations were well-advanced to hit the second-day targets of more than a dozen airfields. The Eighth dispatched 861 heavies supported by 679 fighters. It was a quiet mission for the 352nd Fighter Squadron as they guided their Thunderbolts above the bombers making their way home; some were damaged and limping, while most were lighter and faster after dropping their loads. The bombers and fighters claimed fifty-two e/a, but they lost sixteen and five respectively. The day was almost as successful as the previous, but fatigue was beginning to be evident in both men and machines—and it was only the second day.

Clint was then stood down until the 29th; his 'Big Week' was over as it was time to rotate and bring some fresh flyers into the fray. Both the 'Big' and 'Little Friends' were beginning to feel a bit jaded, but for the Luftwaffe it had been worse. They needed to pull every trick in the book to try to halt the Eighth, and they would have to do it soon, for the bombers were coming back.

Big Week continued, but General Doolittle considered that not enough was being achieved and he wanted more effort. However, the elements conspired to stall the attacks for the following day, as the conditions were terrible and Krick's forecast was beginning to waver. The day started with low cloud providing conditions very unsuitable for bombers to climb through to gather into their formations. In fact, it was downright dangerous, but after receiving information from an RAF reconnaissance pilot that the weather was clear over the targets, General Doolittle determined that the bombers must fly. The sky reverberated once again as inhabitants around the bomber bases were rudely awakened to the mighty sound of throbbing engines; they were going to war once more. The crews were tired and worn from the exhausting battles on the two previous missions, but the job still had to be done. For some the debt would be paid when the Grim Reaper beckoned, and he did so on that day. It turned out to be a disaster for the 3rd BD. As the aircraft rose to spiral round the 'buncher' beacon that assisted the pilots when forming their combat boxes, it needed just one ship to have a problem for the 500-feet maintained height separation to collapse and spell disaster—and it happened. One B-17 lost an engine, fell back, and collided with another on its way up through the murk. There were no survivors. It had a severe knock-on effect and was a fiasco, a confused and frightening mess of bombers not knowing where each other had been positioned in the clouds.

What was it like for those bombers that were mortally damaged and destined to fall? In the excellent book *Big Week*, written by Glenn Infield, the following gives a vivid impression of the horrors that would have been experienced by those young aircrews:

> Bail out! Jump!
>
> The last moments of a dying bomber were always moments of confusion, desperation, and prayer for the men still in the plane. Even after the order to bail out came over the intercom system, it was not a mere matter of walking to the nearest exit and jumping. A crew member had to make certain that his parachute harness was buckled properly, that his parachute pack was attached to that harness, that he had his hand on the metal grip that would open his parachute once he was dropping through space. After he had checked these items, he still had the long walk, crawl, or dive to the nearest exit. If a B-17 was diving vertically or spinning wildly, the centrifugal forces on a man were enough to make it a superhuman effort to lift a foot. When he managed to get started towards the nearest exit, he was often knocked down by a sudden lurch of the doomed plane and had to start all over again—if he wasn't knocked unconscious. Once he reached the exit, he had to fling himself out into space in such a manner that neither his head nor foot hit the tail section. If he did hit the stabilizer or elevators, in all probability he would be killed. And he had approximately two to four minutes to accomplish the above tasks before the plane hit the ground or exploded!

But the airmen were not the lucky ones when the bombers collided that day; they waited, entombed and petrified, for a terrible death thousands of feet below. It was to be similarly repeated too many times in the turbulent skies over Europe, as it more than frequently happened while venomous aerial combats had been swirling around them. Fighting for their lives, some managed by superhuman efforts to extricate themselves from the clinging forces and bail out, but for those who could not, it was a horrible way to die, knowing nothing other than a miracle could save them. It very rarely did—and certainly not on 22 February 1944.

It was a black day as the lives of eighteen young airmen were snuffed out in the terrible mid-air collision before the mission had hardly started, and the Commander of the 3rd BD, Curtis LeMay, had no option; he recalled them.

Although the mission continued, only a few bombers were able to make it into Europe and the forces were depleted and split, the defending fighters highly aggressive, and the Eighth lost a total of forty-one 'Big Friends'. It was also reported that the 15th Air Force heavies that had joined the fray on a shuttle mission from Italy fared little better. For a great majority of the attacking bomber force it had been nothing short of a disaster.

The total e/a claimed destroyed by all fighters was fifty-nine, but it had been a bad day for the 353rd FG as they completed their escort duty for the depleted force over enemy territory. Having cleared with the bombers to leave, Col. Duncan, leading the Group and the 351st FS, had decided to attack an airfield in the vicinity of Bonn. He proceeded to destroy a Ju88—then, when exiting the field, he blasted a hangar and two locomotives. However, he had stirred up a hornet's nest, and the flak was deadly. The multiple 'ace' Major Beckham, of the 351st FS, was badly hit on a strafing run and had to bail out, being taken as a POW for the duration.[3] The highest scorer in the Eighth was down and his Squadron colleagues, Lt Hulburt and Lt Wood, did not survive as they were also hit at low level and lost when their ships smashed to the ground. It was a salutary lesson for the new form of dangerous low-level warfare, and would take plenty of thought as to how best to carry out that type of offensive operation in the future. The 352nd Squadron fared no better. Crossing over the coast near Antwerp, Lt Edison D. Stiff's aircraft was hit by heavy flak at height, and, burning, fell sickeningly to earth. He did not escape from his aircraft.

Col. Duncan was a serious, even compassionate man. Deeply hurt and naturally concerned about the losses, he had to find answers. It has become evident in later years that pilots in the 353rd FG were becoming somewhat disenchanted with their leader during this period. With fuel stretched to the limits and the dangerous game of strafing becoming more prevalent, Duncan, although leading by example, was stretching the abilities of his young pilots; they were unhappy. It would take several weeks before fuel problems and methods of attacking ground targets would be refined and improved. His aggressive exploits were sapping the spirit of the best, and although carrying out his leaders' wish to take the fight to the enemy, Glenn Duncan had some serious thinking to do.

The third mission of Big Week could be termed a fiasco. However, to all extremely tired and stressed combatants the weather then provided a slight interlude, for the following day there was ice on all runways at Metfield and the clouds hung thick and low. It was obvious that there would be no missions flying from anywhere in East Anglia.

The Luftwaffe threw everything they could at the Eighth on the 24th and 25th, and although the bombers got through to their targets, the attrition rate was again high and at great cost to both protagonists. To question if the sacrifice of men and machines was worth it can only be seen by viewing the key result. In simple terms, Doolittle's bombers, together with Fighter Command, had been tasked to weaken, if not eliminate, the ability of the Luftwaffe to seriously threaten an invasion of Europe. Was it achieved? We can only surmise that without Big Week and the continuing air raids, Schmid and his fighter planes would undoubtedly have caused havoc amongst the Allied invasion forces.

It is doubtful that Clint and his fellow pilots would have been fully aware of the ultimate aim of the policy that dictated operations during those few hectic days. However, it is clear that in the period leading up to the invasion they had a great awareness of the implications of failure, as they were intelligent guys and few would waver from that vital commitment.

Following 'Big Week', it now became essential for all of the Air Force to rest, replenish the Squadrons with fresh pilots and aircraft, and be ready for the massive push leading up to D-Day and beyond. The missions continued to be tough, and although Clint was able to record six during the month, it was his operational flying hours that were trailing, even though he added a further sixteen hours during that period. It is possible that he was tending to fall behind the other guys, as the Met flights were usually much shorter than the other operational missions and thus his cumulative total began to get on the drag. If he was aware of this, there was not much he could do about it; Bailey was his boss, and he called the tune.

14

Sorely Tested

The 353rd were not back on operations until 2 March. Bad weather began to stall bombing missions again, and although the Group operated on the 2nd and 3rd, Clint wasn't back on the Squadron roster again until the 4th. As they made their way to briefing, the weather was appalling. All of East Anglia was covered with snow and there were frequent flurries blowing through, making visibility for take-off and landing conditions extremely treacherous. The Squadrons were originally tasked to provide penetration support to bombers heading for Berlin, but because of the prevailing conditions and the mission for the fighters being postponed three times, the orders were changed for them to provide withdrawal support.

Clint made the mission on the 6th. Snow and ice had continued to be a problem on the runways at the base, and the request to clear them had not been fulfilled by 9 a.m. The Squadron briefing was at 9.15 a.m., and in a tense and expectant atmosphere inside the briefing room the map showed the pilots that they were to escort 3rd BD Fortresses to their targets of opportunity around the suburbs of Berlin. As they trudged out into the freezing cold air, the guys could be forgiven for wishing that they were somewhere other than that god-forsaken hole.

Northwest of the Steinhuder Lake area, Col. Duncan, flying with the 352nd FS, was just too late to intercept Fw190s attacking his charges, and picked up the e/a as they came out the rear of the bomber formation. As he still had fuel showing, he dropped one of his tanks and dove after one of the bandits, sending it crashing to earth. Following the chase he got rid of the other tank and was soon on the tail of yet another Fw190, which 'splattered nicely' near Steinhuder Lake. After that bit of frantic excitement, the Squadron headed for home—but the day was not being kind to the Group. Having had his ship badly shot up during that air battle, Lt Ireland of the 350th FS (the only one from that Squadron flying with the 351st FS) was killed when he lost control of his aircraft and crashed on the base.

Having experienced the tragedy of losing one of their own so close to home, the airmen were again spectators to another all-too-common incident that became familiar to Clint, his fellow pilots, and those watching the return of bombers. The 'CTL' recorded at 4.50 p.m.:

A B-17 circled the field approaching and entering the circuit from the north. No.4 engine was observed to be completely shot away and the plane was obviously not under complete control as it see-sawed over the adjacent treetops and could not land on the field. It landed on its belly in meadows just northwest of the airdrome off the end of 15 runway. Landing occurred at 16-52.

Then, at 5.45 p.m., the Log reported:

Pilot of B-17 which crash landed was Lt Schimmel, 452nd Bomb Sq., 3rd Bomb Div. Pilot was flying aircraft alone as the rest of crew had bailed out over the continent. Pilot was uninjured in crash.[1]

The pilot's decision to save his crew by instructing them to bail out was tough. Now he was safe, while they had to see the war out in a prison camp in Germany. The war was full of those kinds of incident. It could happen to any flyer, but on that occasion one made it home and the others didn't.

On the 8th the planners sent the bombers to Berlin/Erkner. When the mission was revealed, no doubt that all the pilots in the Group could see that it was going to be another major effort by the Eighth, as Berlin was the 'Big One'. It was the heart of the German Reich, and the 623 bombers supported by 891 fighters were going to make sure that they would inflict severe damage. Clint didn't make the full trip, as one of his wing tanks failed to feed when a connection broke; the reduced fuel state ensured a frustrating early return.

Clint was on ops again on the 15th, when Headquarters ordered the Group to escort in B-17s and B-24s that were to distribute their loads on industrial areas around Brunswick. Clint has recorded this as a 'Ramrod' escort (i.e. where fighters or fighter-bombers, having completed their escort duties, would carry out attacks on ground targets).[2] After three hours and fifteen minutes in the air, it had not been a very rewarding mission for the Group regarding aerial combat, although the satisfaction was evident that all returned home having shepherded their charges with little loss.

As an addendum to the day, and as an experiment, it had been reported that both Col. Duncan and Col. Rimerman had each shackled up a 1,000-lb bomb, and varying their angles of attack had narrowly missed a barge that they had been targeting in the Zuiderzee. There was no doubt that Col. Duncan had been pursuing all options to take the fight to the enemy with Thunder-bombing, and experimenting with bomb sizes, height, speed, and angles of attack would provide the guidance for others as the months progressed.

Later, back at base, Col. Duncan was presented with a silver cup for having shot down the Group's 100th e/a. The 353rd were becoming a Group to be respected.

352nd Fighter Squadron picture taken in the spring of 1944 at Metfield.
Back row, left to right: Geurtz, Cles, Gonnam, Sperry, Robertson, Corrigan, Bailey, Fogarty, Kipfer, Knoble, Forkin, Jordan, Newman, Callans.
Front row, left to right: Schillinger, Marchant, Johnson, Armstrong, Poindexter, Burlingame, Owens, Juntilla, Morrison, Streit, Dustin, Willits, Keywan. (*Cross*)

From the middle of March 1944, Clint's Flight Record shows an increasing number of missions through to D-Day and until the eventual finish of his operational tour with the 352nd FS. The escalating and threatening events that occurred during that challenging period demonstrate very clearly that experienced pilots were very much in demand as the Allies continued their policy of destruction of the enemy wherever and whenever possible. There was no doubt that the pressure had been building on the Eighth to fulfil all its obligations, and it was the pilots and crews of bombers and fighters who would prepare the ground for the greatest invasion in history.

Progressing from the previously planned and executed initiative during 'Big Week', further 'shuttle' missions began to be operated from various airfields in southern Europe. Following the invasion of Italy in September 1943, the Allies liberated those valuable assets as they advanced slowly towards their ultimate goal—Germany. Foggia became one of those hubs where several airfields surrounding the city were taken over for both bomber and fighter bases for the USAAF, and although being part of a wider brief, the task of those shuttle missions had been handed to the 15th Air Force. They had commenced with their first operation during 'Big Week' on 22 February 1944, and it was now time to hit the enemy from different directions on a regular basis.

The Squadron gathered early at 7.45 a.m. on the 16th; the tension increased as they listened to the Briefing Officer convey details of their mission for the day. It would be an escort for bombers targeting Friedrichshafen, on the shores of Lake Constance (Bodensee), in southern Germany. Clint flew on that operation and recorded a butt-numbing four-hour flight—his longest to date, and also the 353rd FG's most extended mission so far.

The Group were able to catch sight of the awesome and forbidding Alps before they exited from their deep penetration into Germany and made their way back through France. Having fulfilled their uneventful duty to the bombers, the 351st FS, led by Duncan, were seeking out targets of opportunity. Col. Duncan was always ready to attack anything that resembled an enemy stronghold, even though it occasionally turned out to be a costly decision. It wasn't a costly decision for the 351st that day, as he once again elected to strafe an airfield, and camera footage showed that amongst the havoc created by the Squadron was a claim for a twin-engine aircraft.

It was costly for the 352nd FS, who attacked an airfield that had been spotted near Laon. Lt Gonnam, followed by his wingman, Lt Herfurth, led Red flight down, sharing three e/a damaged, but the beat-up ended tragically for two pilots from Yellow flight; Lts Robert Newman and Harry Dustin flew into the hornet's nest that Red Flight had stirred up, and neither returned from the mission. Flak had claimed the lives of two more of Clint's colleagues, as they were later reported as 'killed in action'. It was a bad day for the Squadron and for the families they left behind, and a further reminder to all pilots that the hand of fate constantly followed them as they took the fight to the enemy.

Although the date cannot be confirmed conclusively, it appears that Clint also experienced problems on the 16th.

The story is about one of our longest missions which involved covering B-17s from the 15th AAF based in Italy that were to hit targets in southern Germany on a 'round robin' plan to land and refuel in England then return with targets on the way back to Italy. In this case, we were to pick them up just south of Geneva (keeping clear of air space over neutral Switzerland), and cover them on our return route as long as we could effectively stay with them. The procedure fooled the Luftwaffe for several such missions.

Going in that deep was about the limit of our range, so we hoped that our presence would avoid a fight. I was flying my original SX-E *Mary Jayne* which had just undergone a prop change to the more efficient Paddle blade with the same Curtiss Electric controlled pitch mechanism (my 2nd aircraft had a Hamilton Standard Hydraulic control).

Soon after turning to stay with the bombers toward England, we moved from our 35,000 to a lower altitude closer to the bombers, [and] everything went fine with the prop in automatic pitch adjusting to hold constant rpm as my speed increased on the descent. This means the prop went into a higher pitch. My first clue of a problem was when we leveled off and instead of the prop automatically adjusting to a flatter pitch to hold the same rpm, the rpm dropped. To get the rpm up and manifold pressure down, I had to switch to manual control to bring things where they should be. Nothing happened and I went back to auto to test again. In auto, the slightest descent made things worse so quickly back to manual with repeated attempts to flatten the pitch for more rpm.

Now, I've got a decision to make. My rpm in manual is holding in level flight at 1400 with manifold pressure at 53 inches. I would much rather have a norm of 2525 rpm and 32 inches. I'm concerned about staying with the squadron and the inevitable long term strain on the engine to get all the way back from Geneva, which looked pretty inviting down there on a crystal clear day. The engine seemed to be handling the high manifold pressure without overheating or oil pressure drop, so I kept as close to the group as possible and kept going away from a safe haven toward another safe haven which was unfortunately many miles away.

After leaving the bombers to another fighter group, and keeping a very gradual but long steady descent, I made it to Metfield and was relieved to be on final for what I thought would be an uneventful landing. In my bliss, I failed to realize that with the prop in a high cruise pitch, even with the throttle at idle for landing it had far greater pulling power than the normal flat pitch for landing. This didn't really show up until I was happily rolling down the runway which I was fast running out of.

I rolled to the very end and was slow enough to unlock the tail wheel, apply modest braking to one main gear wheel, and ground loop instead of rolling onto the soft ground beyond the runway end. Now, with the prop in such a high pitch, it took a lot of power to taxi in to the flight line and shut the engine down. On disassembling the Curtiss electric drive (a new drive assembly that was part of the new prop), they discovered a metal washer about ½ inch in diameter that would jam the motor armature as it reversed for lower pitch (higher rpm) but would allow the armature to slide by for higher pitch (lower rpm). Fortunately, with no manual demand for any pitch change the brake held and I was very lucky to get home.

It's hard to imagine that a small metal washer could virtually cripple a 2000-horsepower engine if not caught in time. Interestingly, the long steady climb all the way to the Swiss border allowed the prop control to hold climbing and level settings automatically until for the first time in the flight I started to let down to bomber level. This, as we now know, was when the little washer was pushed the other way and decided to act as a brake.

A malfunction that deep in enemy territory had been a very traumatic experience, but with calm and reasoned airmanship Clint was able to save himself from an uncertain fate. Trust in his own ability and the knowledge of his aircraft enabled him to make it safely back to Metfield. Sadly, if Clint's problem did occur on that date, he had lost two good friends, and the Squadron had lost two valuable pilots.

On 17 March the tactics were certainly beginning to vary for the Fighter Groups, as the 353rd FG, together with the 78th, 359th, and 361st FGs, were once again briefed to go Thunder-bombing against airfields in France. The Group had been carrying out those types of operation for quite a while, and it was becoming very evident that they weren't very good for the health of the pilots. Sure, it also wasn't too healthy for those on the receiving end, but so what? They were the enemy.

Following briefing at 1.48 p.m., thirty-one ships took off for the Continent at 3.10 p.m. Their target was Soesterberg Airfield, Holland. Probably as a result of various experiments by Col. Duncan with dive-bombing techniques, the 350th and 351st FSs adopted the glide-bombing method as they dove at the target at a 45-degree angle. Some, having unloaded their bombs, also strafed dispersals. With Capt. Hoey leading the 352nd FS, Clint's SX-R was one of eight ships that carried out their dive at a 70-degree angle, leaving four up top as cover. The results were not initially observed in the turmoil they were creating on the ground, but they would have been analyzed later from gun-camera footage back at base. Although quite unusual, all the Thunder-bombers were awarded a double credit for a good job carried out at the airfield, while the four escorts were only awarded single credit—probably because the powers that be considered that they had an easy time of it with a free grandstand view!

It was back to escorting on the 18th as Clint was among the pilots chalked up on the Squadron Flight Board, listening in anticipation and perhaps no little apprehension to the briefing at 9.20 that morning. The Group were to carry out another 'Ramrod' but also to escort out the 1st, 2nd, and 3rd BDs after they dropped their loads on many different targets over central-southern Germany. The Group were to operate in the Strasbourg/Friedrichshafen area. The heavies were very severely mauled by e/a, losing an unsustainable forty-three bombers, yet they had at least been able to claim forty-five German fighters destroyed. As previously observed, in the swirling and deadly attacking phase, with Luftwaffe fighters flashing past through the bombers, it was understandable that, with the number of guns pointing at the enemy from the defending bomber formation, several gunners would be firing at the same aircraft and each claiming a hit or victory. That did not diminish their efforts, though over-claiming became inevitable. The Fighter Groups accounted for thirty-nine e/a, but thirteen of their number failed to return. Major Bailey had been leading the 352nd FS, and he and his flight had been unable to join up with the Group. Clint commented: 'March 18—Appalling weather: Led flight of 4, 2:45mins and 45mins instruments'. He was not with Bailey's flight, but by recording a flying time of only two hours and forty-five minutes, his flight was also unable to rendezvous with the bombers,

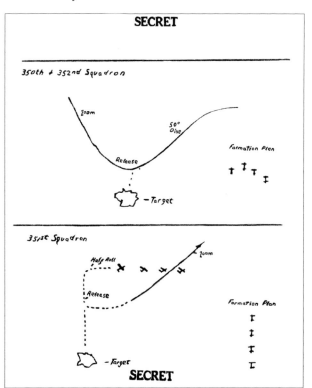

Taken from the 353rd Fighter Group microfilm, this diagram graphically shows the two dive-bombing techniques on a different mission. This time, the 350th and 352nd Fighter Squadrons are adopting the shallower angle of attack with a 'finger-four' formation flight approach, while the 351st is using the steep dive angle of attack with the aircraft flight approaching the target with an 'in-line' formation. However, the 351st aircraft about to bomb look as if they are flying the wrong way! (*USAF*)

who had been considerably strung out when forming up, probably caused by the weather. It appeared the Squadron and the 353rd FG did not have a good day. At least all eventually returned safely to base—that was a plus.

The operation on 20 March appears to be Clint's last for several days. In fact, it ended on a sour note as the briefed mission for the bombers to target Frankfurt was abandoned due to high cloud, with some of the 'Big Friends' well into the continent and friendly fighters trying to shepherd them through the difficult conditions. Clint had marked this as a 'Ramrod', but it turned out to be abortive as all the Squadrons were recalled due to the unsuitable weather, and a single mission credit was given to all who participated. The 'CTL' reported that 'Ops says our guys have been recalled and will return early'. Clint had flown for one hour and fifty minutes—twenty of those on instruments. A frustrating day and a waste of resources for the Eighth as it was recorded that they lost seven bombers and eight valuable fighters—about eighty guys who wouldn't be back for chow that night.

Having finished the mission on the 20th, it appeared that Clint was due to go on a 'Week's Leave' as he had handwritten it on the Group Mission List. He was involved with seven out of the twelve missions leading up to the 20th and had totaled seventeen hours and twenty-five minutes of operational flying time. Clint had probably realized that he had passed the halfway mark for his tour, and the missions were getting more frenetic as the pressure on the German infrastructure intensified. It would get even busier when he returned from his furlough.

Whilst air combat operations were proceeding during late winter and very early spring, Glenn Duncan had been giving a great deal of thought as to how to progress his earlier initiative of ground strafing. It was therefore no coincidence that some special visitors just happened to arrive at Metfield back on 14 March.

Group commanders weren't particularly keen to entertain the top brass on active fighter bases as it usually meant 'bull' and being subjected to unwelcome scrutiny. That day was different at Metfield, for Glenn Duncan was welcoming a hatful of brass with open arms. He had been keeping his boss, Major General William 'Bill' Kepner, well briefed on the 'occasional' ground-strafing attacks that the Group were carrying out, and although they had incurred losses (including Beckham), they were certainly stirring up the enemy. Kepner had been in favor of new initiatives, and to introduce the possibilities to General Carl 'Tooey' Spaatz, a bunch of Generals visited Metfield.[3] It turned out to be a fruitful visit.

Duncan had a good working relationship with his boss at Fighter Command, and he was not short in coming forward with his aggressive ideas for hunting the enemy wherever he could find them. After consultation with his fellow Generals following their visit on the 14th, Kepner gave the official go-ahead the following day to consolidate the new ground-attack role. The raid back on 21 January was a precursor of things to come, and Duncan wasted no time in forming another Squadron. It was designated 'C' Squadron, with orders to accept volunteers from throughout Fighter Command; it was aptly named 'Bill's Buzz Boys' after the support given by General Kepner to the project. Training commenced on 18 March, and the first 'official' raid took place on 26 March.

As a result of the new policy, several ground-strafing missions were flown in the spring of '44, causing severe damage and disruption to airfields, rail networks, rolling stock, road, river and canal traffic, enemy installations, and anything that moved that had the hint of a black swastika on it.

Much was being learned from those ground-attack missions during this period, and it was becoming evident that the method first pioneered by Col. Duncan was becoming widespread throughout Fighter Command. However, since Duncan's initial foray into that deadly game of ground strafing, the fighter boys were beginning to see that low-level operations were an extremely dangerous occupation. Sure, the attacks were more precise than bombing, and it could be productive being able to sweep across an airfield, picking out the targets, each P-47 packing six or eight Browning .50-caliber machine guns—but the whole concept needed more thought and guile. Guys were getting killed down there and the German flak gunners were beginning to learn how to effectively knock them down, not only by firing directly at them or 'leading' them, but also by putting up a curtain of fire that they were almost bound to fly into.

Col. Duncan entertains the Generals at Metfield on 14 March 1944 in front of a rather shabby Nissen hut. The visit was to propose the formation of a ground-attack squadron, which after authorisation became 'Bill's Buzz Boys'. *Left to right*: Maj. Gen. 'Bill' Kepner, Lt Gen. 'Tooey' Spaatz, Col. Duncan, Maj. Gen. Doolittle, unknown, and Brig. Gen. Woodbury. (*Cross*)

This picture at Metfield may have been taken on 23 March 1944 or earlier. The group shown after the medal ceremony had taken place are, standing left to right: Corrigan, Johnson, Knoble, Juntilla; kneeling are: Streit, Marchant, Sperry. (*Sperry*)

Attacking trains was also a dicey occupation. The fighters first had to stop the train by targeting the locomotive, then commencing the destruction of the freight cars holding war materials while trying not to hit the carriages that may well have held innocent civilians. The Germans were initially unprepared, but eventually they hid flak cars along the trains. At the first sign of attack, screens would be pulled back and flak guns commenced firing, thus providing a lethal welcome to the incoming fighters. Just as dangerous, when hit the ammunition trains and trucks would violently explode and occasionally smash the aircraft to the ground with the blast. Life had become roulette for the low-level fighter jocks.[4]

Gradually, as the ground attack missions rolled on, the tactics changed. No longer did they just dive down and strafe, for they began to try and confuse the enemy by indicating that they weren't interested in their target. The fighters would fly way beyond, then circle round and hit the deck to come on in at zero feet to gain the element of surprise. After the first pilots went in to take out the more aggressive flak batteries, those following would change direction of attack and criss-cross the area to hit identified ground targets and make one pass only if the sky was too hot with lead. If the target was hot, one pass would be enough, two could be foolhardy, and three would mean a letter from the Air Force to the folks back home. So they learned on the job, but it was still expensive as the flak had been lethal. The guys had to be fast, low, and lucky to survive, and many were not. All the same, it was also very expensive for the Germans, and the destruction of aircraft, manpower, and materials by smashing the Luftwaffe before it could take to the skies had been vital to the Allied cause. Those raids were essential to the success of the forthcoming invasion, and Glenn Duncan and the 'Buzz Boys' gave them credibility. Ground strafing had become part of the Air Force armory.

Although significantly successful, it transpired that General Kepner formally disbanded the 'Buzz Boys' on 12 April 1944. The whole Air Force had, by then, adopted the stance of 'wherever they are, we'll find and destroy them', and destroy them they did—in abundance.

15

Raydon

So where did Clint take his leave? His family are fortunate that Clint took some rare cine-film during his operational period, and there are some fine views of his visits to Wales, where friends were made and relaxation became a valuable commodity. There is no doubt that his pictures taken of the hills and estuaries under dour Welsh skies were a lifetime away from the stress of battle. It was atmospheric and uplifting for anyone seeking peace, away from action. Although little was shown of the sun he so loved, the freedom and sanity of a new part of the world gave him the ability to shut off the war and relax in the freshness of the new environment. It was what he needed, and it would refresh him for the coming momentous weeks of combat. But that was looking into the unknown, and for the time being he was happy with the change of scenery and the welcome given to him by his friends in Wales.

On 1 April, Clint was back in the air. Even though he was a spare for his first sortie of the day, a colleague dropped out and he eventually flew with the Squadron, who were tasked with escorting B-17s of the 3rd Bomb Division.

It was a miserable early morning at 6.18 a.m. as the pilots gathered to hear the Briefing Officer show the route, flak areas, and strength of enemy air cover. Also of great importance was the weather, as it was definitely pretty darned poor in England. The forecast in France was also very bad for the mission, and the 3rd BD encountered heavy cloud and were forced to turn back to their bases. Of the bombers that remained, B-24s from the 2nd BD made for Strasbourg and other targets of opportunity. However, the day did not go well for them as a result of navigational problems. The city of Schaffhausen in Switzerland was bombed in error by some loose ships, killing some forty civilians, and the United States later had to pay $1 million in compensation. It turned out to be a costly and embarrassing situation; as a neutral country, Switzerland was somewhere to avoid, and there were several occasions during the war when bombers in trouble had to land there and were even shot at by the Swiss Air Force to ensure that they were captured. Unfortunately, as was the ruling, all aircrews were held for

The beautiful coastline of Wales. (*Sperry*)

the duration of the war as the Swiss were playing the neutral card absolutely to the letter, as agreed by the warring countries. Those aircrew finding themselves interned were occasionally (but unfairly) criticized for taking the 'easy' option when trying to get damaged bombers to safety. They were out of the war; that was the deal, and the internment wasn't exactly tough. Boredom was probably the biggest problem, and although the Alps and the Jura were in the way if they wanted to head for home, some tried; a few eventually made it back to England through France and also via other tortuous routes.

However, the 353rd Squadrons fulfilled their mission without any incident, and soon after passing Brussels both bombers and fighters headed back to England. Clint was thus able to recommence his operational flying after his leave and was given a full credit for the mission.

The day of 8 April turned out to be a busy one for the Squadron. On the second mission of the day, Clint, flying SX-E again, was one of fifty-six 353rd Group pilots briefed to provide high-cover escort to fifty-nine Fortresses of the 1st BD, who were tasked to deposit their loads onto their primary target of Oldenburg airfield in Germany. The weather didn't play ball as there was heavy, lingering fog at the bomber bases, and most of the 1st BD mission was cancelled—although the Group covered those remaining and carried out their duty with distinction, losing none of their charges. During the mission, Capt. Hoey, leading the Group and also 352nd FS, temporally departed the bombers and took the Squadron down on the deck to hit targets of opportunity. They found them initially at Hoperhofen airfield, where they damaged three e/a and a locomotive before heading back to their prime task of protecting the bombers.

The 9th brought no respite. The briefing was at 8.15 a.m. and take-off at 9.16. The Group Squadrons, led by Major Christian, were tasked to provide high-cover escort to 1st BD B-17s into their primary targets of Rahmel and Marienburg; they were centers of aircraft industry. Unfortunately, two Thunderbolts were lost, but on that occasion both pilots survived. The 350th FS had an interesting time, as they flew low over the Channel, going out to meet the bombers, and were shot at by an enemy convoy—which was most unwelcome. They attacked a lone E-boat to exact a bit of revenge, which they subsequently damaged. Following completion of escort duties, Lt Tanner strafed a locomotive and then attacked a Heinkel He115 flying boat as he exited out of enemy territory. Unfortunately, he lost his wingman when diving down to attack a target. Lt Stearns' aircraft appeared to be hit and he bailed out to spend the rest of his war in Stalag Luft I.

With Major Christian leading the 351st FS, Lt 'Jake' Terzian experienced fuel difficulties, and although fearing fumes would leak into his oxygen system, he decided to carry on. He got in a mix-up with a Fw190, and after the e/a broke off he decided that it would be best to head for home, nursing his fuel problem—but things began to deteriorate. Out of oxygen and having a terrible time with the fumes, he decided to bail out about 70 miles off the coast of England. However, he was a tough cookie and didn't panic, for as soon as he landed in those cold, dark waters, he managed to haul himself straight into his dinghy. He had to be mighty fast at that time of year to survive. The 'CTL' subsequently reported the event at 6.45 p.m.:

> R/T transmission from Pipeful 28 (who was hunting Lt Terzian) explains that he has observed Lt Terzian being rescued from his dinghy by a launch after leading it to the scene.

There is no doubt that Terzian owed a great deal to Lt Tom 'Pinky' Lorance of the 350th FS, flying as Pipeful 28 on that day, for the Channel waters would have taken another victim if he, and no doubt others, had not kept watch over their buddy.

As for the 352nd FS, they suffered six aborts. Clint had flown the full mission for three hours and fifteen minutes, and having returned to base he may have refueled and taken off again to assist in the search for Lt Terzian.

The missions on 10 April provide the authors with a slight dilemma, for there are conflicting indications as to which of the two missions Clint joined. He has marked on the '353rd Fighter Group Mission List' that he was with 'Bill's Buzz Boys', but on his 'Flight Record' he has marked 'High Cover Escort'. However, he had been on one of the BBB missions when he reported his observations relating to this type of operation:

An RAF Air Sea Rescue launch at Great Yarmouth docks. These craft would be the saviour of many airmen during the Second World War. It was an invaluable service, and sometimes quite dangerous if the Luftwaffe or E-boats took exception to their task of rescuing downed aircrew. (*Petticrew, via Cross*)

I flew as a replacement pilot with Bill's Buzz Boys. Kepner (General) ordered the concept closed 12 April '44. They flew 8 missions—2 of them uneventful— lost 3 planes and 2 pilots. Big problem picking up targets from tree-top levels. Virtually no air to air combat … just destroy them on the ground and run. A great disruptive concept but less effective than anticipated.

With Clint flying SX-E, it is quite likely that he was a last-minute replacement pilot for BBB. His remarks for 'high cover escort' might fit with the BBB mission that day as they were initially tasked to provide high-cover support for 'Droop Snoot' P-38s (with a bomb aimer in the nose) from 20th FG. They failed to rendezvous and went strafing instead, so it is possible that Clint filled in, but the outcome is still inconclusive, with no firm evidence of written support as the missions were coming thick and fast. As a result, the increased action has not enabled accurate reporting of Group records on a few of their operations. Some days subsequently turned out short on information or were (sometimes inaccurately) recorded retrospectively.

The final mission on the 12th was the last one for the 'Buzz Boys'. It was evident that ground strafing had offered new opportunities to the aggressive tactics adopted by the Eighth and Ninth Air Forces, and Kepner had determined that there was now no need for a 'specialist' group of aircraft to carry out those operations. It had become the domain of all Fighter Groups—although as ascendancy of the air evolved so did the casualties, for the flak thrown up (and sometimes down!) at the fighters as they screamed across airfields would take a severe toll. It was therefore a final farewell on the 12th to the 'Buzz Boys' as Capt. Starr led them on their last official operation to strafe airfields in Germany, where they were able to destroy six locomotives during their attacks. Regardless of their perceived effectiveness, they had fulfilled their original brief prepared by Col. Duncan and had led the way for the thousands of others who would follow the dictate of eliminating the enemy on the ground. They had succeeded in their overall mission and written a little history of air warfare; BBB had become a small legend in the Eighth Air Force, and their legacy was invaluable.

Having returned from a high-cover escort mission on the 12th, Clint and the Group were in full swing preparing to move to a new base several miles to the south. Also in Suffolk and in sight of the Essex border, it was Station F-157, and it was situated next to the village of Raydon.

By 13 April, preparations were well-advanced for the Group to finalize the move. Forward parties had been very busy making ready for the considerable logistical exercise of moving men, machinery, aircraft, and the thousands of

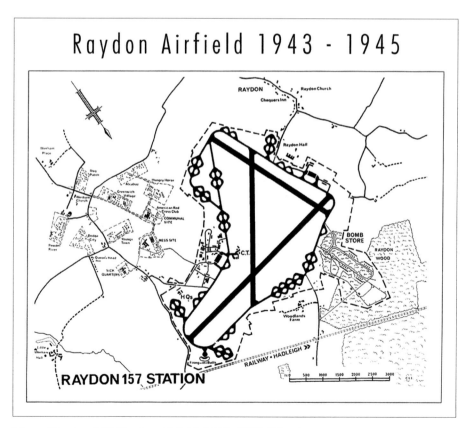

Map of Station 157, Raydon Airfield, 1943–1945. (*Elsey*)

different inventories that made an airfield tick. The previous incumbents, the IX Air Force Thunderbolts of the 358th Fighter Group, had moved to High Halden in the county of Kent, leaving their residue of chattels to the 353rd FG. It would take some time for the 'Slybirds' to settle down, and it was time for another change of call sign. No doubt the guys were well used to those they had been allocated for many months at Metfield, and it is possible that there was confusion until the pilots became used to them when operating on early missions from Raydon. The 350th FS were allocated 'Seldom', the 351st FS 'Lawyer', and the 352nd FS 'Jockey'.

Nevertheless, missions still had to be flown, and 13 April would find the Group providing high-cover escort again to the 2nd and 3rd BD Fortresses and Liberators as they exited their primary targets at Oberpfaffenhofen and Augsburg. That day, and very likely as a result of the increasing strength of pilots and planes, the 353rd FG operated as two Groups—'A', led by Capt. Lefebre, and 'B', led by Capt. Hoey. It was a three-hour mission for Clint (flying in Group 'B') and his fellow pilots, as they sought rendezvous with the bombers that were straggling out from their targets. It was not an easy task because the whole area was overcast with heavy thunderclouds, all the way up to 30,000 feet. The bombers had lost a distressing thirty-eight of their number to flak and enemy fighters, but the 871 P-38s, P-47s, and P-51s wrapped around the Bomb Divisions had knocked hell out of the Luftwaffe yet again. They claimed forty-two air combat victories and thirty-five destroyed on the ground, losing just nine of their own in return. 'Just nine' was nine too many, but the Luftwaffe were suffering far greater losses, and would continue to proportionately lose many more as the war and the battles in the air progressed.

There were no bombing missions and the Group did not operate on the 14th as they finalized their move to their new home. It would be the last time they relocated until the end of hostilities. Clint's comments were brief and to the point relating to that event, as he took a short forty-five minute non-operational flight from Metfield to their new base: 'Completed move to Raydon 14th April 44. Didn't realize that 353rd didn't arrive 'til then'. He would experience just ten more weeks of intense and dangerous missions before being released from operations, though had he been aware of it at the time, it would probably have seemed a lifetime away.

So what did the Group inherit at Station F-157, Raydon? Putting it mildly, it was dirty and in bad repair. The Unit History for April went into somewhat greater detail:

... [the inhabitants could] feel the breezes blow through the cracks around the window sills. The insulation on the inside of the buildings is falling down. Windows were covered with dust and paint. The paint job that had been done was woefully inadequate so each unit set about doing it all over again. It is not

With a Nissen hut as a typical backdrop, the Stars and Stripes are raised for the handover ceremony at Station 157, Raydon. The Group departed Metfield leaving the base in excellent condition, which is more than can be said for the previous occupants at Raydon—who left facilities in a very bad state. (*Cross*)

uncommon to have a leaky roof. In some areas the buildings were fumigated. Latrines as a whole were in a deplorable state, and had to be thoroughly cleaned immediately. Many of the drains were stopped up as no attempt was ever made to clean them out. Light fixtures were cut off and light bulbs were missing. It was most gratifying to see each organization move in and make the very most of the situation. Grass had to be cut—posts put in—walks replaced—orderly rooms rearranged—mess halls cleaned.

At the end of one week most of the dirt was cleaned up so that Units could now get down to the finer details and work them out one at a time as they came up. Planes were operational in two days. The Fighter Squadrons operate their own mess halls and the other Units eat at the Consolidated Mess—half of which houses the Post theater. A particularly fine job was done at the Officer's Club with 1st Lt Coy Fisher in charge. The long bar was moved and the partition which makes a bar room out of one end of the lounge. A grass rug was laid and the many comfortable chairs were neatly arranged. At the end of one week we were comfortably fixed at our new Club, which is bigger than our Metfield Club. Much could be said as to the policing that was necessary to put this field in good shape. The construction of the buildings does not make the situation any easier but are a handicap. Many have jokingly called the Group the 353rd Engineer Co. However, when we saw the mess we were moving into, everyone said: 'Changes will be made when the 353rd moves in'.

The 352nd Squadron monthly summary had been somewhat milder in its appraisal, and reported:

> After several mobility reports were hastily submitted this Squadron began making preparations to move, the first week in April. On 11th April 1944 seven men and two trucks load of equipment left Metfield for our new base at Raydon. The men remained to act as guards for the equipment, which was sent daily until Friday 14th April when all remaining equipment and personnel left the old base for our present home. The new base was left in very poor condition but the men pitched in and by working long hours finally have it looking much better. The Enlisted men now have their own Squadron Mess, which has boosted morale greatly. The living area is only some three hundred yards from the flying line, which is most convenient. The Red Cross Aero Club has much larger and better facilities than our old one.

So the Group Squadrons were now ready to carry out operations from an airfield in the beautiful but sleepy rolling countryside surrounding the small village of Raydon.[1] In that location they would see out their operations until the end of the war. However, for many there would be little time to enjoy the surroundings, but for some it would be the last home they would ever see.

By the middle of April 1944 it was getting very noticeable to those in command in England that the policy of destroying the ability of the Luftwaffe to operate from their severely damaged airfields was beginning to pay off. The Mustangs, with their impressive long range, were now able to roam at will throughout the Reich, and although they were being knocked down with tragic regularity, the Luftwaffe knew that very few places would be safe from their attention. The tough and uncompromising Thunderbolts, together with the P-38 Lightnings (the 'fork-tail devils'), had forged the way for the long-legged little guys to break new ground well into the German heartland. To counter that, the Germans had considerably increased both heavy and light gun batteries around all airfields, major industrialized areas, and other critical points, and were still very capable of filling the sky with a deadly barrage of lead. Even though the Luftwaffe was becoming severely depleted, they were not yet a spent force, and their ability to protect vital targets, together with formidable flak barriers, continued to provide a viable and deadly defense.

The 15th saw the first operation from Raydon, as the Group was briefed to carry out a 'Jackpot' mission. This entailed all Fighter Groups being allocated a sector within a grid system throughout enemy occupied territory, studying it carefully, and then carrying out what may be termed as organized mayhem. As 'Bill's Buzz Boys' had ceased to operate and ground attacks were becoming more prevalent, General Kepner did not want disorganized and rampaging fighters getting in each other's way and causing potential disasters—hence the grid system.

The allocated grouping for those operations was either in designated target areas I or II; it was decided that a Jackpot II would be carried out around the Hildesheim area on the 15th, but it was not to be. That first mission from Raydon was aborted due to inclement weather just before they cleared the enemy coast, which made the prospects of success nearly zero. As for Clint, it was reported: 'Lt Sperry—emergency landing at Martlesham Heath'. He was not the only one, and it was not a good start from the Group's new base.

Led by Major Robertson, the 353rd FG experienced yet another type of mission on 17 April. They provided a close escort to 2nd BD B-24s, who were ordered to operate in conjunction with five Pathfinder Force (PFF) aircraft in an experiment to drop 1,000-lb general-purpose bombs on a 'No-ball' V-weapon launching site at Wizernes, near St Omer, in France.[2] Having completed this single-credit mission in poor weather conditions and returning home, 352nd FS White Flight suffered an annoying and rather dangerous event when the tail gunners of the bombers opened fire on them! One can only guess what Col. Duncan suggested to the Commanding Officer of the B24s that evening—maybe a recommendation to smarten up on aircraft identification would have been the more palatable of his suggestions? At least nothing was damaged—just the pride of the Squadron. Although Clint flew on that mission, he made no comment on the occurrence; the only item of note was that he was twenty minutes on instruments flying SX-I, probably because his usual mount was declared unserviceable from the previous mission.

On 18 April Col. Rimerman led the Group on an extended mission of four hours and fifteen minutes deep into Germany. They were tasked to provide high-

This still photograph has come from Clint's personal cine-film, and although the clip only lasts for a few seconds, he was in formation with the P-38 whilst flying his P-47. It is not known when it was filmed, but it's a P-38H Lockheed Lightning from the 343rd FS, 55th FG based at Wormingford, near Colchester, in Essex. (*Sperry*)

cover support for all three Bomb Divisions, totaling 776 ships carrying 1,645 tons of bombs to their planned targets around the Berlin area. The 'Big Friends' came under attack by fighters and flak and lost nineteen of their number. It is not recorded if the Group were in contact with e/a, and there was nothing to suggest that it occurred; however, reports do indicate that the rendezvous was not successful, and the meeting failed to take place with the bombers on the return journey. A couple of locomotives were damaged by the 351st FS, but although some e/a were spotted on Zwischenahner airfield, Yellow Flight leader of the 352nd FS was unable to call them in as he had lost his radio. Lt Mueller, of the 350th FS, was sent off to search for a crew of a B-17 down in the Channel, but he only found a single person in a dinghy and passed over the responsibility to an Air Sea Rescue boat.

Clint was flying SX-F on the mission, his ninth of the month, and the Squadrons were carrying out their tasks with great discipline—though the pickings were particularly thin. It seemed to be enemy trains and boats, and not so many planes, on that particular mission.

According to a postscript on that day, there was a further item of 'misunderstanding'. This time it was apparently self-inflicted by Col. Bailey. The 'CTL' stated:

> Last evening at 17-47, Col Bailey in SX-B landed on the runway in use, 05, and before reaching its end, turned to the left and taxied down 27 runway. Before reaching the end of 27, the plane turned left again down 17 runway, crossing 05, the runway in use. SX-B was without radio contact with the tower and no permission was given to taxi on the runway.

The following day would be another bad one for the German aircraft industries and airfields. The 772 heavies hit multiple targets in north-west Germany, with Kassel, Bettenhausen, Eschwege, Lippstadt, and Werl all being primary targets, together with several others marked out as secondary or 'targets of opportunity'.[3] It would be another day of attrition as, once again, Fighter Command sent out nearly 700 aircraft to escort the 'Big Friends'. It was noted that it was a hugely impressive spectacle to see the massive fleet of American aerial invincibility forge its way towards the industrial heartland of the Reich. The sight was truly awesome.

Although the pilots were briefed relatively early at 7 a.m., Major Christian led the Group and Lt Juntilla the 352nd FS to rendezvous with the bombers in the vicinity of Paderborn and Gütersloh as they headed home from their various targets. The big guys were battered and full of holes, with at least 150 of them reporting damage from e/a and flak. In spite of that, all but six made it home—a remarkable record for Bomber Command. It appears that the fighters kept the Luftwaffe at arm's length, for all of those 'Big Friends' only managed to shoot down one enemy aircraft. The 'Little Friends', however, claimed sixteen, which tends to imply that there wasn't too much action for them. Indeed, a few of the 350th FS hit the deck to see what they could find, and managed to shoot up a train. So, for Clint and the Squadron it turned out to be a long and relatively quiet trip, but still very exhausting—dry mouth, cramped, weak, and bushed!

Incidents still continued to occur back at Raydon, as another item of interest was reported in the 'CTL' at 2.02 p.m.:

Oxford has been taxied off the edge of its dispersal into soft mud. Until such time as it can be pulled out (a crew is now at work), an M.P. has been instructed to have taxiing aircraft taxi through an adjacent dispersal in order to avoid hitting a wing of the Oxford which sticks out over the perimeter track.

Life was never simple.

16

Threatening Skies

It happened to be a very eventful day for the Squadron and the Group on 22 April (their call sign changed from 'Slybird' to 'Jonah' on this day), but for different reasons it was to be extremely unsettling for the Eighth Air Force.

The day kicked off with a report received at Raydon at 9.30 a.m. that a P-47 had crashed near Lindsey. The Hadleigh constable reported that the fire service and a doctor had been summoned, and that crash action had been taken. Two ambulances were sent to the scene, finding the smashed remains of a Thunderbolt from the 56th FG at Boxted—down the road and just over the county border in Essex. The pilot had managed to bail out, receiving a broken leg for his troubles. After rendering assistance at the site, the crash party returned to Raydon at 11.52 a.m., probably relieved that it wasn't a ship from the 353rd FG; of greater importance, no one was killed. For many others on that day, they would not be so fortunate.

Over 800 bombers were sent to Hamm in Germany, where marshalling yards and various targets of opportunity were the recipients of a massive hail of bombs. Nearly 2,000 tons of high explosive had been offloaded by the three Bomb Divisions as they droned over the objective, their sole aim being to decimate the supply lines of German military support. Lt Frank Emory later reported:

We saw the bombs falling on Hamm. The whole city sparkled with bursts. A large oil reservoir in the center of the city went up in a great sheet of flame and smoke. The railway yards were a mass of wreckage. As each wave of bombers passed over, many more sparkles lit up, and more smoke and fire shot up.

Once more it had been a vivid and frightening reminder to the enemy that the Allied war machine would fight through to the target, regardless of the flak and fighters that were protecting the lifeblood of the Reich.

Clint was filling in as a spare on the mission, and it didn't start well for the 352nd FS, who were briefed to provide a high-cover escort to the bombers. It was a late-afternoon take-off from Raydon at 5.33 p.m., heading for the skies over Germany. Lt Robert Geurtz was on his take-off run when his left tire blew. Unable to control his skittish ship, it veered off the runway and tipped over on its back, trapping him inside the cockpit. Fortunately, the rescue crews were soon on hand to lever him out of his predicament, after which he was taken to a medic who stitched up a nasty head wound caused by a shard of broken canopy. However, for Robert Geurtz it was a lucky day. Clint recalled:

> I was on same mission but missed the excitement. Bob Geurtz was a very lucky guy. I think I recall a takeoff accident when he ended up on his back with plenty of fuel around.

Having located the vast aerial armada, the 351st FS then clashed with e/a as they endeavored to get through to the bombers. Lt Hunter destroyed a Fw190 (later reduced to a probable) and Lt Herbert Field also claimed as his Squadron performed an excellent task of protection for their 'Big Friends'. Hunter's wingman, Lt Crampton, was badly shot up during the swirling mêlée, but on a wing and a prayer he managed to drag his aircraft home to land safely back at Raydon. 2nd Lt Paul 'Mickey' Trudeau was not as lucky as he stretched out his return to base. With his P-47 badly riddled with flak, he was able to coax it as far as the Dutch coast. However, he had just made it over the shoreline when he was forced to bail out. The weather and seas in the Channel were relatively quiet, but the shock and sudden awareness that he was down in that inhospitable and life-ebbing expanse of water was no comfort to him in his unfortunate location. Frank Emory, aware of his predicament, had stayed over him, giving constant radio fixes to bring in some kind of rescue before dark, even though the dinghy was floating dangerously close to the enemy beaches—but it wasn't to be. Paul just hunkered down, soaked and insignificant, with just his Mae West life-saver for reassurance, listening to the RAF going about their nocturnal business throughout the dark and foreboding hours.

By morning, after a wet and miserably lonely night, his buddies were buzzing him to ensure that a rescue could be attempted. It was around noon when he heard the welcome crackle of the Air Sea Rescue Walrus biplane as it alighted on the dangerous coastal waters and picked him up. Yet that kind of operation wasn't simple; the Walrus couldn't lift off, as the seas were by that time too choppy and extensively mined around the coast. They had to hang around for an RAF rescue launch, which eventually took the exhausted pilot into its care and then hitched up the Walrus, towing it back to more friendly waters. For strictly 'medicinal' purposes, Paul was given several shots of whiskey that had a pleasant reaction, and he found that sufficient quantity would render him rather more cheerful than the situation demanded! The 23rd turned out to also be a good day for Paul, and it was reassuring to Clint and others that there were brave souls prepared to risk their lives to save them from the forbidding Channel waters.

The Squadron also performed their protective duty that day, driving off bandits that were harrying the bombers; together with the 350th FS (having been released from their orders), they had a rewarding time attacking and damaging some rolling stock before heading home. Clint—with three landings credited, the last in virtual darkness—had probably located at another base prior to the mission with the rest of the Group before eventually landing back at Raydon. For all those participating in events on the 22nd it had certainly been quite an interesting and intensive day.

However, for the returning bombers, the night would be deadly; the 'Big Friends' were in for a very nasty surprise. Following another well-executed mission, and exiting their target and heading back towards the Channel, the tension in the ships was beginning to ease—but it was soon rudely and tragically shattered.

It was inevitable that at some time or other the Luftwaffe would endeavor to find new ways of inflicting damage on the growing number of bombers unleashed upon their Fatherland. On that late mission on April 22nd, and in the gathering gloom, they took the fight into the Eighth's back yard. It was a disaster for the returning bombers, for, as they prepared to land in near darkness, German fighters got in amongst them. One can only imagine the crews being tired, emotionally drained, and probably with their 'eye off the ball', looking forward to 'home' as the Luftwaffe infiltrated the stream. This resulted in fourteen aircraft being shot down or crash-landing, and a large number of the crews being killed or wounded. Many were not lucky that night; a relaxing smoke prior to touchdown turned out to be their last, as they smashed down to earth in flames. Those who did survive did not make the same mistake again, for a bitter and bloody lesson was learned that evening. The funeral pyres of planes and men were a sad reminder of the brutality of war.

The Group Squadrons carried out a sweep and strafing mission in the Ems/ Weser canal and Bramsche areas on the 23rd. However, Clint's bad luck surfaced again as the Mission Report recorded: 'Lt Sperry—glass elbow broke on wing tank'. Flying SX-Y, Clint put in five hours and fifteen minutes, with three landings, but where he was when the problem occurred is not noted. To record all of that flying time with no result must have been extremely frustrating for him; it was a perfectly flyable and fully armed ship left with no legs to carry out the task because of the breakage of a small, glass component. It was happening very regularly to many pilots and had been costing the USAAF valuable time on operations, also weakening their vital bomber protection.

Meanwhile, although the Group was causing some disturbance to barges and airfields, the inherent danger of that type of mission would again be experienced as two 353rd FG pilots found themselves 'off ops' for the duration—honored guests of the Third Reich. Lt Peterson of the 351st FS had been hit and bellied in to be captured, and a colleague of Clint's, Capt. Jesse Gonnam (leading the

352nd FS), was also hit by flak when attacking an airfield; he was lucky to bail out low and survive as a POW for the rest of the war. The Group had created some havoc, but the loss of two experienced pilots (Gonnam being an 'ace') was hardly a good trade-off. The whittling down of the German defenses continued to be very expensive, but the Air Force was doing a magnificent job of keeping Jerry heads down as the days drew nearer to the expected invasion of the Continent.

The 24th turned out badly for the Group and also for the bombers, even though the 'Little Friends' from the Eighth and Ninth caused massive losses of aircraft to the enemy. Briefed at 11.50 a.m., the Squadrons eventually lifted off at 1.22 p.m. to provide high-cover escort as the 250-plus B-17s of the 1st BD made their way to the Karlsruhe area to drop their high explosives on aircraft depots, airfields, and associated industries at Oberpfaffenhofen, Landsburg, and Erding.

The 352nd FS sighted several Fw190s near the rendezvous point, but the recently promoted Lt Col. Bailey did not engage the Squadron. Yet again, with problems probably caused by belly tanks not feeding fuel, the 350th and 352nd FSs suffered twelve aborts between them. Although the Squadrons reported an e/a probable, one P-47 was lost, with yet another pilot becoming a 'Kriegie' (short for '*kriegsgefangen*'—POW) for the duration.

The 1st BD suffered badly, losing twenty-seven of their number to fighters and flak; they were seen to crash and burn on the mottled landscape far below. Many young men lost their lives on that mission, and it would have been little comfort that their 'Little Friends' had handed out some heavy retribution for their loss. The fighters protecting all three Bomb Divisions (1st 2nd & 3rd) that day accounted for an amazing sixty-six air 'kills' and fifty-eight ground 'kills'—a total loss to the Luftwaffe of 124 valuable aircraft and no doubt many more valuable pilots, whose loss was almost impossible to replace at that point in the war.

Clint had recorded four hours and ten minutes of operational time, with a further thirty minutes non-operational—tending to indicate that he may have landed away from base, probably short of gas.

The missions rolled on. The following day, 25 April, all pilots were roused early for briefing and a 7.45 a.m. take-off. The Squadron, with Clint as a Flight Leader in SX-H, joined with the 351st FS to form 'A' Group, and aircraft from the 350th FS formed 'B' Group. They were to escort bombers onto their airfield targets at Nancy, Essay, Metz, Frescaty, Dijon, and Longvic. The bombers were aiming to destroy all the aircraft and facilities that would provide succor and support to the enemy, and the total fighter force were to pursue the same task—which they did, with excellent results. The 719 fighters that left their bases that day claimed twenty-nine ground and five air 'kills' to rack up more problems for the Germans. Clint recorded a mission time of three hours and ten minutes and a further one hour and thirty minutes non-operational—although the reason was not recorded. However, it was definitely not Clint to whom the 'CTL' referred at 11.40 a.m.: 'Called 350th Sqdn re ship LH-L taxiing into Hangar #1 and towing 4 cyclists'.

Thorpe Abbotts was the base for the 'Bloody 100th' Bomber Group, and Col. Duncan would do anything possible to extend the range of the P-47's to protect the bombers. However, Clint's sense of humour took it a bit too far! (*USAF*)

Come on now, some guys gotta have fun! For the other pilots, there was a note of interest: 'Boxted called re German a/c being sent here for identification purposes. All concerned notified'. One can only guess that the P-47 jockeys had more than enough time to study them in recent months; however, they could now get up real close if those captured enemy aircraft weren't shot down by an over-eager P-47 *en route*!

Heavy overcast prevented the bombing force from targeting their primary objectives on the 26th as the 353rd FG covered them out from their respective objectives around Brunswick, although nearly half of the force failed to bomb due to lack of pathfinders. On a day fraught with weather and location problems, it could only be termed very satisfactory that all of the 651 bombers made it home—although the little guys lost five and only claimed two ground 'kills'. In a sense, it was a strange day that would have been concerning for the Air Force Generals due to the lack of total success and the lack of aggression from the Luftwaffe, who were notable by their absence. However, there had been

The Me109G in this picture was captured and taken on charge by the RAF. It was flown into Allied air bases by an RAF pilot from the Fighter Development Unit at Farnborough to let the British and American pilots familiarise themselves up close with this agile little fighter. Highly manoeuvrable and versatile, it was a worthy opponent. (*Sperry*)

The Focke Wulf Fw190 arrived at Raydon with other captured German aircraft from the Fighter Development Unit at Farnborough. This excellent fighter packed a real punch and was soon jumped on by the 353rd pilots, who were pretty darned impressed with its appearance and cockpit layout. It was a formidable combatant that they had seen close enough over Europe—but not this close. (*Cross*)

a disturbing incident; one item in the Squadron report stated that a couple of unidentified B-17s were seen orbiting over the Channel. It was long suspected that Allied aircraft, previously captured by the Luftwaffe, were being sent to spy on missions, for they were spotted in the proximity of raids on several occasions as the pressure intensified on the German defenders. There were even reports of some 'unfriendly' fire from them. In time it was verified, and Allied planes were given permission to knock down any aircraft that had been confirmed as 'non-friendly'—which they did.[1]

With Clint participating in his familiar SX-E as Flight Leader, the 353rd Squadrons flew two missions on the 27th. The first took off at 9.48 p.m. to provide escort support for bombers out to inflict serious damage to 'No-Ball' V1 launch sites in the Pas de Calais area. With the flak unusually inaccurate, no action had been reported and they landed back at base at noon. As noted on the previous day, a B-17 was again seen to be making a series of orbits over the Channel, once more raising suspicions of 'enemy' infiltration to gain intelligence for the Luftwaffe. Whether it made it 'home' is not known.

Although the Squadron flew four more missions to end the month, Clint did not record any until 7 May. He had written '56:25 HRS COMBAT IN APRIL' on his Flight Record to complete his personal record of operational time for the

B-17s from the 390th Bomber Group, based at Framlingham (Parham), dropping their bombs on V1 sites around the Pas de Calais region. (*Sperry*)

month. That combat time would increase significantly for him in the next two months, and serviceability of his aircraft would begin to improve, but for the moment Clint had a three-day pass, and whether he had been on or off-base, the break was needed pretty badly.

Stress on its own was probably controllable during those tumultuous days of war. For a pilot involved in constant operations, with constant danger, constant tiredness, and constant aggression of an enemy out to kill him, stress was an ever-present specter. Day after day, the pressure increased. There would be times when the guys would be scared out of their skins, hyped up by constant missions, the weather that accompanied them, and the loss of fellow flyers to flak, fighters, or accidents. All these losses would have a deep and profound effect on them, consciously or otherwise; to see their buddies there one minute and gone the next, to see the 'Big Friends' writhe and fall or explode in one blazing catastrophic flash, with no evidence remaining that they ever existed, must have ground them down. However, those guys were young. They had some form of ability to shut off those terrible and painful happenings most of the time—but shut off was all they could do.[2] Clint was one of the lucky ones, as he had good control of his emotions:

> Amongst my closest friends, after a mission briefing, we would ride out to our aircraft together and joyfully discuss on the way what we'd do tonight. Which Pub, what party, and tease one another about the likelihood of crashing on the way down the hill to Hadleigh on our bikes ... or more likely, on the way home. We at least took off on a mission with a light hearted (however fictional) urge to get the job done, get back home and do what we talked of doing on our way out. Of course, there were many sad interruptions to our plans, but one had to store those memories and sadness for a time when they could be thoughtfully and peacefully explored with deserving tribute and reverence.

Taken on face value, it had been a pretty lean time for the Group Squadrons during April, only claiming one air victory and seven destroyed on the ground. It appeared that although they were greatly involved with many missions, they weren't in opportune positions at the time the big air battles took place. But appearances can deceive, as their overall contribution had been more than respectable, even though the abort rates were unacceptably high (predominantly caused by those fuel-feed problems). For Clint, it was his busiest month to date, as he had been involved in sixteen missions and had added fifty-six hours to his operational combat time. Regardless, he was still a long way from the magic 200 hours he needed to finish his tour; it seemed like a lifetime away. The authors are unable to confirm this, but it was sometime during April or May that Clint was given a new P-47D-22-RE. His original *Mary Jayne*, SX-E, was eventually re-coded, and Clint was able to transfer the SX-E coding to his new natural-

Although not very clear, this picture shows Clint in SX-E, about to lift off from Raydon with a teardrop tank, indicating another long mission. This was before he received his new P47D-22-RE. (*Sperry*)

metal finish (NMF) Thunderbolt. In this new aircraft he was able to complete his combat missions. However, there was a great deal more action to see before his tour would finally end.

There should be an awareness that, by April, the long-legged P-51 Mustangs were beginning to roam further into the German heartland and hit the defenders hard. As previously stated, it had been the brutally tough and uncompromising P-47s and P-38s, together with their shorter-range counterparts in the RAF, who had initially paved the way, clearing the skies for the massive air armadas of heavy bombers who were pounding targets by day and by night. Therefore, as the United States Army Air Force and the Royal Air Force gradually weakened the Luftwaffe in Western Europe, the apparently solid German defense line was being inexorably forced back, ever deeper, towards their homeland.

It must also be remembered that apart from destroying Germany's ability to wage war, the Allies had to prepare the area designated for Operation 'Overlord'— the final invasion of Europe.[3] The date for D-Day was yet to be finally agreed, and all but a handful of very senior officers were aware of details, but it would come soon—and the weakening of defenses and infrastructure would intensify.

Many months before, Allied Generals had planned for the vital prerequisites to enable the invasion to proceed. This would firstly be control of the air, and then the destruction of all forms of ground targets: airfields, communication centers, supply lines, and V1 missile sites. It continued to be a bloody battle of attrition that the Allied air forces were very slowly winning—they had to.

Build-up to the Invasion

The month of May was originally favored for the invasion. However, the Generals and Heads of State were concerned that the Allied Air Forces were still not doing enough damage to the Luftwaffe and the enemy infrastructure to ensure that 'Overlord' would be successful; they were just not ready.[1] Control of the skies over Europe was certainly being won, although there was still much that had to be done to protect the ground troops and the armaments that would enable them to fight off the beaches. Of equal importance, it was vital to expand the bridge-head, hold the ground, and then break out and wipe out any resistance as they fought deeper into enemy territory. The task would be formidable and dangerous, and many lives would be lost in its execution, but the soldiers just had to be able to hang on in there and do it. Any thoughts of failure would be monumentally frightening.

Having participated in what could only be termed as a 'quiet' mission on the 7th, the following day brought another escort mission for the Group—this time led by Col. Duncan and the 352nd FS by Lt Col. Bailey. Clint was a Flight Leader in SX-E as the Squadrons provided another high-cover escort to 500 B-17s of the 1st and 3rd BDs. Their targets were spread around the Berlin area again, but 8 May wouldn't turn out as easy as the mission from the previous day. The Fortresses lost twenty-five of their number as e/a got amongst them with heavy and aggressive attacks, as if they were making up for their non-appearance the day before.

The 351st and 352nd FSs had brief encounters with Me109s that dove past them trying to get to the bombers, and the P-47s chased them down. However, no direct contact was made and all Group ships made for home, escorting some beat up B-17s as far as the English coast.

It was under those kinds of confused conditions that the Air Force continued to search for ways of disrupting the German defenses. Although first used during 1943, 'Carpet', an electronic device for jamming Würzburg range-finding radar for the German flak batteries, was operating on heavies that day.

Even though they lost more bombers to the German fighters than the previous day, when 'Carpet' was not operating, the flak damage on 8 May was less. It was subsequently concluded that the installation of the device in a number of bombers offered some protection by dislocating the flak radar system. Although slight improvements were noted, the damage inflicted by flak was still substantial.

With Capt. Lefebre leading the Group and Capt. Juntilla the 352nd FS on the 11th, it was a late afternoon take-off to provide an escort to 3rd Air Tactical Force, 3rd Bomber Division B-17s specifically targeting loco sheds and marshalling yards in Brussels. The bombers were once more hitting the transport structure to disrupt the supplies destined for the German Army. They were part of a mighty force of over 600 that day, targeting many marshalling yards spread throughout north-west Europe. The flak was flying thick and fast as the bombers swept onto their targets, unloading their high explosives over the rail networks and causing a great amount of destruction and dislocation. Although many aircraft were damaged by flak, only eight of their number were lost. The Group chaperoned their own force of about 100 'Big Friends' without loss, and excellent bombing was recorded through difficult hazy conditions. Escorting the force out, all the P-47s eventually landed back at Raydon at 7.51 p.m. Clint had racked up another two hours and forty-five minutes and the Squadron had completed another successful mission, but where were the German fighters again? Were their spasmodic appearances a sign of weakening?

It didn't take long for the answer. They turned up the next day—swarms of them.

Oil was a vital target for the Allies and a critical target to protect for the Luftwaffe, for without oil there could be no defense. Just like the raids on the ball-bearing factories earlier, those in high office sensibly considered that oil production and its storage facilities had to be another 'panacea' target for bomber commands of both the RAF and USAAF. It was the Mighty Eighth who were first to pick up the challenge to destroy oil production, as it was also seen to be the means to an end—effectively destroy those installations, and the German forces would eventually run out of oil-based products to power their vehicles, both on land, sea, and in the air. The Eighth swung at yet another curve-ball.

The Squadrons lifted off at 10.22 a.m. on 12 May to provide high-cover escort to B-17s of 3rd BD that had set out to destroy synthetic oil installations at Brüx and Zwickau. The weather was good for visual bombing that day, but it also allowed German fighters to spot the bombers. There was no doubt that the Luftwaffe had been protecting the oilfields to great effect, and there was a strong enemy fighter reaction against the leading bomber elements. There were terrible losses on both sides, showing further confirmation (if it were needed) that this method of weakening Germany's resolve was not going to be easy; forty-one bombers were lost and 162 damaged, with 377 casualties. It was a bad day for the attackers, in spite of the protecting Fighter Groups accounting for twenty-six e/a destroyed. It was recorded:

The contrails tell the story. The fighters manoeuvre to cover the bombers. (*Sperry*)

A superb picture of Clint standing on the wing and waving while crew chief Leo Katterhenry prepares to settle him into the cockpit prior to another mission. The artwork showing Clint's painting of Mary Jayne on the front of the aircraft would have been in stark contrast to the distinctive black-and-yellow chequers on the nacelle, which had been adopted by the 353rd after they moved to Raydon. Extra fuel in a teardrop tank and no bombs indicate an escort mission. (*Sperry*)

It is believed that this picture was taken in late spring 1944. Clint attached the following information to the photograph: 'This was my old aircraft, which was painted olive drab. It was a flat porous finish, which I spent hours wet sanding and finally waxing to gain nearly 15 kts. You can see the shiny surface of the wing in the foreground. The crew didn't like it because they'd slide off while trying to lay in .50-cal. ammunition. Great fighter pilot and friend Paul Cles to on my left (to right in photo). (*Sperry*)

> After the 350th dispersed the first attack, the 352nd witnessed e/a 'like a swarm of bees.' 50 e/a made an attack on the second combat wing, with several bombers and enemy fighters believed to have collided. Another 50 e/a made a third pass at the bombers while a further 20 kept at 30,000 ft for top cover.

It must have been a very sobering experience for the P-47s, as they struggled to protect the bombers and survive themselves. Emotions ran high, with fear and aggression evident as men fought for their lives in that aerial maelstrom.

Clint had again been flying SX-E during the mission, and with a time of three hours and forty-five minutes (much filled with unbroken high tension) he and the rest of the Squadron were most relieved when they eventually returned to base. They would be unaware that apart from an incident the following day, there would be no missions for a clear five days. The Eighth needed the time to recover.

Although Clint had flown several times non-operationally during that period, there was one event on 16 May that caused a bit of a panic. It was reported that the

352nd FS were allocated as the evening 'alert flight', and as a result of confusion over change of runway there was a delay, and then a misheard 'scramble' call. The flight was in the air for seventeen minutes when it was determined that the original call was to line up the ships for dispersal, so they were somewhat hastily recalled back to base. Clint may well have been involved in this debacle, but it was not reported as operational time—it was perhaps just too embarrassing.

One can only imagine whether all flying crew considered their own mortality. A short period away from operations may have prompted them to think about what the future held for them; did they think that there even was a future? It has often been recorded that many actually resigned themselves to the fact that they would not survive a tour. Some thought that it relieved them of their responsibilities, while others feared the outcome and became more cautious or even irresponsible in their actions. Whichever was the case, the Air Force gave some guidance. So, would Clint have considered or heeded any advice? It is very probable that he did make a will, and if so may have consulted the Judge Advocate General's Department. Many did and a great number were not present when the will had to be executed. They were young men still in their teens or very early twenties, and a large majority thought they were immortal—before war shook that theory.

However, those young guys were far from home, and there were many distractions to take their minds off the stress of combat. Some were liable to 'forget' that they had responsibilities back in the States; yup, they took a great shine to the British girls. Some were wild and abandoned, but others were more discreet, managing to keep a lid on their indiscretions. Marriages, divorce, and the birth of children became a sudden reality for many young airmen serving in England during the Second World War, and the effects of that period of excitement and disruption to the British way of life are still encountered to this day.

'Did you know your father was an American airman...?'

On returning to operations, the mission on the 19th severely tested Clint's flying ability and his nerve. The following has been related by him in report form:

May 19, 1944: Target Escort Brunswick.

353 Fighter Group Leader: Col Glenn Duncan. (48 aircraft)

Briefing: B-17 [B-24] Bomber escort to target, Brunswick.

Weather: Clear over continent, haze North Sea & Channel area.

T.O. 11-36—Form up to climb on course 93d to cross coast of continent south of The Hague at 25,000+. Bomber rendezvous estimate, 13-15.
Mission duration, est. 4-50 hrs. External fuel 216 gals.
Assigned position: Leader of 8 aircraft, 2nd Section 352nd Squadron.

Report: During smooth air climb of 600 ft/min with the coast of Holland not yet visible, at about 11-55 proceeded to switch to alternate wing tank. While checking fuel pressure during the switch I noticed the oil temperature running higher than normal. Opened oil cooler doors, but temperature continued to climb into the red. I then partially opened the engine cowl flaps hoping to cool things down. With constant attention to engine gauges the oil pressure was now dropping steadily and it became evident I would have to turn back.

At just over 12,000 ft and a guess of 40-50 miles from the English coast, I broke radio silence to report, 'Slybird [Jonah] Red Leader leaving formation'. Breaking out to the left clear of others and dropping the nose for more speed at reduced power, I opened oil coolers fully and adjusted engine cowl flaps to full open. On the return course, descent to minimum, but within minutes the engine temperature was all the way in the red and oil pressure dropped to zero. At this point the engine became violently rough with the engine cowling twisting dangerously and the entire aircraft being seriously shaken. As I pulled the throttle all the way back with mixture full rich in an attempt to smooth things enough to keep the engine from tearing away from the aircraft, it came to a wrenching stop.

Because I was fearful the engine would literally be torn from the aircraft, this silence and final stability was a great relief. Again, in consideration of radio silence, I reported, 'Slybird Red, I've lost my engine.' The immediate response from the Group Leader was simply, 'Get out.'

Because I was not yet ready to test the waters of the North Sea, I wisely ignored the suggestion and applied every skill I had learned about this highly respected aircraft. I was determined to at least get as close to the home coast as possible.

I was now descending through 9,000 ft estimated to be about 25 miles from a visible but hazy coastline. I kept my speed at between 270-300, with oil cooler and cowl flaps now fully closed, but with a decision still to be made about the external tanks. I decided to keep them with me. I did not want to risk having one release and the other hang up causing more aerodynamic problems than I already had. (A release malfunction would not normally be of concern, but it bothered me at the time.)

By holding my speed up I could comfortably control the aircraft and hold my descent close to 1000 ft/min. I briefly tried slowing down but the sink rate and loss of forward progress toward the beach resulted in a quick return to speed. It was encouraging to feel that I could at least get close to the beach. In seconds I found that I could easily make the beach and now hopefully belly into the marshes somewhere between Orford Ness and Felixstowe.

Just over the beach I still had nearly 2000 ft and about 300 mph with time to think. (I can thank a very helpful upper air tail wind for this welcome miscalculation.) I can't belly in with external tanks, but can wait to last minute.

Dead ahead was Martlesham Heath (356 Fighter Group Base). Thoughts about saving the aircraft were real but another very urgent decision had to be made. All three runways were lined with one squadron each as 356 Group was just starting their take-off to pick up the return escort of bombers on the Brunswick raid. I had time for about a 90d positioning turn for a parallel approach to the runway with lead aircraft just starting their take-off roll. The approach turn was adjusted to land as short as possible on the grass without crossing any runway intersection if I got that far. I was at ease with my approach and rapid descent and confident of impact possibly short of the airfield boundary, but the terrain and approach were clear of any serious obstructions.

I would guess at about 300 ft and still in my turn with a few degrees to go to line up for final, I was now committed to keep tanks on. A quick glance at hydraulic pressure assured enough for gear and maybe flaps. The gear was down in seconds quickly followed by full flaps. Still holding at 125-130 because I needed solid control with a final descent line estimated to put me on the very edge of the field boundary. It was important to compensate for a very heavy aircraft, i.e., full load of ammunition, full internal and external fuel (less 20 minutes), plus four stationary wide Hamilton prop blades.

Rotation from a very steep approach was going to have to be smooth and steady to avoid stalling either wing for I'm very committed. Rotation was complete and in spite of much higher than normal touch-down speed SX-E dropped hard into the soft boundary turf and rolled no more than 1500 ft to a stop well short of the intersection and parallel to the squadron whose lead elements were continuing their take-off roll.

A jeep monitoring the 356 departures arrived beside the aircraft simultaneously as I came to a stop. As soon as the flaps made it all the way up, a Colonel climbed onto my left wing to the cockpit, lit a cigarette and handing it to me simply said, 'I never would have believed it'. At the same time his driver was tugging at the prop and confirmed that it was frozen solid. The Colonel asked where it quit and I told him, 'About 40 miles due east at 12000 ft.' With a simple thumb's up gesture and a slap on the back he went back to the runway observation point and another vehicle took me to Operations. I then learned that my greeting was made by Col Phillip Tukey, CO of 356 Fighter Group, who was obviously not flying that mission.

Later, Col Tukey told me that the final approach (which he was very concerned about) was spectacular. Disappointingly, he was not referring to my flying, but the condensation streaming off the wing tips all the way. During the final seconds of landing rotation he told me there was a sheet of white from the tips to the wing roots (somehow I missed seeing that).

A new P&W R-2800 engine was installed at 356 and three days later I flew out of Martlesham Heath happy to have my own aircraft back. I asked about what caused an obvious oil starvation since there was no visible sign of leakage. The crew that changed the engine were fortunately also curious and in their investigation discovered that a rag had somehow gotten into the oil tank (reservoir) and completely blocked the flow of oil to the engine. This was a thorough crew, for to simply change engines the oil tank would not ordinarily have been disturbed. The result could have been another engine failure with possible disastrous results.

To my knowledge, no enquiry was ever conducted, and other than my warning about the practice of the time-saving rag techniques at fuelling time, to this day I don't think anyone in operations knew of my problem. Only the guys at 356 who nervously watched my approach knew that it wasn't just a routine emergency landing.

There is absolutely no doubt that Clint's experience and competence saved both the aircraft and himself during that incident. His immediate and controlled reaction when confronted with a dead engine had been the result of extensive training and combat. Without that previous background experience, Clint would almost certainly have ended up in the North Sea. Sadly, many pilots would not have had that advantage, but Clint was an exception; his knowledge and awareness of the P-47 and its handling characteristics, together with his valuable accumulated flying hours, resulted in a successful conclusion. It was an incredible feat of flying that very few could or would accomplish in a 7-ton glider! As his Crew Chief, Leroy Katterhenry, stated in his letter to Mary following Clint's final combat mission: 'Lt Sperry can fly anything that has wings on it.'

It is rather strange that apparently nothing was officially recorded about the potentially grievous error during the fueling process, but it was a time of great pressure on the Squadron, and as no aircraft or pilot was lost, it is likely that just a verbal admonishment and recommendations to take more caution were issued. Regardless, Clint was back in the air the next day, but without SX-E.

18

Unrelenting Pressure

The dawn of 20 May was marked by heavy ground mists and poor visibility. Following briefing, the Group P-47s lifted off at 8.28 p.m. to provide a high-cover escort to 1st BD B-17s targeting Orly and Villacoublay airfields. All three Bomb Divisions were operational that day, the aim being to disrupt enemy movements around airfields and marshalling yards. Regrettably, as a result of the very poor visibility, eight bombers were lost either in taxiing collisions or forming up, so the initial omens were not good. R/V with the B-17s was ten minutes later than scheduled, but the Group picked them up and followed them through to their bombing runs. The results were later pronounced as fair to poor, and although those that took part picked up some flak damage, it was a relief that no aircraft were lost. It had been noted, while on their way in, some P-51s were seen to join up with the bombers, giving an indication that the introduction into the ETO of that fine fighter was well-advanced. In fact, they had been contributing small numbers to escort duty since December '43. Since then there had been several Groups operating the Mustangs, and they were supposed to be taking the ache out of the butts of the P-47 pilots as they commenced the longer missions—or so the Thunderbolt pilots thought! However, it didn't always work out that way, as the P-47 guys were still flying some stretched escort jobs—if fuel continued to feed from the tanks.

The operations were now coming thick and fast, both for the Squadron and for Clint, and 21 May was no exception. Capt. Dewey Newhart was leading the Group and Capt. Poindexter the 352nd FS as they took off at 10.20 a.m. for a 'Chattanooga Plan 1' dive-bombing mission in the Bremen area.[1] Clint was leading 'Jockey' (the 352nd Squadron call sign) Red Flight flying SX-E, now with a new engine installed as a result of his aborted mission from a couple of days ago. They were looking for targets of opportunity along the rail networks in order to do as much damage as possible to disrupt enemy transport networks—they targeted rolling stock, junctions, bridges, and anything that had steam or smoke blowing out of it. As they crossed the coast and headed out over the North Sea, the sky was a forbidding overcast with heavy rain showers, and peering down

This picture is taken at Raydon following the Group conversion to P-51Ds, which began at the end of September 1944. It is the personal mount of Lt Col. William 'Bill' Bailey, and carried the name *Double Trouble*. (*Cross*)

from 15,000 feet the sea looked ominous and rough with mountainous waves. It would not be good to have a problem during that crossing; little did they know that one of their number would feel the wrath of those elements on the way home. To compound their concerns, ground attacks were not a safe occupation. Trains laden with explosives and ammunition could destroy attacking aircraft, so they guessed the operation was going to be a hairy affair.

The Squadron scored well. The trains were found and attacked, with Clint claiming the destruction of two, and his 'Jockey' Red Flight were able to share in the destruction of another locomotive with 'Lawyer' White Flight. Clint remembers: 'If the engines saw us coming in from the side, I could watch them jump clear while underway. Always hoped they survived'. He also destroyed '...a small factory (which was written up in 'Stars and Stripes') for it was discovered to be a brick factory of little strategic value—it was excused because with the other 500-lb bomb [he] took out a major bridge'. In later years he also remembered that moment when his bomb hit the factory, for when it disintegrated the bricks were hurtling up and around him, and it was a minor miracle that his own bombing did not bring SX-E down. But, as for a bridge, Clint recalled:

My one most successful bombing (other than the brick factory) was skipping a 500 lb into the shore end abutment of a good-sized bridge thus dropping the end into the river. Skip bombing was very effective on bridges and into short railway tunnels. I say 'short' because there could not be a high rise from the tunnel opening. You had to get down just off the tracks approaching the opening, release the bomb and pull up in a hard turn real quick to clear the rise over the tunnel.

Clint's gun-camera footage shows strikes on a train on 21 May 1944. (*Sperry*)

With a very necessary 10-second fuse delay you could drive the bomb right into the tunnel, pull-up and away and watch the dust blow out of both ends; actually skipping off a river is much cleaner and often more accurate. The hill in front of you at tunnel end is a distraction, and release can be a bit hurried. Skip bombing was certainly not my invention. I suspect it came from the Navy. Torpedo bombers used to launch torpedoes at surface level and found that the torpedo would skip before submerging slightly to propel itself to the target. Actually, the longer 1000# bomb had more surface for skipping and as I recall, that's what we used.

Clint had skill and a little good fortune that day—there had to be an element of luck for a precise hit, for wind, angle of attack, bomb flight, and other distractions had to come together at the same time. Then there was flak.

Also fortunate was Squadron pilot 2nd Lt Raymond Eluhow. The weather had been closing in as he flew back across the Channel, short of gas. He didn't get far; his engine died, he rapidly gave a fix, and then he bailed out into a very uninviting sea, running with 20-foot waves. Managing to crawl into his waterlogged dinghy, seasick and holding his small Bible, his prayers were answered when the Squadron found him and stayed with him until the watch was taken over by an RAF Spitfire pilot, who guided a rescue boat to pick him up.

Clint, meanwhile, was not exactly home and dry. Following the action-packed four-hour mission, he recorded: 'I had to land my flight on an airfield under construction, which accounts for the two landings and added 30 minutes'.

The pressure on the enemy was intensifying. The constant battering of all vulnerable facilities that were their lifeline was beginning to have an effect on their ability to mount an efficient and coordinated defense. The Allied attacks were ferocious and, more importantly, sustained.

The mission on the 22nd was yet another attempt to disrupt the transportation network by targeting the railroad bridge at Liège. Clint was again flying SX-E as the Group Squadrons took off from Raydon at 1.40 p.m. Unfortunately, he hadn't been able to complete the mission; he was an early return, recorded in the Mission Report as 'prop out', and landed away from base before eventually returning to Raydon. This poses a confusing dilemma, for when his prop gave out on the 19th it was officially reported as 'Lt Sperry—generator out', yet Clint stated the problem to be 'prop out'. Did Clint confuse the dates? It appears more likely that the Mission Reports, which were not always completed on the day of the event, may have confused the two, as often happened. Evidence indicates the latter scenario, but one thing was certain—Clint was only in the air for about thirty minutes on the 19th and showed one landing. That stacks up correctly, as he would not have been able to make more than one! Also, on the 22nd he recorded three hours and thirty minutes (of which one hour and forty-five minutes were marked as operational) and he made two landings. On that timing he could have still managed to get back over the Channel, even with a generator problem. It could then have been fixed, thus enabling him to carry out a test flight and return to home base; conversely, he could have taken an earlier flight before the mission. Regardless, this theory of

Taken from Clint's cine-film, this is a superb picture of Clint in SX-E, taxiing from hard-stand to runway at Raydon. (*Sperry*)

confused dates is conjecture, but the facts do tend to support Clint's recall. We are therefore, in this instance, going to go with the dates he recorded.

The mission continued, the defenses were alert, the weather conditions were poor, and the bridge could not be located. The Group subsequently looked for and attacked targets of opportunity. Although a 350th FS ship bellied in near Raydon, the one loss was Lt Jack Terzian of the 351st FS, who took some 20-mm hits and had to belly in near Brussels. He was able to evade, but was then captured and handed to the Gestapo; after managing to escape, he was eventually liberated in Brussels on 3 September 1944. Lt Terzian certainly had a tale to tell when he arrived back at Raydon, and he told it to the guys as it was. It had been a story of courage and endurance, and he'd had a tough time.[2]

The Mission Report on the 23rd effectively sums up the Group's next action:

> Escort to 3rd ATF under Type 16 Beachy Head Ref PO # 348'. Lt. Colonel BAILEY leading Group. Up RAYDON 0707 hours, down 0932. Due to insufficient time for preparation after receipt of Field Order, plus weather conditions at takeoff time, Group twenty (20) minutes late setting course. When Leader learned that R/V with 3rd TF would be extremely late and that they already had escort, decision was made to pick up 1st Div bombers. R/V 0805 hours, 20,000 feet over solid undercast. Left bombers 0835 hours when P-51s came in. L/F out north Cayeux 0856 hours, 18,000 feet. No vectors from Snackbar. No e/a seen.

Clint had been leading a Flight in SX-W. It was not a very satisfactory mission, but at least the Group's Squadrons sustained no losses. He was off missions for a few days and remained on base, taking on other flying duties. He put in a few short flights, including taking up the Percival Proctor again. Did Clint like it? Was it duty, just stooging around, or just another type to add to his growing list? At least it was quicker than a bike.

It was an early briefing on the 30th that heralded two missions for the Group Squadrons, the first being a high-cover penetration support for B-17s bound for Halberstadt. Capt. Poindexter was leading the 352nd FS, with Clint making up a Flight with Lts Armstrong, Johnston, and Newton.

Before the withdrawal from the well-formed bomber stream, about seventy e/a appeared, and as 352nd 'Jockey' Squadron dispersed them, Capt. Poindexter sent down two Fw190s to a fiery end on the ground below. It was apparent that P-51s were also in the area to give further support, and probably accounted for others. Following that action, and in yet another skirmish, Capt. Poindexter endeavored to chase a Fw190 off the tail of his wingman, 1st Lt Francis Edwards. He was too late—the young pilot went down to his death. He had recently married an English girl, and it was a tragedy for his new wife and his family when they received the sad news. It would be one of those occasions when the Judge Advocate General's Department would be activated; that formality was not wanted by anyone.

A little over three hours later, following the extended four-hours-and-forty-five-minute mission during the morning, the Group Squadrons lifted off for a Thunder-bombing raid, looking for rail and canal targets around Verberie and Compiègne. They soon found trade. Col. Duncan had been leading the Group and 352nd FS as they attacked a bridge 6 miles south of Compiègne, with twelve P-47s carrying two 1,000-lb bombs each. Flying in at ground level, they skipped the bombs onto the target, recording one direct hit. Five bombs exploded very close to the structure, damaging ten freight cars that were caught in the blasts. The bombs were so close that barges near the bridge were seen to blow up. Strafing targets on their way out, the Squadron subsequently claimed one loco and four damaged, together with ten goods wagons, leaving behind a mess of steaming and tangled metal littering the area.

Curiously, the 352nd Squadron Mission Report showed that twelve ships were down for the mission, but Clint had been listed as a single at the bottom on the list, flying SX-E as an extra. He definitely flew that second mission of the day as he has recorded it in his IFR, and his camera footage was proof that he was involved in the attack on locos claimed by the Squadron. Clint totaled eight hours of flying that day, and the pilots on both missions were exhausted after all that time in the cockpit—especially since sitting on a parachute and dinghy was tough on a certain part of the anatomy! At least they had a few hours of rest in between operations—enough to get the creases out of their pants.

Striking rail and road junction on 30 May 1944. The steam rises as the boiler blows on a locomotive when Clint's machine guns bracket the target. (*Sperry*)

The pressure on the enemy intensified as the last day of May saw the Group taking on two more missions. Poor weather predictions for Bomber Command were prompting Met flights, and reported cloud cover over Germany, France, and Belgium caused them to abandon bombing several primary targets.

There is no record to indicate Clint was on the first mission, and the reason for uncertainty is that he had recorded on his IFR that he flew a total of seven hours and thirty minutes, with two landings that day. Although it is confirmed that he entered '3:45 - Dive bombing' on the afternoon mission, there is no positive indication of his contribution during the initial three hours and forty-five minutes, as it was not recorded as operational. It is possible that Clint carried out a Met flight as requested by the Eighth Air Force, for at some time during his seven and a half hours of flying he spent an hour on instruments. In this instance it is pure speculation, and places further confusion on the issue of Met flights being logged as an 'Operation' or not. Judging by the value to all Commands and the danger to the pilot, they certainly should have been. Although there is no firm evidence that Clint carried out a Met flight during the morning of the 31st, the following story does indicate that the unaccounted three hours and forty-five minutes may well have led to his following recollection:

Weather reconnaissance mission for Bomber Command with a negative report to them and a near miss for us.

We took off in lousy weather. 'We' because I was to go in hopefully as far as Antwerp and needed a radio relay pilot in another P-47 to hold at the Belgian coast and relay my weather reports to Bomber Command. The controller would vector me to him for rendezvous on my return leg. I left him at the estimated coastal position at 30,000 on top of a very solid overcast which we were in during our climb from 6,000 to 18,000. After estimating my penetration (for the ground was not visible as far ahead as I could see), I received a rather strange vector for the rendezvous, but picked him up at the designated 20,000 just above the overcast tops and promptly lost my radio (we never flew combat operational aircraft on weather flights and some were not that well attended to because of it). The radio loss was not a major problem because England has got to be to the west. My partner tucked in close and I made a rapid descent until, through rain, I could detect ocean white caps at about 6,000.

In terms of time, I thought we should be virtually over the coast of England and picked up a hazy coast line just south of our position (off to my left). Although several miles south of where I expected to be, it had to be Margate with London to the west. With a fairly rapid deterioration of weather I turned south with a stop at Manston on the outer Kent peninsular. We let down to 4,000 and as we crossed the coast were greeted by anti-aircraft bursts and turned to sea again.

In terms of time, we had to be nearing the English coast, but the first landfall in the rain and poor visibility was Calais, France, the northern most tip of France … and we were not welcome.

I thought I was ... just south of intended course, however quite a bit south. With a weather deterioration I intended to land at Manston, but we were actually ... just off Calais.

I had no visible landmarks during my entire penetration of enemy territory and must have flown directly over Brussels on top at 30,000. No AA until we were an easy target over Calais at 5,000. A newly assigned replacement pilot saved the day. He was our 'Shepherd' on that particular day.

It's a sure thing that Clint and his colleague were flying along the Belgian coast. However, when heading home he was under the illusion that it was friendly fire that they were receiving from the British, and they were firing real ordnance at them! With his radio out, poor visibility, and feeling somewhat concerned, they both took the flak. However, Clint later found out that the unknown factor that caused the problem was a wind exceeding 60 mph from the north-west, blowing them off their route home.

So, who was the 'Shepherd'? There had been several that may have fitted a 'newly assigned replacement...', but unfortunately the authors are unable to resolve who it was or if the date is correct.

Steve adds a footnote to the mission:

Dad read a short story in the mid-1990s by Frederick Forsyth ('The Shepherd') about a de Havilland Vampire pilot flying to his home base on Christmas Eve of 1957. The aircraft developed a complete electrical failure, was low on fuel and lost in fog. He's met by a de Havilland Mosquito (WWII fighter/bomber); is led to an unused RAF field and safely lands. It's an enjoyable read of fiction but I believe Dad identified with the Vampire pilot to some degree having found himself in a similar situation in fact. My father is not alone in such otherworldly encounters in the air. Many pilots (including this one) have closely held stories that follow a similar thread. Easier and more fun to attribute a positive resolution to great skill and luck.

There is no doubt that Clint was very much involved in the second mission that day. The target was Gütersloh airfield, and the Group departed Raydon at 5.31 p.m.; the 350th FS was laden with bombs and the 351st and 352nd were loaded with fragmentation clusters. After they dove down from 6,000 feet, through the vicious flak thrown up by defenders, the bombs caused significant damage to hangars and barracks, and the frag clusters spread around the parked enemy aircraft, destroying five Me410 twin-engine fighters. Conclusive evidence of Clint's involvement came with the Mission Report, which stated: '2 no 410s destroyed on ground by Lts Sperry & Mayhew'.

It had been a successful mission, ensuring that a few less Luftwaffe aircraft would be able to interfere with the approaching 'big event'. The Group were keeping the bad guys heads down. Clint later reflected:

Between April 1st and May 31st, I flew 136 hours and 20 minutes of combat [flying] time (which reflects much the same flight time of all in the Squadron). This was a solid indication of the pending invasion. Although carefully witnessing ground activities in coastal areas it was never discussed.

As the saying on every billboard warned, 'Loose lips sink ships'.

It had been a significantly busy month for Clint, as he flew on fourteen missions and recorded over forty-eight hours of combat time at that point. However, on 15 May there had been a very unwelcome message from Eighth Air Force high command. For those who had not reached 180 hours of operational time by that date, they had raised the bar to 300 hours, and Clint was one caught by the new dictate. He would have been close to finishing his tour as he totaled just over 200 hours by the end of May, but that was just too late. He would now have to start thinking about how he could reach the new total, and it gave him an unpleasant feeling. Why had they changed the rules? Could it be that they wanted to keep the experienced ones held back for the forthcoming invasion? Were they finding it difficult to get replacements? In fact the problem had arisen much earlier, as many of the experienced pilots in Fighter Command had become time-expired and headed for the States, either taking a thirty-day leave to return or being reassigned on home territory. Whatever the case, these pilots needed replacing, and the 353rd FG alone took in forty-six new pilots during April and May. That's a lot of inexperience and even more pressure on those experienced guys who were left to carry on the fight during the critical days ahead.[3] The pilots had to grin and bear it, as no one could argue with those in command; there were plenty of long-faced fighter jocks in Fighter Command.

The month of May had seen many changes and renovations around the base at Raydon. Col. Duncan had been quick to praise the improvements that had been carried out by the efforts of all the airmen. They had made a start on a base theatre, had established a well-stocked library, and the building and decorating work resulted in a transformation of the living accommodation and working facilities. The state of the base as a complete entity had been enhanced way beyond the sorry condition that had been left by the previous incumbents. Yes, the boss was impressed.

Of a more unfortunate nature, there had been poaching around the country estates—a pastime not acceptable to the local inhabitants, some of whom were poor folks who relied on the illegal fare, regarded as a necessity to their families in those difficult years of austerity. The airmen generally mixed well with the local communities, though situations sometimes got out of hand, and many was the guy who would roll up (and off) his bicycle returning from the local pubs. Celebrating was common to both airmen and locals, and it has to be said that most pastimes were carried out with good intent and in the best of humor. However, pinching pheasants and rabbits from the poacher just wasn't fair play—besides, poaching was against Air Force rules.

Of a more serious and military nature, there had been frequent exercises to consolidate the defense of the station, and the alerts from occasional 'visiting' night raiders kept everyone sharp and ready to defend their airfield.

What was more acceptable were the parties, which saw ladies visiting from Colchester; there were also cycle rides to Flatford Mill and Dedham to learn about and savor the area's heritage. It is certain that many airmen had ancestors from Suffolk, who had made a perilous journey across the Atlantic to become the first settlers on the eastern seaboard of what is now the United States of America. In fact, many towns in the eastern States have common names taken from those in East Anglia.

The cause of 'good versus bad' was probably not debated in depth by pilots of the Air Force, for guys like Clint mainly fought for each other and enjoyed a sense of 'belonging'; their values were tuned accordingly. A few had hate for the Nazis, but many thought those on the other side were just doing their job. It must be said that there can be a very fine line between those who believe that their cause is just and those who go beyond it with evil intent. There were many in Germany who thought that Hitler would enhance their lives, just as there were many in Russia who felt similarly about Stalin. However, from the Allied perspective Germany was clearly the enemy, and although Russia was now fighting with the Allies, the dividing lines would become clearer as the war neared its end and Stalin began defining his intent—but that time had yet to come.[4] Despite the awareness of those in power of the possible difficulties that would arise at the eventual cessation of hostilities, victory over Germany had to take precedence for the time being, and so the fighter boys fought on. The first major step was about to commence—the invasion of Europe.

Flatford Mill is situated on the River Stour, near Dedham, in Essex, and has been a beauty spot for many years. The very well-known landmark, Willy Lott's Cottage, is positioned behind the camera in the picture taken. (*Sperry*)

Operation 'Overlord'

With all the preparations for D-Day evident to those in the south and east of England, the inevitability of the invasion was beginning to get all participants high with anticipation. Where there had been space, it was soon filled with transports, tanks, weapons, and men. Tens of thousands of servicemen of all Allied nationalities were temporally placed in any spare buildings, tents, and shelters, awaiting the call to duty—but the date for the beginning of the invasion remained unknown. The waiting hours for those guys passed like days, and the days passed like weeks as time dragged. Some would never see their homes again; for those who would live to see the end of the war, it would be something to tell the kids. The waiting continued to be very wearing for those prepared to give their lives for a just cause. Sadly, many would pay that costly price in the days that followed.

There were no missions for the Group or Eighth Bomber Command on 1 June, though the complex and critical build-up to the invasion advanced apace the following day as the Squadrons flew two missions. It was the continuation of Operation 'Fortitude', aiming to deceive the Germans into thinking that an invasion would be in the Pas de Calais region, which had been the anticipated shortest route to the Continent.[1] It would be an elaborate and complicated deception, and many stories have been related as to how it was carried out. The Mighty Eighth were part of that plan, and to ensure maximum security, all Group personnel were restricted to within 25 miles of the base, as were personnel at all other airfields. As Clint alluded to earlier, it paid not to talk about what was very obviously about to happen.

Both missions that day were to provide protection for B-17s targeting coastal gun batteries and 'No-Ball' flying bomb sites; the latter were of very serious concern to High Command. The weapons had yet to make a significant impact, but the evaluation of their threat was proved to be accurate when they appeared in their hundreds. The Allied air forces tried hard to wipe out the launching sites, although they were difficult to find and destroy. It had to be pinpoint targeting to eliminate them, and although some sites were wiped out, many others sprung up to cause great destruction to London and the surrounding areas as the months progressed.

Clint did not participate on either of those missions on 2 June, although he was in the air for two hours and forty-five minutes and recorded three landings. He had also marked his IFR as 'Operational', so he was involved in the proceedings in some form; it is possible that one flight was Met, because the cloud conditions for the 'Big Friends' threatened to prevent accurate bombing.

There was another anomaly on the 3rd, as it was recorded in Squadron records that Clint was listed as having flown a mission covering bombers targeting gun positions around the French town of Rouen, although the Unit History reports it as Pas de Calais. Regardless, his IFR shows he carried out no flights that day, so it is possible that he was replaced and the records not amended. It is also possible that he was involved in the Practice Ground Defense Alert, keenly contested between defenders and attackers. The pressure was surely on every man to be on the highest state of readiness for the coming days—nothing could be left to chance. However, the following day he participated in both planned operations carried out by the 353rd FG.

There was a late-morning start on the 4th as the Group, led by Lt Col. Christian, and 352nd Squadron, led by Lt Cles, took off at 11.14 a.m. to escort B-17s and B-24s that were attacking coastal defenses around Pas de Calais and Saint-Quentin. Pathfinders led the raids as the targets were plastered with high explosives by nearly 228 'Big Friends', who were not subject to any form of attack by e/a or flak. All ships landed back at base at 2.04 p.m., after what could only be termed as another rare 'milk run'.

They were back in the air again later that day for an early-evening mission, escorting B-24s from the 2nd and 3rd BDs that were to target airfields at Bourges, Romorantin, and St Avord. Major Hoey was leading the Group and 352nd FS as they protected the bombers, who were spread over a wide area. They did their job well as no bombers were lost, although several took some hefty damage from flak. Of the nearly 400 fighters sent to guard them, one e/a was destroyed, but three 'Little Friends' were lost. The Group ships were all safely down at 9.46 p.m.

It was the original intention that 'Operation Overlord', the code name for D-Day, would commence on the early morning of 5 June. Advising General Eisenhower was a small committee of meteorological experts, led by RAF Group Captain James Stagg.[2] He and his advisers had an enormous responsibility to accurately evaluate the weather patterns that were evolving for that critical day. They needed a window of opportunity, but the weather wasn't cooperating. It was a tremendous blow to the whole plan of 'Overlord', as so much was at stake. The rain slashed down, the wind blew hard, and the seas were running high during the night of the 4th, and High Command had been in an agonizing debate to decide whether or not the invasion would proceed. With tension mounting, and the weather forecast to slightly improve within the next twenty-four hours, General Eisenhower had a hell of a decision to make. With the guidance from Stagg, he made the right one—he postponed the invasion for a day.

It is difficult to imagine the thoughts of the tens of thousands of soldiers, sailors, and airmen, keyed up to 'go', who were then told to stand down. Naturally, Clint was one of many to appreciate the meaning of all the activity, but there was no doubt they were lucky not to have to make that critical decision. Lives were at risk, and the risk was considered too great.

While the General was ruminating on the colossal implications of his final decision, aircraft of all three Squadrons of the 353rd FG took off on 5 June to escort bombers battering targets around Boulogne, thus continuing the deception to the bitter end of the build-up to the invasion. Other bombers, meanwhile, were attacking further down the French coast, at Le Havre, Caen, and Cherbourg—a vital task to weaken the German defenses that would soon feel the full might and fury of the invaders.

On landing back at base at 11.08 p.m., no personnel were allowed to leave the Station, and the aircraft were immediately attacked by guys with paint-brushes and spray guns! Their beautifully polished and painted Thunderbolts were rapidly (and sometimes not too carefully) adorned with black and white stripes. They were painted with black and white bands around the wing roots, both above and

A US Army Signal Corps photograph of General Eisenhower in England on 18 January 1944. Although there were several months to go until D-Day, his workload would have been immense. (*Eisenhower Presidential Library and Museum*)

below the wing, and also just in front of the tail, around the fuselage. Some were still drying the following morning. The pilots were none too pleased to have those aerodynamic negatives slung round their ships, as they reckoned that they would get an increase in weight and a reduction in airflow—and thus speed. Whether or not that would be a serious hindrance could only be determined during combat. But fly them they did, for those in command considered clear identification of paramount importance. With all the pilots' nerves jangling on a knife-edge, they could quite clearly deduce that it was imperative that 'friendly fire' should not be a major contributor to losses.

At 11.30 p.m. pilots from all three Squadrons were called to a briefing that lasted two and a half hours, where they were told by Col. Duncan what was expected of them in the coming days. At last, this was it; the invasion was on the morrow!

General Eisenhower had made the most important decision of the war; 6 June was to be D-Day, and Operation 'Overlord' would take place on the beaches of Normandy.[3] He sent a heartfelt message to all who would risk their lives that momentous day, as he was sure that many would not return:

Soldiers, Sailors and Airmen of the Allied Expeditionary Force!

You are about to embark upon the Great Crusade, toward which we have striven these many months.

The eyes of the world are upon you. The hopes and prayers of liberty-loving people everywhere march with you.

In company with our brave Allies and brothers-in-arms on other Fronts, you will bring about the destruction of the German war machine, the elimination of Nazi tyranny over the oppressed peoples of Europe, and security for ourselves in a free world.

Your task will not be an easy one. Your enemy is well trained, well equipped and battle hardened. He will fight savagely.

But this is the year 1944! Much has happened since the Nazi triumphs of 1940-41. The United Nations have inflicted upon the Germans great defeats, in open battle, man-to-man. Our air offensive has seriously reduced their strength in the air and their capacity to wage war on the ground.

Our Home Fronts have given us an overwhelming superiority in weapons and munitions of war, and placed at our disposal great reserves of trained fighting men.

The tide has turned! The free men of the world are marching together to Victory!

I have full confidence in your courage and devotion to duty and skill in battle. We will accept nothing less than full Victory!

Good luck! And let us beseech the blessing of Almighty God upon this great and noble undertaking.

SIGNED: Dwight D. Eisenhower

The 353rd Fighter Group Unit History records:

> At about 0300 hours on the 6th many of the personnel were up to see the planes take off... The planes were overhead in great number. It was a sight many of us will remember as one of the most outstanding things in the war. Flares were being dropped by bombers who were using them to get into formation. The flares were of many colors and made the whole sky look like a Christmas Tree Decoration. Our own planes took off about 3:30 and were quite a sight as they circled the field with their lights on. Shortly thereafter our friends at Boxted took off. We only saw the port lights of our planes but we could see both the red and the green lights on the planes of the 56th Fighter Group.
>
> Our first mission was led by Colonel Duncan who managed to bring them all back safely. After flying over enemy occupied territory while it was still dark. That is a new experience for the Group. The second mission of the day was led by Colonel Rimerman. At the end of the day the Group had participated in seven missions, some being done by single Squadrons. We saw no enemy aircraft. Our missions were area cover and later dive bombing missions. The boys saw very little on the ground because of cloud.
>
> The Group feels somewhat elated that the invasion came on our first anniversary in this theater. A celebration had been planned in the way of a party at the Officer's Club, but not many gave it further thought when the invasion came. We celebrated our anniversary by helping invade Normandy. What more fun could a Fighter Group have on its anniversary in this theater.

The D-Day commitment by all Allied Air Forces provided massive air coverage of the Normandy beach areas and beyond. It had been a day to remember, as East Anglia and the southern counties of England shook. If there had been an earthquake, who would have known the difference as the mass of Allied aircraft roared into life? The sights and sounds were mesmerizing. With engines straining, they rose into the air in support of the greatest land assault the world had ever seen—the invasion of Europe to defeat the evil force of Nazism.

From the early morning the weather had been dark and unbroken, with cloud down to about 1,500 feet, and the sea in the Channel was rough, somber, and uninviting. With naval escorts guiding them to their destiny in flimsy landing craft, what those soldiers were experiencing was beyond imagination. Many did not make it, as the German gun batteries found their range and blasted the landing craft out of the water.[4] Although some beaches had it better than others, it was at 'Omaha' that those who did manage to make the shore were cut down on the beach, in many hundreds, as they fought to seek shelter from the hail of machine-gun and small-arms fire that raked through their ranks. Then, at Pointe du Hoc, they had to scale the cliffs.

If the pilots had managed to catch a distant glimpse of the beach-heads, they would have seen the Allied troops struggling ashore on 'Utah' (US), 'Omaha'

Troops on board a ship heading for the Normandy beaches. (*Franklin D. Roosevelt Library Archives*)

'Into the Jaws of Death'—US troops wading through water and Nazi gunfire. (*Franklin D. Roosevelt Library Archives*)

(US), 'Gold' (British), 'Juno' (Canadian), and 'Sword' (British). Looking down, the pilots could only imagine and hope for the soldiers' survival, for it could only be seen as frighteningly immense and inspiring.

Clint's abiding memory was the sight of the invasion in action, as he recalled:

As a flight leader, taking off in the dark under a low overcast was no sweat, but keeping the exhaust flames of the flight ahead at proper distance was tricky. Formation within the flight was fine because tight formation kept exhausts very visible. We stayed below the overcast which was low over England but we gained more room as we got over the water. Crossing from the south coast of England to the Normandy beachhead was an awesome sight of hundreds and hundreds of marine craft of all sizes streaming towards the beaches.

So, how did he feel about his own reservations and what he had seen?

No complaints—after seeing the Normandy beaches. My heart and prayers were for those guys. When I think of how concerned we were about meeting the massive air defense as we met this morning for mission briefing, I felt ashamed and more determined than ever to do my best to hit anything the Germans had moving up to hit our guys on the beach.

Tending to the injured on the beaches. (*Franklin D. Roosevelt Library Archives*)

The Group carried out seven missions supporting 'Overlord', with operations commencing at 3.30 a.m. and the last plane touching down in complete darkness at 11.11 p.m. The 352nd FS was on three of those, led consecutively by Major Hoey (Area patrol), Lt Col. Bailey (Area patrol), and Bailey again (Transport bombing). There were no e/a claims during those missions, but there was one loss—F/O Green, of the 352nd FS, whose aircraft sustained blast damage. Despite suffering from burns, he managed to bail out and successfully evade capture.

The authors are able to confirm the mission Clint flew on D-Day; it is recorded in the Short Mission Report that he was on the third Group operation led by Lt Col. Bailey. Consisting of just the 352nd Squadron, they took off at 9.29 a.m. in a dark, murky sky, landing back at 1.40 p.m. The Squadron did have sight of some trains around Clermont, and eight Thunderbolts dropped their bombs—but they only reported near misses. One pilot strafed and stopped a train, but as there was no further trade, the Squadron returned to base.

The sky was fraught with danger, with just about every Allied pilot wanting to be on the invasion that day. Unknown to the majority, even General Doolittle had conspired to be there by grabbing a spare P-38 Lightning and flying around the invasion beaches to see how the battle was progressing. He was very satisfied to observe that the Luftwaffe had decided to stay at home. Clint remarked, 'I certainly anticipated being greeted by the entire Luftwaffe on June 6, but did not see a single enemy fighter.' Any sightings by the fighters were fleeting, and very

P-47s taxi round the perimeter track at Raydon prior to take-off. The black and white 'invasion' stripes are clearly seen. (*Cross*)

few e/a wished to risk any form of combat. Seeing the thousands of aircraft from the Allied nations roaming the skies, who would have dared?[5]

Group and Squadron records were sparse on that momentous day, because every airman around the base was entirely focused on making sure that all aircraft remained serviceable. The greatest effort by all personnel was just getting the aircraft out and back in one piece, and to hell with the paperwork! However, the patrols the 353rd FG carried out were not as frantic as most expected, and although all aircraft were allotted different heights and areas of patrol, with so many in the air at any given time mid-air collisions were still a hazard. Therefore, most aircraft tried to keep their distance. During the seven missions carried out by the Group, the Squadrons bombed and strafed designated targets around the periphery of the action. Just one P-47 was lost, and, as previously noted, the pilot eventually made it home.

It had been a day to remember—the day when the free world made the giant step to free those who were oppressed by the Nazis for more than five years. Clint, reflecting on the event many years later, wrote:

Sad thoughts today, and continued wonder that I'm sitting here writing about an historic event during which so many gave their lives. Raydon was welcome sight on every return.

It most certainly was on D-Day—and the Allies had landed on the Continent, intending to stay.

The Invasion Prevails

The Group flew an incredible nine separate Squadron missions on D-Day + 1. The Squadrons took it in turns to operate independently, and at no time did the Group fly together. It is presumed that the reasoning behind that decision had been to provide continuous coverage of the battleground; always having planes attacking targets as they appeared, and never letting the enemy rest. The pilots owed it to the guys on the ground that they could keep German heads down.

The first mission on the 7th started with a very early wake-up for the 352nd FS pilots, who were trying to get some shut-eye in the Ops Room; they had slept little that night because of their efforts the previous day. Any thoughts of exhaustion soon disappeared as they discovered that Lt Col. Rimerman would be leading the Squadron on its own for a Thunder-bombing mission, hitting rail networks north-west of Paris. It was imperative that the Allies stopped any German reinforcements and materials reaching the battlefront, and absolutely every single sortie was vital to ensure the soldiers at Normandy had the very best chance to break out and gain that major foothold on the Continent.

It was a god-forsaken hour for flying, and still dark at 5 a.m. as the aircraft swept up through the early morning mist and joined up with their leader. Crossing the coast near Le Tréport, they were eager for action. The Squadron then split up into sections and went looking for targets of opportunity. Breaking down from 25,000 feet, and out the bottom of the cloud at 2,000 feet, they bombed and machine-gunned anything they could find, and at the end of the mission they had claimed one Me410 damaged and one loco and an army truck destroyed, and all by strafing. They also claimed one train with flat cars and goods wagons damaged and two oil cars destroyed. When carrying out those attacks, they had been surprised to note that the enemy were even resorting to using horses to pull some wagons in their frantic efforts to support the German Army (the Wehrmacht). The pilots didn't like shooting horses, but the Germans were beginning to feel the pain.

The conditions were recorded as 'fair to poor' as the Squadron made their way back to Raydon, touching down from a successful early morning's work at 7.58

On 7 June 1944, the 352nd Fighter Squadron were tasked to go Thunder-bombing. Clint was able to strafe and destroy a truck, and multiple strikes can be seen lighting up the vehicle from his gun-camera footage. (*Sperry*)

a.m. The guys headed to the Mess for a deserved breakfast and then to prepare for the next mission. As a Flight Leader, Clint was more comfortable than most in those early morning conditions, and he entered thirty minutes of night flying and one hour on instruments in his IFR.

A few minutes before the return of that first mission on the 7th, Capt. Blickenstaff led the 350th FS on another Thunder-bombing mission. Unfortunately, after dropping their bombs on rail traffic in the same area as the 352nd FS, they lost one pilot, Capt. Francis Walsh, on the way out of France. It was a bitter pill to swallow, but the 350th FS would be up again in the afternoon and also later in the evening.

The 351st FS lifted off at 8.52 a.m. for a further Thunder-bombing strike around Amiens and Creil, and before they landed back at base, the 352nd FS took off again with sixteen ships on their second mission of the day (and the Group's fourth). Clint was not on that operation as Bailey led the Squadron to seek out targets of opportunity around the Verberie and Amiens area. The mission was successful. Marshalling yards were bombed, trains, bridges and tunnels were attacked and severely damaged, and three Me109s were destroyed and three damaged when Yellow Flight, led by Capt. Poindexter, strafed Margny/Compiègne airfield.

Capt. Newhart led the 350th FS on their second raid of the day, with each of the sixteen aircraft carrying two 1,000-lb bombs. They unleashed them on two railway tunnels, completely destroying both—one at Sonnery, the other wiped out at Malaunay. It was a very successful strike.

As far as the elimination of e/a was concerned, the most fruitful mission of the 7th was the sixth 353rd Group mission, carried out by the 351st FS. When the Luftwaffe eventually made an appearance, the Squadron accounted for nine air victories and six damaged on the ground. 2nd Lt Hartley (1), Lt Maguire (2), 2nd Lt Franklin (1), 2nd Lt Cobb (1), Lt Hungate (1), Lt Field (1), and 2nd Lt McLaughlin (2) made the air claims.

Grover McLaughlin had a great time, but with potentially fatal consequences. After disposing of his two Me109s, he found himself over an airfield dotted with a few e/a. He dove down and was given damaged credits for three more Me109s and a twin-engine job, but he was a lucky guy; as he rejoined his flight to make their way home, someone called up on the radio to observe, 'One P-47 is still carrying two bombs.' Looking around, no-one else had bombs hung up, so he soon realized it was himself. He was the dummy, and through all that combat he had forgotten to jettison his bombs. He was lucky that day, and when he later recalled it he said, 'I don't believe I'll ever forget that ride on a powder keg over France.' It's probable several of his buddies in the 351st wouldn't let him forget, either!

The mission wasn't without its tragedy. During his frantic moments of combat, and following the downing of a Me109, Lt. Herbert Field reported that he'd been hit and was bailing out. It was later presumed that he did so, after giving a position fix about 5 miles off the Kent coast; a search launch could find no trace of him, and he was subsequently reported MIA (missing in action). There always seemed to be a tragic downside to a raid, causing more people to grieve at home.

The seventh mission that day, and the last for the 352nd FS, ended yet again with a tragic loss. After a 3.45 p.m. take-off, the Squadron made landfall forty minutes later over Tréport, setting a heading for Beauvais/Tillé airfield. Clint, flying SX-E, had been leading a flight with Lts Keywan, Greenwood, and Johnston, although it had been Blue Flight who took the honors as they strafed the field, taking out several parked e/a. Lt Cles (1 x Me109 and 1 x Me110), Lt Waggoner (1 x Fw190 and 2 x Me109s damaged), Lt Mayhew (1 x Fw190 damaged), and Lt McGarry (1 x Fw190 damaged) were those who submitted claims. The Squadron didn't stop there, for they also dropped bombs on the airfield and destroyed a Ju88 and damaged two others. Seeking yet further targets, they severely damaged a bridge near Beauvais, together with a hapless truck nearby, and then flew on to bomb and damage another bridge and more marshalling yards near Rouen. It was a busy and fruitful mission. On their way out, pleased but never relaxed, and continually weaving, they were straddled by flak south of Le Tréport. A young newcomer to the Squadron, 2nd Lt Luther Avakian, was hit and went down in his P-47 to smash and explode into the ground near the coast. Survival was a lottery during the war, and yet another young life had been snuffed out in the fight.

Apart from the first mission of 7 June, when fifteen ships took off to unleash their weapons on the enemy infrastructure, the rest of the missions on that day consisted of sixteen P-47s. The penultimate was no different, as sixteen aircraft of the 350th FS, fully laden with ammunition and two 500-lb bombs, headed again for Beauvais, this time to attack and destroy a railway tunnel and a train that had been caught as a bonus at the tunnel entrance. The Squadron then swept the area, destroying yet another train, a fuel storage tank, and finished off by strafing and bombing marshalling yards at Fourges. It was another successful mission, and thankfully there were no Squadron losses.

This continued on the last mission of the day, led by Lt Col. Christian. The 351st FS was still out for blood, and they continued from where the 350th FS had left off by destroying and damaging trains and freight rolling stock at the marshalling yards at Creil and Fourges. Blue and Yellow Flights were led by Col. Duncan on that late-evening mission, and they were bombing marshalling yards at Ribécourt when attacked by an Me109. Naturally, as was his aggressive way, Col. Duncan had been involved when Capt. Gordon Compton chased the Me109 off Lt Biddy's tail. Capt. Compton inflicted some damage on it, and after a short chase Col. Duncan sent it down to crash and burn—yet he hadn't quite finished, for on the way out he sidled up to a lumbering old Ju52 and swatted it out of the sky. As he later recounted:

> Such a beautiful sight—flames and blood all over the place. He ruined a nice section of woods when he crashed. I am hoping he had a lot of infantry square heads on board going up to see the invasion.

It was the character of the man that for him the war was absolutely black or white, and he had little sympathy for the enemy. He wasn't alone, but others, like Clint, didn't necessarily savor the death of another human being at that time. Although it was war, taking a human life was still difficult. In the heat of battle he didn't waver, but during quiet, off-duty reflection he couldn't relish the thought that lives were lost by his own hands. However, Clint and the majority of the Allied fighting forces certainly would have hardened their perspective when the horrors in the 'Death Camps' were eventually revealed.[1] It would be yet another reason why the Nazi regime just had to be destroyed.

D-Day + 1 had been a very damaging one for the Germans. The Squadrons of the 353rd FG, together with many other fighter and bomber Groups and the RAF, were fulfilling their tasks of keeping enemy armaments, supplies, and reinforcements away from the boys on the beaches, who were still struggling to fight their way inland from very tenuous positions. That they managed to achieve it was a remarkable victory in its own right, and the Combined Air Force played their part in helping to keep the ground they had fought so bravely and bloodily to gain.

All Allied nations fighting off the beaches were grateful that the Air Forces would be their shield as they progressed in the coming days. The days of 6–7 June 1944 had been critical, and they were slowly winning ground. Now they had to drive deeper into France.

On 8 June the Group reverted back to joint squadron missions. Clint was not on the board on the first of three that day, as Lt Col. Bailey led the Group and the 352nd FS off from Raydon just before 6 a.m. to escort B-24s tasked to bomb rail targets and airfields in France. The Squadrons were also ordered to carry out their own Thunder-bombing raids in the Le Mans area once their escort duty had been completed.

Although hampered by fog, each of the sixteen 350th FS Thunderbolts were able to offload both of their 100-lb bombs on an armored column, inflicting damage on tanks and trucks; on heading home they strafed an airfield, possibly near Breteuil, claiming two e/a destroyed.

The 351st FS started their aggression by dropping their bombs rather inconclusively on a bridge, but it was the battles in the air that were rewarding, as they claimed four Fw190s, attributed to 351st leader Capt. Compton, Lt Weaver, Capt. Emory, and 2nd Lt Hatch. They also claimed a Fw190 and an Me109 destroyed on the ground.

Meanwhile, the 352nd FS, led by Lt Col. Bailey, had found its own targets. With 500-lb bombs hitched up to their bellies, they gave Angers airfield a going-over, unleashing their bombs and strafing e/a spread around the field. In Red Flight, led by Lt Clifford Armstrong, the final claims for e/a were by F/O Hicks (2 x Me109s and 1 x single-engine e/a), Lt Armstrong (1 x Fw190, 1 x Fw190—shared with Lt Waggoner, 1 x Ju52—shared with Lt Miller), Lt Miller (1 x Fw190, 1 x Ju52 shared with Lt Armstrong), and Lt Waggoner (1 x Fw190, 1 x Fw190—shared with Lt Armstrong). Together with the vehicles, locos, and freight cars destroyed around marshalling yards, it certainly was a very profitable mission for the Squadron.

The second mission that day saw the Group Thunder-bombing all forms of transportation targets in France. The 350th FS was hitched up with 500-lb bombs, and the 351st FS with 250-lb bombs. They struck rail tracks and marshalling yards, and destroyed several trucks on a convoy that they happened upon. However, the 351st had to cut short their attacks and jettison their bombs when ten Me109s and Fw190s interrupted them at around 10,000 feet. They engaged, damaging three, and 2nd Lt Carbonneau managed to destroy a Me109 as the rest sought cover in the clouds and fled.

With Clint leading a flight in SX-F, the 352nd FS bombed marshalling yards at Tinténiac and St Brice, damaging goods wagons, rail junctions, truck convoys, and a bridge. The targets had been many and varied, and although there were no e/a destroyed by the Squadron, the contribution of damage they inflicted on the transportation network had been vital. When they made it back to base at

3.20 p.m., Clint was found to have expended 514 shells on some of those various enemy installations.

Clint wasn't on the last mission of the day, when the Group carried out Thunder-bombing during the evening in the vicinity of Dreux. The 350th and 351st FSs were able to damage and destroy a locomotive, lock gates, radar installation, and a flak battery (a very satisfying target!). Not all were involved, for Lt Col. Bailey, who had been leading the 352nd FS, decided that the weather was too poor for action and the Squadron returned to base at 7.15 p.m.

There were no missions on 9 June, and this was a most welcome break for all airmen at Station 157 Raydon. However, one or two senior officers just happened to be paying a visit when P-38s of the 479th FG, who were returning from an escort mission, decided to buzz the field. As they did so, Lt 'Bill' Tanner and a colleague happened to be up on a test hop, and the inference of the 'buzz' job had been accepted as a form of challenge. It was taken up by one of the Lightning pilots, and after several tight and hairy maneuvers, the P-38 clipped some wires and crashed into the fortunately unoccupied 'Alcatraz' living quarters on the base. The pilot was killed outright. The Brass were not impressed, and the boss of the 479th wanted Tanner court-martialed. After a few days he was rapidly shipped off back to the States for a 'rest', leaving Col. Duncan to confirm to the authorities that the 479th enticed Tanner into the mock dog-fight.

A low pass by a Thunderbolt at Raydon. In the background in front of the Nissen huts is a watching crowd, probably senior officers, and further right is a B-24 Liberator. The essential cycle rack can be seen outside the hut on the far right. (*Cross*)

The break so richly deserved was tainted—though it had also been evident for quite a while that the boys were pretty stressed out with the continuous mission activities, and badly needed time to recover. There had been no doubt that some needed to recharge more than others, and in the previous happening it clearly showed that guys like Bill Tanner were still up for competition in the air, be it deadly serious, in combat, or just deadly, as with that incident.

It was not only the pilots who were feeling beaten up—the ground-crews were working their butts off to keep as many ships flying as humanly possible. The maintenance record had certainly improved in recent weeks and was a vast difference from the early part of the year, when aborts caused by fuel tanks and other problems soured their efforts. However, other vital tasks on the ground had also created massive problems in manpower, logistics, transport, ground handling, and the pain of everyone's workday—paperwork! There was one word to sum up the constant pressure of missions, and that was stress. As the 'CTL' recorded: 'Aircraft continued to try to land wheels up and flaps down. Red flares fired to warn them'.

For several months leading up to that period, Col. Duncan was seeking ideas for causing further distress to the Germans by enhancing the effects of Thunder-bombing. At the 353rd FG Reunion in 1983, the following conversation explained how his grisly idea for eliminating the enemy evolved:

Wheeler: At Metfield ... Duncan told me one day, he said, 'I want you to put a thousand-pound bomb on each wing of the P-47. You get me a P-47 fixed up with a thousand-pound bomb on each wing. And put a 165-gallon ... you know, the metal tank, the one we put up underneath, 165 gallon.'

Cope: Paper tank.

Wheeler: Paper tanks on the side, but he was going to put a thousand pound bomb on ... each one of the wings. And this was there and start bombing. So, I looked up the tech order on those wing shackles and called him back and I said, 'Colonel, the tech order says that these wing shackles are supposed to only hold 683 pounds,' and I said, 'And you want us to put a thousand-pound bomb on there?' He said, 'Well, you know how they are.' He said, 'They probably have at least a 50 percent margin of error anyway' [chuckles]. And we put on the bombs with a 165-gallon tank up underneath. Full, but not hooked up. Full of gas but not hooked up...

The idea later progressed to strapping grenades onto the gas tanks topped up with oil, primed to explode three seconds after release—a real low-level and dangerous method of attack. In effect, the fiery and unpleasant weapon was the precursor of the napalm bomb used later in the conflict and in future wars. Although initially a crude and rather dangerous weapon to the carrier (if hit by flak or tagged by an enemy aircraft), it caused great distress, terror, and death on the ground to those caught in the clinging and flaming solution that burned everything in its path. It was not at all pleasant; in fact, it was lethal. It would later be used to devastating effect.

Having had a day off for some form of recovery, the Group Squadrons were back on operations on the 10th, putting in three more missions. Clint didn't participate on the first Thunder-bombing operation, targeting transport in the area of L'Aigle, although he was down for the second mission of the day (also Thunder-bombing). This time the Group were ordered to hit the Vannes/Guer area. Led by Lt Col. Rimerman, they did an excellent job knocking out a truck convoy, rail-yards, locomotives, bridges, and roads. However, the 352nd FS had a bad time at Rennes airfield. As they made their attack, intense light flak sprayed up, down, and around them, and as a result two P-47s and their pilots, Lt Marchant and 2nd Lt Johnston, were lost. Hit at a very low level, Johnston had no chance and was killed in the inevitable crash. Although the Group completed their task, the success of the raids was marred by the loss of those two valuable lives. It was subsequently reported that Lt Marchant successfully bailed out after his ship was hit, but was killed by enemy fire while still in his chute. There were those who operated by the unsavory rule that an aircraft could be destroyed and replaced, yet pilots were valuable and should not be allowed to return to action. Many were to abhor this practice, but it happened. Maybe the young Lieutenant was hit inadvertently by ground fire, or maybe it was deliberate? Whatever the case may be, he was yet another victim of the aggressive policy operated by the Group. War was a random killer.

The last mission of the day lifted off at 8 p.m. and made landfall over the French coast fifty-five minutes later. The weather in the target area of Rouen and Paris was good and enabled Col. Duncan, leading the Group and the 352nd FS, to pick out targets clearly. Clint, as a Flight Leader, was again flying SX-E as the flights split, with White Flight bombing a tunnel and destroying a train, and Red, Blue, and Yellow dropping their loads on yet another tunnel. That certainly messed up the transport system in that area for a while, and the Group continued bombing tracks, bridges, and other targets of opportunity before heading for home. Lt Armstrong of the 352nd FS managed to engage and destroy a Fw190 to round off a successful mission for the Group, and they were down, with engines off, by 10.35 p.m., all logging an hour in the gathering darkness with at least half that time on instruments. It had all been wearing on the nerves, bodies, and butts!

There was an early morning start for Clint (leading a Flight in SX-E) and the Squadrons at 5.58 a.m. on 11 June, as they lifted off on the first operation of the day to go Thunder-bombing and provide air support for 2nd BD B-24s in the Beauvais area. While the Group made the rendezvous point on time, the bombers were unfortunately late, and the 'Little Friends' had to wait until the

Clint's gun-camera footage shows train busting at Nogent on 11 June 1944. Strikes are clearly seen through smoke rising from the attack. (*Sperry*)

B-24s dropped their loads and departed before they could get down on the deck to do some damage. They did just that, and eleven aircraft of the 350th FS each unleashed two 250-lb bombs on Moyencourt airfield with good results, although the 351st FS in their sector weren't able to join the fun as it was apparently 'not permitted under Type 16 control' to attack trains—only enemy aircraft.[2] Regardless, with Lt Col. Bailey leading the Group and the 352nd, a thirty-car train was destroyed at Nogent, with Clint's gun camera footage catching his contribution to the destruction. Blue Flight attacked a bridge with little result, although they did claim one further locomotive destroyed. Whilst not a wildly successful mission, the guys had performed as expected, and were pleased to hit the plate back at base at 9.48 a.m. for an anticipated late breakfast.

Catastrophe and Retribution

12 June 1944 was a day that Clint would never forget; there were bad days, but then there were very bad days. For the group, the 12th went beyond 'very bad' to 'disastrous', as they lost eight pilots during that fateful mission. There is no doubt that the success of the Allied landings at Normandy had encouraged complacency in Eighth Fighter Command. Ten Groups of Luftwaffe fighters had been deployed into the area in recent days, and their build-up had given a warning two days before, when the 78th FG had lost several of their number to large formations of e/a. It was a portent of what was to come.

Col. Duncan had been leading as they took off in the growing light at a very early kick-start time of 4.34 a.m. They were tasked to Thunder-bomb targets of opportunity in the vicinity of Dreux. The three Squadrons hit problems as soon as they had started bombing and strafing targets; they were all bounced by e/a in numbers that indicated that there were some highly skilled *experten* leading their attacks, and it was soon evident that at least two of the Squadrons were in deep trouble. The 352nd FS had split up to select targets, and Clint was leading a Flight with Lts Gabriel, Keywan, and Reinhardt. Clint relates the story:

June 12, 1944: A personally devastating day, and a terrible day for 353rd. Weather conditions reported during the mission briefing were for clear skies all day across the British Isles and to the south east. There were cloud layers reported over southern France, but not heavy enough to disrupt low level fighter operations. Missions flown following the invasion were relatively void of enemy aircraft. The Luftwaffe was still desperately trying to move fighter operations closer to the invasion area, but to this point in time there had been little to indicate any major fighter concentrations.

Briefing reflected an easy-going complacency which raised the spirits of the group in their effort to keep the German troops from any advances or establishment of defensive concentrations. Our objectives for this mission, as in previous post invasion missions, was to hit any obvious or suspected movement of troops, equipment or supplies to the invasion front, to concentrate on vehicular movement of any kind and eliminate as many routes of supply as possible. This included bridges, major roads, rail facilities and airfields whether operational or not.

The 353rd Fighter Group despatched three squadrons of P-47 aircraft each for a total of 48 fighters leaving Raydon Airfield in clear skies. Each aircraft armed with 3,500 rounds of 50 caliber API ammunition, plus two 500-lb bombs carried under the wings, but no external fuel.[1] On a climbing course to the south we left the coast of England and within minutes picked up the Normandy coast. The long slow climb was to terminate at a relatively low 20,000 as we crossed over the beach-head. Altitude was still considered necessary to prevent surprise interception. With no enemy aircraft reported by Control, and no activity sighted in the air, we broke up as planned into individual flights of four aircraft for greater flexibility in low level search of targets. The cloud layer to the south was evident at about 4-5,000.

In retrospect, it was a pretty cocky decision, but much to the liking of flight leaders, since we could individually decide about targets without cumbersome squadron maneuvering.

As 'Jockey' Red flight leader, I penetrated deeper into the area southwest of Paris hoping to pick up some enemy ground movement.[2] We stayed in the clear paralleling the edge of the lower cloud layer, which lay to the south. No movement could be seen, so I chose a major rail junction just outside the village of Dreux. (Our group presence had obviously been detected early, thus convoys or movement of any kind was well hidden).

At this stage in our bombing experience, we had discovered the accuracy of near vertical dive bombing by flying directly over the target and rolling the aircraft onto its back and pulling the nose through the target. The gun sight could then be used to line up with the target. Corrections could be made for drift if any, and pressing the release set the bombs on course with amazing accuracy.

Concentration in the dive had to be of short duration, for the P-47 had rapid acceleration when heading for the ground. The roll into the dive had to be made from at least 9,000, with quick work getting on target for release no lower than 4,000 at about 400 mph. Pullout start even at that altitude was often very close with plenty of G's and condensation off the wingtips. One can watch from above with great anxiety as the fighter and its shadow seem to converge at the bottom of the pullout curve. (Instantaneous fused bombs could be used because the release and bomb track line were quickly left behind.)

That was the strategy today as we separated enough to allow observation and separation in the pass. I pulled over the target, rolled over and got the gun-sight on the northern most intersection of the railroad. The rest of the flight would act as top cover, and my wingman would start his dive as soon as my recovery was started. This allowed me to get back up there to cover the last man down. The flat of my pull out was fine at about 300ft (I nearly always had momentary blackout from G forces, but vision was back in seconds in the initial pull). At that moment I could look south underneath the thin stratus cloud layer. Visibility under the thin cloud cover was excellent with a sort of diffused amber glow well in underneath the clouds where the sun penetrated a thinner layer 15 or 20 miles beyond.

This very background glow beneath the overcast allowed my instant sighting of silhouetted dark specks streaking together in a mass low turning climb. They were enemy fighters. At first 15 or 20, then, more like 30 or 40 of them. I was certain they were not ours, for I had gone in deeper than the other flights. Within seconds my judgment was confirmed as they closed rapidly in a shallow climb from under the cloud layer into the clear. They were Me109s in bunches without any discernible flight formation.

With my wingman John Gabriel (#2) probably on his way down, and Dick Keywan and Ed Reinhardt lining up, I pressed the mike button and gave the warning which I remember very clearly: 'Jockey Red Flight, break off the target, break it off. We have 20 or 30 109s coming up from under the cloud deck—use the clouds if it gets too hot—I'll pull them up with me if I can—keep your eyes open.' At that point, I had the throttle to the wall with water injection on. I simply had to pull them up with me and actually climbed through three of them before they knew I was there. They were fortunately new and very confused ... except for the leaders who were turning in as I maintained a near vertical high speed climb, holding well with the momentum of my dive, as opposed to the 109s climb from level flight.

I kept going straight up to clear as many as possible until I virtually stopped and kicked left rudder in the stall for the journey down and to gain maneuverable speed. I did little firing, but did scatter them enough to cause what appeared to be a collision (a collision was reported from someone in the group, but not confirmed) between two EA with a result I was in no position to watch. I had no idea where the rest of my flight were. There was no radio talk from them, which was encouraging at the moment, but they were very capable and disciplined pilots about radio talk in an emergency.

With what seemed like half the Luftwaffe around, I pulled a tight screaming turn into the overcast and was relieved for a breather in the comparative shelter. Still no word, and I kept off the air. I felt my initial broadcast was sufficient warning to other flights in the Group.

Silence was broken by Redford White Leader [350th Sqdn] who was now being hit by the same group. Flight Leader Dewey yelled, 'Fifty plus hitting us, we're in trouble!' There were a few radio yells for help or direction, but otherwise only distant chatter. All this took place in very few minutes and I then pulled up on top. I immediately spotted three 109s in a wide turn just above the clouds in front of me and to the west at about 5000. They had a lot of speed and

I turned well inside them still undetected since I had just broken out on top. I could not close any more at this speed but was in a good position for a very long shot (I would guess a good 1000 feet). I got him quickly lined up and pulled through for a big lead at that distance and fired a relatively short burst.

At that point another 109, which I could not see, was pulling in on my underside. Although at that instant unaware of his position, he fortunately gave himself away by firing from underneath but outside of my turn, missing completely but coming into view now ahead and below my turn. A tight turn at my speed would have put him behind me in the turn and I was not sure who else was back there so slipped again into the overcast hoping for reappearance in better position.

With the hope that they had left, I pulled up again in a wide turn toward home and found probably the same 109 also breaking out behind me eager to start again, but I could turn inside him sticking close to the cloud tops and actually watch him fire with tracers going well underneath me. He just could not get his nose ahead of my turn to even come close. With fuel getting to be a problem, I had to lose him and slid into the overcast making an immediate level instrument turn to a northerly heading. As the cloud layer ran out, I was much relieved that I had finally shaken him and headed straight for a fuel stop at Manston.

This is Clint's own sketch from memory of his battle with Me109s on 12 June 1944. After subsequent analysis of his gun camera footage he was awarded a 'probably destroyed'. (*Sperry*)

I was alone crossing the English coast to the southeast corner of England. It would have been comforting to have friendly company, but far better than being followed by the enemy. At Manston (a major emergency air strip for refueling and other more serious difficulties), in spite of very busy refueling crews, I needed to top off only one tank so was quickly served and took off for the short flight to Raydon. Lack of radio chatter on the short run gave me a false sense of encouragement.

There was not the usual group traffic for landing, but of course I had stopped to refuel. There were two aircraft just breaking away for landing as I approached the field. I prayed they were two of mine. Transportation was waiting at my aircraft revetment as I shut down, but the mood was not encouraging. In operations, a very sad group were waiting hopefully for some relieving news, which in fact I was hoping to hear from them. Neither Dick Keywan, Ed Reinhardt or John Gabriel had returned, and there were no reports to verify their safety.

I presented my brief of the initial engagement, then watched the sky, waiting for calls from possible fuel stops as time ran out. To add to this devastating loss, I learned that five others were not back. All of Dewey's Flight were lost in that single encounter, which started just minutes following our engagement. Less preoccupied pilots listening to transmissions reported that Dewey's flight was caught on the deck, a big fight ensued, and all evidently were shot down. There were no reports of enemy losses, for I was the only one home to report. I reported that I fired on an Me109 and knew that I had hit him, but could not divert my attention to determine final result so claimed a 'probable'. The film would have to be assessed for determination.

Time helped to soften my flight losses with reports that two had managed to bail out and are thankfully alive today. Dick Keywan was killed in action, and in the massive confusion of so many aircraft, I have no idea as to how he was attacked. I only knew that he was a close friend and very able pilot who lost only to the tremendous numbers against him. I could not report on the results of my bomb drop at the railroad intersection, for my attention was on the approaching enemy aircraft.

I had a very hard time dealing with such a loss from my own flight. My only wish was that they all got out. It was my 84th mission, during which a cloud layer and a powerful and amazingly maneuverable aircraft got me home.

Clint desperately tried to distract the attackers from the rest of the flight, facing several passes. In his combat report he stated that what saved him was the fact that the enemy aircraft got in each other's way, rather than a few getting at him more effectively. He made no claim, but he was awarded a probable on assessment of his combat film a few days later.

Lt John Gabriel was not able to avoid the bounce by those Me109s. He later related:

Clint's gun-camera picture taken on 12 June 1944, from a sequence of cine footage of the initial strike as it lights up the fuselage of the Me109. (Sperry)

The Messerschmitt starts smoking as it tries to draw away from Clint's fire. (Sperry)

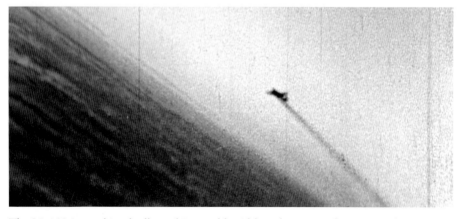

The Me109 is smoking badly and in trouble. Although apparently in control, it appears that the aircraft is badly damaged and heading for the ground. This action led to Clint being awarded a 'probably destroyed'. (Sperry)

We were on a low level bombing run on some railroad junctions when a gaggle of 20 or more German fighters dove on us. The German fighter blew the whole empennage off the tail of my plane (a/c 42-26011) so I was out of control. I parachuted from about 300 meters. Lt Keywan was also forced to bail out but was too low and hit the ground before his chute opened, killing him. I only know this because three days later I met the French people who had buried him.

Lt Gabriel was hidden by the resistance until liberated by advancing American infantry. Blue Three, 1st Lt Richard V. Keywan, was killed, but not before he had destroyed one Me109 and damaged two others—as confirmed by his wingman, 2nd Lt Edwin D Reinhardt, who was awarded the Purple Heart. He related:

In the vicinity of Dreux and Évreux, France, our flight was bounced by 50 plus Me109s. I was just on my bombing run, dropped my tanks and bombs, and immediately started a steep climbing spiral to the right. When I reached cloud level at approximately 8000 ft I had three 109s on my tail. Continuing my tight turn to the right, I was called by a member of my flight to turn left and help him. I believe this to be 1st Lt Richard V. Keywan as he had the only other painted P-47 in our flight. Just prior to reversing my turn to the left, when I received many bad hits, I observed this P-47 destroying a 109 which went down in flames, and getting hits on two more. My plane was on fire and I had to take evasive action and try to extinguish the flames on my left wing. I hit the deck in violent maneuvers and proceeded home where I was instructed to proceed to Wattisham and crash land my aircraft.

There is no doubt in my mind that Lt Keywan destroyed one and damaged two E/A. The last time I saw this P-47 there were two 109s on his tail and he was heading for the cloud layer. They were shooting at him and I observed their tracers going below Lt Keywan's aircraft and I judged them out of range.

While Clint and his flight had been fighting for their lives, the 350th FS were in great danger, as it appeared that the gaggle of Me109s were targeting them also. There is no doubt that the Luftwaffe pilots were out to regain the initiative and achieve air supremacy, and in doing so clear the skies to give their threatened transport system some support. The 12th also happened to be the opening day of the V1 campaign, and they would be aware that the launch sites would also need protection. Regardless, the outcome had been devastating for the 350th and 352nd FSs. The 350th were being led by Major Newhart, and they, like the 352nd, were caught as they bombed and strafed ground targets. Dewey Newhart's ship had been badly hit, and he perished when his aircraft crashed. He was a great loss to the Group, but also shot down that day were Lt Main (POW), Lt Bedford (POW), Lt Phelan (KIA), Lt Moretto (evaded), and Lt Peters (WIA). Together with Lt Keywan (KIA) and Lt Gabriel (POW) of the 352nd, it had been the worst day of the war for the Group. Yes, they would recover—they had to, and fast—but the wounds were deep and Col. Duncan was adamant that the Luftwaffe would pay.

Glenn Duncan was a very angry man, and his hate for the Germans drove him to request Fighter Command for a 'Revenge Sweep' later that day. The guys were certainly well prepared for a fight. They were after nothing but the fighters who had mauled the Group a few hours before, and they were now after their blood. Although the 352nd FS were unable to locate e/a, the 350th and 351st FS avenged their colleagues—every one of them, and one extra for the Colonel. They were expecting the enemy to bite, and bite they did; the two Squadrons downed nine in short order as the German fighters felt the full force of their attacks. Every man was dog-fighting as they split up large forces of Me109s, who must have thought that they were in for more easy pickings. The reverse was the case, and the Group didn't lose one plane or pilot.[3] Those who were lost that day had been avenged; it wouldn't be sufficient restitution for those who died, but that afternoon mission sent the message to the Luftwaffe that they were not to mess with the 353rd Fighter Group.

After the war, Clint wrote to Ed Reinhardt to ask what became of John Gabriel and Richard Keywan. It is an example of how little the guys knew of what went on as one day rolled into another, and combat situations had to be pushed to the back of their minds. Much later, back home and trying to adjust to a normal life, they began to recall and ask the questions and look for the answers that had eluded them during their operational period. With Clint, the sadness descended upon him when he received the final story of the tragedy. There is no doubt that this was his worst day during his operational tour.

Clint's narrative is vivid, and the consequences of four P-47s mixing it with around forty Me109s is too dire to contemplate. However, that only one pilot was killed from his Flight was a tribute to the training, skills, and luck, both good and bad, of the pilots concerned—and their tough P-47s. When Clint recounted that terrible day for the Group and his Flight a few years ago, he was still choked and had tears in his eyes as he told the story. It had hurt him badly, and the death of his personal friend, Richard Keywan, was a great loss. Being Flight Leader made him feel very responsible for his three colleagues, and he never really got over that mission. In hindsight, it is impossible to blame anyone. Clint, however, felt this responsibility deeply.

Just having returned from a disastrous mission, the Group were probably not in the right frame of mind to accept appreciation for what they had achieved both before and after D-Day. Nevertheless, the following messages were received by Colonel Duncan from the Commanding General, 66th Fighter Wing, and were for the attention of all personnel.

First was a message from the Air Commander-in-Chief, Allied Expeditionary Air Force:

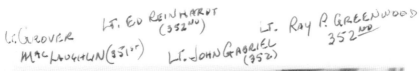

A fine group photograph of good friends, two of whom were with Clint on the fateful mission on 12 June 1944. *Left to right*: Lt Grover McLaughlin (351st), Lt Ed Reinhardt (352nd), Lt John Gabriel (352nd) and Lt Ray Greenwood (352nd). (*Jean Luc Gruson, via Cross*)

Lt Richard P. Keywan and his aircraft, *Little Hotsy*, with ground crew. Fighting bravely against great odds, he destroyed one Me109 and damaged two others before being killed in action on the mission with Clint on 12 June 1944. (*Streit, via Cross*)

I would much appreciate it if you would convey my heartiest congratulations to the VIII Fighter Command for the magnificent efforts they have made since the beginning of the battle. I am certain that they have made a great contribution in delaying the German Army by their low flying attacks in the strategical area, especially in the area west of Paris and the Brest Peninsular. I wish to thank them for their magnificent response, and wish them the best of luck in their future operations.

Signed: Leigh Mallory.

This was followed by:

I am pleased to relay the above message and add my own appreciation for such superior performance.

Signed: Doolittle.

And also:

I add my personal commendation and am extremely proud of every member of this command for their tremendous contribution to the invasion efforts.

Signed: Kepner.

And finally:

Enough said—Woodbury.[4]

In the cold light of day, and digging deep into the Group's torn emotions, the airman knew that the only way to get through that period had been to knuckle down and avenge not only those lost that day, but every single person who gave their lives for the cause of freedom. The ultimate response could only be a collective and disciplined breaking down of the Nazi infrastructure and the demoralizing and destruction of their forces; they knew they were succeeding, although the cost would still be great.

Tour Finale

Clint wasn't on the first mission on the 13th, and whether or not he had a discussion with Jim Cope regarding the previous day can only be guessed. However, it must be reasonably certain that the Doc had been around the pilots of his Squadron when they returned from that devastating mission, and would probably have assessed their condition before giving them the OK for further operations.

The Group were back on the line and loaded up with 250-lb and 1,000-lb bombs to carry out another Thunder-bombing raid. The 350th FS scared anyone who happened to be in the vicinity of two bridges at Tours, and the 352nd FS, encountering substantial amounts of flak, straddled another bridge in the same area. Lt Jones' Thunderbolt was hit, but he managed to get it down on a beachhead strip and get out of the wreckage with the plane in flames. He survived. The 351st FS had to drop their bombs and head home as a result of being attacked by some unfriendly P-47s; they managed to avoid damage, but were mighty chewed off with the bounce.

In the late evening, the Group pressed starters at 6.05 p.m., and all three Squadrons were briefed to attack a vital target for transportation—Le Port Boulet Bridge across the Loire River, near Tours. With the 350th and 351st FS aircraft loaded up with 1,000-lb bombs, the 352nd FS were to provide top cover. A light mist had been gathering over the target, and with cloud at 3,000 feet and only a slight cross-wind, the conditions were nearly ideal for the attack. The 350th FS had several near misses, and it was left to Col. Duncan, leading the Group and the 351st FS, to finish the job with four direct hits. With Clint flying his regular mount, SX-E, and leading a flight, the protective cover circling at 17,000 feet wasn't required. Lt Eluhow experienced an oil leak and subsequently had to make a forced landing on an advanced landing strip, while the rest of the 352nd FS made a heading for base, landing in the growing darkness at 10 p.m. It was a quiet mission for Clint, and would have helped to restore his confidence—but he wouldn't have been the only one suffering…

In the period around D-Day, Clint's original P-47, *Mary Jayne* (seen here) was passed on to another pilot. Clint had taken charge of a new, natural-metal-finish SX-E. (*Cross*)

Clint did not fly when the Squadron carried out an area patrol on the early mission of the 14th. Lt Reinhardt, having recovered from the mission on the 12th, did call in a gaggle of approximately forty Me109s heading in the direction of Brussels, but the Squadron didn't engage.

Having gathered for a late briefing, the final mission for the Group that day had been to dive-bomb special targets in an assigned area near Compiègne, in France. Flying inbound at 16,000 feet, they made landfall at 8.04 p.m., and although the Group arrived in the designated area they failed to find the briefed targets. With the 350th FS providing top cover, the 351st FS went off to bomb and strafe marshalling yards and trains, while the 352nd FS, with Lt Col. Bailey leading and Clint in his flight, set out to bomb Beauvais/Nivilliers airfield. With Clint and Lt Reinhardt covering, Bailey and his wingman, Lt Miller, dropped fragmentation bombs. The results were poor. No e/a were seen; although the air controller reported that 'Little Friends' to the north (356th FG) were being attacked, contact with them proved otherwise. There being no more trade, the Group returned to Raydon, landing back once more in the gathering gloom. It appeared to be yet another relatively quiet mission, but not for those on the receiving end, on the ground.

Mission, after mission, after mission—the strain on the pilots was constant, and although they were unaware of the total strategy of 'Overlord' they were pretty darned sure that they were fighting for the guys on the ground. It was no different on 15 June, as the pilots were up early again for briefing; their mission that day was to provide tactical support to a large group of B-17s from the 3rd

BD, who were bombing many targets throughout France and Germany. The 353rd FG were satisfied to note that the Fortresses they had been protecting were in good, solid formation, and their bombing pattern well and truly plastered the chosen target—the bridge at Chalonnes on the Loire. It also pleased all the 'Big' and 'Little Friends' that there had been no flak or e/a reported in their sector. Exiting out near Le Tréport at 9.55 a.m., they touched down safely at 10.25. The rest of the day would be spent catching up on their other duties. In later years, Clint referred to the mission on this day by recording a few interesting facts.

> June 15, 1944; Single (1 landing) mission: 4 hours:30 min: At normal 65% power, the P-47 consumed 130 gallons of fuel per hour (130 x 5 = 585 gallons): Mission fuel: 370 internal gallons: Plus: 216 external gallons = 586 gallons on board: Note: At full military power, fuel consumption: 275 gph: At emergency war power (water injection): 315 gph.

It is worth observing that if the Group were flying at normal, 65 per cent power throughout the flight, there wouldn't be much gas left in their tanks when they hit base—indicating they would have been 'flying on fumes'!

Although poor weather restricted operations on the 16th, the Group went Thunder-bombing, attacking the many targets still available (and necessary) in support of the invasion. Although it cannot be confirmed, it appears that Clint carried out a Met flight for two hours and fifteen minutes. He had marked it down in his IFR as 'operational', with two landings and fifteen minutes on instruments. It would almost seem like a welcome break, continuing the next day when he missed out on any flying.

Clint was back on operations again as Flight Leader when the pilots were briefed for a Thunder-bombing raid on the bridge at Ham in the late afternoon of 18 June. The following dialogue has been taken from the 352nd FS Mission Report:

> Squadron upon reaching target area overcast conditions prevailing and group leader thought it inadvisable to continue mission. Overcast was too bad from 11 to 13,000 feet. Very heavy haze layer. All bombs returned to base…

Relieved? Frustrated? Flying over the Continent for two hours and thirty minutes, with time on instruments, was not the best way to spend the evening, but it was a rare occasion when they were not able to carry out their allotted task. The determination to succeed was the most vital part of their combat psyche.

Clint would surely be aware that his time in the 353rd and his own Squadron would soon be at an end. Did he consider the implications? He may well have

A line of 352nd FS Thunderbolts waits to take off on another mission. The front plane is Bud Tordoff's SX-L *Anne*, a/c 42-75247. Behind is Hal Miller's SX-S *Sniffles*, probably a/c 42-75691. (*Petticrew, via Cross*)

done, but he also had to be very aware that mistakes so near to completion might prove fatal—and to have gone through all those months of combat and then fail would be unthinkable. It is therefore almost certain that after filtering those thoughts through his mind, he filed them for later, as he had to continue until the day he would be told that he was tour-expired and going home. However, it wouldn't happen quite yet as there would be many hours of combat ahead.

Of the two missions scheduled for 21 June 1944, Clint would participate in both. Col. Duncan led the Group as they lifted off with full wing tanks at 6.46 a.m. to escort 2BD B-24s into their target in the Stendal area, Berlin. They made landfall at 27,000 feet after achieving their rendezvous at 8.31 a.m., encountering 'moderate heavy accurate flak' coming up from the Frisian Islands and Bremerhaven. Before leaving their charges, the Group observed overcast all the way to the east of Berlin and back to Bremen, where the sky became clear. They were then able to get down on the deck and carry out strafing of some rail targets, claiming a train near Neustadt. However, their mission to escort the aptly named Liberators was the main task. It was carried out without contact with the Luftwaffe, but in spite of the 'no show' by e/a, the bombers did take some punishment from the flak, losing several of their number. Although the Group were capable of countering any e/a that happened to intercept bombers, they could do nothing about the flak, and both the 'Big' and 'Little Friends' just had to run the gauntlet, regardless of the outcome. Clint had been flying SX-E, with Lt Col. Bailey leading the 352nd FS. They touched down without loss at 11.58 a.m., although Lt McGarry had to land away from base, apparently short on fuel after the five-hour-and-twelve-minute operation; it was the longest to date—real sore butts again!

It wasn't, however, the finish of what was to be the longest day in the air for the pilots. Exhaustion must have been evident in some as they took on their next challenge in the early evening of the 21st. They were back in the air at 4.30 p.m. to again provide an escort to 2nd BD B-24s as they targeted V-1 sites in the Pas de Calais region. The 'Doodlebugs' were now causing a great deal of damage, and many people were being killed or injured in and around London. In fact, only the previous day the CTL recorded that at 8.53 p.m. 'Ops had called to say Diver reported heading their way. 20-55—Diver reported crashed ... south of Wormingford'. It was also noted that, even 7 miles away, 'it shook every building on the base'. There had been no doubt that the V-1 (Doodlebug, Diver, or Buzz-bomb) was becoming more than just a hindrance to the defenders, for when that evil-sounding pulse-jet cut out, everyone hit the nearest shelter. It was a deadly weapon that had to be destroyed, and that day had been yet another attempt by the heavies to extinguish the launching sites. The 353rd 'Jonah' escort had been uneventful, and no e/a were seen in spite of the controller trying to direct them several times. The B-24s were flying between 20,000 and 23,000 feet, but the Group were unable to observe the bombing results—although they did observe many RAF Lancasters in the area, presumably on the same mission.

It had been a long and tiring day for the 353rd FG, and with another three hours and thirty-six minutes in the air, sitting on his parachute and dinghy, Clint would certainly have been relieved when they all finally returned to base at 7.56 p.m. Flying for over eight hours and forty minutes, under constant tension, he had been grateful that SX-E was performing flawlessly. Anything different could have been unpleasant to say the least.

Although there had been a late-morning mission, Clint (flying a different ship, SX-Y) continued his combat time on the second operation on 22 June. The Group provided support escort to three combat wings of B-24s planning to hit targets in the vicinity of Le Havre. It had been the 352nd FS who found the action when White Leader, Major Hoey, dove down to investigate four 'bogies'. Lts Miller and McGarry got separated when following down to check them out and spotted fifteen to twenty more, and Lt Miller was able to hit and claim a Me109.

It was after that action that several B-24s were escorted back to the English coast. They would be extremely grateful. Bomber crews shared great camaraderie in combat, and it wasn't easy for those men to imagine dying alone in a P-38 'Fork-tail', a little P-51 'Spam Can', or a big 'Jug' fighter. In a bomber crew, although they might not be the closest of friends, the fact that they had several men in the same aircraft gave a form of security that could be interpreted as 'togetherness'. Consequently, the 'Little Friends' continued to be hailed as heroes

Although a poor photograph, this shows Clint flying in formation in his new SX-E, P-47D-22-RE, 42-26121, NMF (Natural Metal Finish, and one of the first in the Group). It is also the only picture of Clint in the air on operations. (*Sperry*)

by those many crewmen in the heavies. But it was also very much reciprocated, as the little guys thought that those who flew the bombers were the real heroes. They never wavered until beyond control, were never able to maneuver rapidly out of harm's way, and they always endeavored to fly on doggedly to their targets, some with terrible damage and mortally wounded crewmen, and some to plummet, blazing and out of control, to explode in a terrible and intense conflagration on the ground below. For both the 'Big' and 'Little Friends' it was an extended period of highly deserved mutual respect that they carried through until the end of hostilities.

It was another escort job again on the 23rd; the bombers were after 'No-ball' sites and more visual targets on airfields and rail networks in eastern France. Clint was once again flying SX-E, and as Flight Leader had Lts Harris, Andrews, and Eluhow in tow as Col. Duncan led the Group to provide penetration and withdrawal support for their 'Big Friends'. Because of the difficulty of 10/10s cloud topping at around 6,000 feet, checkpoints were not observed over almost the entire route. Consequently, the outcome of the bombing couldn't be seen. Seven bombers were lost to flak, although no e/a were encountered. The Squadrons hit the plate at dusk after an uneventful mission.

Following another escort mission on the 23rd, the next day 340 Flying Fortresses of the 1st and 3rd BD had another tough haul to Bremen, where the main thrust of their attack was oil installations, while other B-17s with the raid hit the city center and aviation industries. Col. Rimerman led the Group and Capt. Poindexter the 352nd FS. Clint was again leading a flight as the aircraft, with wing tanks fully fueled and heavy, lifted off from Raydon at 10.56 a.m. to head for their rendezvous over Norderney Island at 22,000 feet. The bombers were flying in good, tight formation, making the job of the fighters a great deal easier as they shepherded them to their destination. Intense, heavy, and accurate flak was seen to hit the bombers over the target at 25,000 feet, though the Group remained unscathed. Only one bomber was lost, but several were observed to have taken hits, those being escorted home by flights of the 352nd FS. The rest of the Group went hunting low down and claimed two e/a destroyed on Deelen airfield, together with locomotives and trains in various scattered locations. Due to those incidents, the Squadrons straggled back to base, with the last down at 3.47 p.m. Clint later commented that the official mission time had been recorded as five hours, and they were concerned about their fuel state:

[I led my] flight of four ships to an emergency landing at [a] field under construction. Following fuel delivery for the flight, the added 15 mins was from emergency field to home base. We could not have made home base without the stop.

It's fascinating to review some of the stuff that we didn't have time to think about then. Probably a good thing we didn't! Fuel and weather were sometimes as worrisome as flak and fighters. The North Sea didn't deliver any flak, but in spite of its beauty, it looked pretty mean at times when fuel was low.

The day, however, was not at an end, for something nearly as dangerous got the guys full of excitement that evening. The Unit History for June 1944 reported:

> The Officers party on the twenty-fourth was the usual success. The girls seemed prettier (spring maybe) and the arrangements made at the club were even better than at previous dances. Capt. Fisher does a good job. Our usual friends from Boxted and the engineers returned to take part in the festivities.

Unfortunately, it appeared that some got carried away with the occasion. Whether it was the booze or the influence of the opposite sex or both, the following situation occurred:

> At 22-25 hrs the control tower reported that YJ-E, one of the ships on alert flight, was seen to taxi and rapidly take off. Lt Claville, the scheduled pilot, had got into another ship. YJ-E engaged in a number of aerobatics for 15 minutes. The ship landed, returned to the dispersal, and spun round a dozen times. The pilot then got out of the plane staggering badly. He was helped off with his parachute and taken to the station Hospital.

As YJ happened to be the code sign for the 351st FS, it can only be assumed that it was a pilot from that Squadron. It had to be appreciated that those guys were under intense pressure for long periods, and although not a valid excuse, it was almost understandable that he should let off some steam. But what if he had crashed? No doubt there were plenty ready to tell him in a more sober moment.

For those with hangovers, it was a bad start to the next day. There were guys in briefing who probably regretted a surfeit of alcohol, food, and perhaps 'prettier girls'. Others were just capable of regretting, while the majority were probably fairly responsible—as aviators, they had to be. The minority, with due consideration to their own perceived condition, had to shake themselves, head for the flight-line, stick their head into the cockpit, and suck in some life-giving oxygen, swearing that they'd never, ever, do it again. It was one way of relieving tension and dealing with stress.

The morning mission required the Group to provide withdrawal support to B-17s hitting special targets south of Paris. Airfields, power and transformer stations, and an oil dump were listed. As the Squadron staggered into the air, Clint, as Flight Leader, and Lts Reinhardt, Greenwood, and Hunt were ready for battle. Having rendezvoused with the three B17 Combat Wings near Argent at 25,000 feet, they escorted them into their targets and out, finally releasing them to head on down to strafe targets of their own. The 351st FS had the

The guys looking pretty laid back in the 352nd FS Ready Room at Raydon, with Jim Cope sitting middle front. On his left is Lt Hal Miller and seated opposite is Lt Raymond Eluhow. Capt Fred L. Uttenweiler is standing by the bookcase—the others are unidentified. Clint's artwork and printing are clearly evident. (*Cross*)

privilege of attacking an airfield at Bourges, destroying four and damaging three e/a, while the 350th and 352nd Squadrons provided cover until the Group made its way back to base, to make ready for the next mission a few hours later.

The day continued with a Thunder-bombing mission attacking airfields at Evreux/Fauville. The 350th and 351st Squadrons made for Fauville and the surrounding area; the results of their bombing and strafing were inconclusive, although the 352nd FS did manage to cause some damage at Evreux. The Group arrived back at Raydon by 7.32 p.m., and with no missions the following day, Clint and the rest of the Group were granted a hard-earned break. Certainly, Col. Duncan had been setting a remarkable standard leading those missions, and his stamina was described as 'amazing'. He was a great inspiration to his pilots and a remarkable leader, although at times some thought him over-aggressive. However, there is no doubt that the pilots respected him.

The pilots had a little longer than expected before the next mission on the 27th, as it had been a late briefing for an evening take-off at 6.30 p.m. Again they went

Thunder-bombing, this time hitting airfields around Épernay. Making landfall at Gravelines, they soon made out the recognized target, but as there were no enemy aircraft visible they started to seek other options. Some Me109s were chased and lost in cloud to be engaged by other Squadrons, although Major Gallup, leading the 350th FS, managed to destroy one before they disappeared. After orbiting a known landing ground, a further e/a was destroyed by the Squadron. The 351st FS were able to engage a few more Me109s and claim one destroyed and two damaged, but the 352nd FS, despite sighting about six e/a, failed to engage; they were instead able to drop their bombs on Villeneuve Vertus airfield. It had been a mixed bag of destroyed and damaged aircraft, and even though moderate to light flak had been encountered, all made it safely back to base late in the evening. For Clint and the Squadron it had been a satisfying mission, but the guys wouldn't call it spectacular—it was just getting the job done. More would follow on the morrow.

However, before the Group settled for the night, the CTL reported that a certain Senior Officer had been 'caught on occasions walking (in this case on the evening of the 27th with another flyer), and also previously, taxiing the wrong way and generally upsetting those in the tower, as he had not asked permission'. No names, but it was noted that there had been a certain lack of respect for the authority that he was supposed to represent. There may, of course, have been good reasons for those alleged misdemeanors.

On 28 June the Group escorted B-17s as they bombed the airfields at Juvincourt and Laon. They could see that the 'Big Friends' had made a good job of damaging the targets, and with all Fighter Groups participating there was little to stir the 353rd FG into action. It was a day when the aerial power of the 'Mighty Eighth' could be seen at its zenith. With over 1,500 aircraft crowding out the skies, it was an awesome sight.

It was the last day of the month, and it was that deadly Thunder-bombing again. The mission would bring the momentous month of June 1944 to a close.

As the Group lifted off at 6.26 p.m., one can only wonder if, having evidenced the recent invasion of the Continent, they had a sense of achievement, of history, or of impending victory. As alluded to earlier, they knew they were destroying the vital infrastructure of Germany and German occupied territory, but if High Command couldn't judge when the war would end, how could the fighting man be expected to know what was going on in the broader picture?[1] To the fighter pilots, 30 June had been just another day. All the same, they did have hopes, and they were the ones at the pointed end who could see the fruits of their efforts. At least they could guess what the future might bring when the war was won—if they survived.

Clint was getting close to finishing his tour when his name came up on the pilots list for the late mission on that last day of June. It turned out to be a real corker for the Squadrons, as they spread mayhem around Nogent Bridge and

Another one bites the dust. Clint's gun-camera footage captures the demise of another German vehicle—probably a staff or reconnaissance car. (*Sperry*)

other targets of opportunity. Having made landfall over the Continent at 7.12 p.m., and north of Cayeux at 14,000 feet, the attackers racked up one hell of a score. Although the 350th and 351st FS hit bridges, marshalling yards, trains with freight cars, and trucks, together with catching and damaging some Me109s, it had been the 352nd FS that made a significant dent in the German air and ground transport and communication system. It claimed one damaged and four destroyed locos, fifteen destroyed trucks, eight damaged freight cars, six destroyed oil cars and one staff car, one reconnaissance car, and one damaged tank and one transmission station. Finally, 2nd Lt Miller was awarded two Me109s damaged on the ground north of Troyes.

It had been a great day's work by the Group and especially 352nd Squadron, and Clint was there mixing it with his flight of Lts Greenwood, Newton, and Parker as they strafed their targets. The Group had expended a great deal of ammunition, together with twenty-four 500-lb general-purpose bombs; all were dropped on target. They did good work on that last day of June. Would it be Clint's last mission, and then home? Did he dare think of it? Did he want to think of it? Had anyone told him? Maybe. He had racked up a further twenty-three missions and nearly 102 hours of operational time in those previous weeks. He must have been close to that magic 300-hour total.

It cannot be confirmed that Clint knew that he would finish his combat tour before he went on the mission on 1 July 1944, but if he did, he'd have probably been pretty darned screwed up. If he didn't, it would be just another mission. It turned out to be a Thunder-bombing raid, and to add a sour note, the weather was gradually deteriorating as the Group lifted off from Raydon for that late evening mission at 6.53 p.m. They were heading for the Compiègne, Noyon, and Soissons areas to find and attack barges on the canals. The method of water transport had become increasingly important as the much faster and more efficient road and rail networks had been severely damaged by low-level bombing and strafing by the Air Force. With Lt Col. Bailey leading both the Group and 352nd FS, most ships had been carrying 250-lb bombs.

The 352nd FS were the first to locate the target area and proceeded to seek out the trade on the waterways. They found several barges on the Compiègne to St Quentin route and let loose their bombs, causing one or two barges to be severely damaged. Seeking further targets of opportunity, the Squadron then destroyed trucks and a locomotive before finally heading for home.

Clint had been leading his Flight that evening and was one short for the raid, as Lt Andrews had to land back early at base because his wheels wouldn't retract. So, down to three ships, Clint and Lts Nance and Eluhow made sure that the flight caused some dislocation to the transport system. It appears that whilst the Squadron was strafing and bombing, Clint stayed up as top cover. Lt Col. Bailey almost certainly knew that Clint's tour finish was imminent and probably gave him the safer option, as usually happened to a pilot on his final mission. There were too many stories of guys 'buying the farm' on their last one before going home, and that was just the worst of bad luck. Whatever the case, the Squadron did a fine job, and with the 350th and 351st FS contributing several more barges and rolling stock, they made landfall out at 12,000 feet before crossing the Channel and landing back at Raydon at 9.47 p.m.

With ninety-four combat missions, thirteen Met flights, and just over 300 hours of operational time, Clint was told, 'That's it, Sperry. You're tour-expired.'

Clint hung around base, waiting for orders. He had made his last flight in his favorite P-47 Thunderbolt, SX-E. No doubt he'd also paid his greatest respects and heartfelt thanks to his faithful ground-crew, who, apart from the fuel tank problems (and a few more), had kept both his SX-E ships flying throughout his combat tour. To them, he would be eternally grateful. They obviously had great affection for their pilot and sweated him home on every occasion. As Clint mentioned earlier, following his final mission, his crew chief, Leroy Katterhenry, wrote to Mary Jayne:

Dear Friend,

Received your letter the other day and want to try to thank you, for the crew of the *Mary Jayne*, and the others you spoke of.

'Sweating him out', during his long tour of operations, we really got to know Lt Sperry, and can realize, how you at home must have worried about him. He is one swell person and it was a pleasure and privilege to be a member of his crew. We like to think that he believed in us and needed us but we have agreed among members that Lt Sperry can fly anything that has wings on it.

Danny Kilb suggested some pictures of Clint some time ago and am sending you two that he gave me.

The close-up is no good but the other was taken just before he took off in that last, long, 'finishing up' mission. Boy, we really did sweat him out on that trip. He only needed little over an hour to finish but being the fighter pilot he is, he stayed for the whole trip and gave us a real buzz job on returning home.

The picture of you and little Steve was an added incentive, too, I think. The day he got 'it' he had me make a frame for it and fasten it in the cockpit so you can say you have spent some time over Germany by proxy 'Ha Ha'.

Things are looking better and better over here. Possibly it will end soon and we can all be home again.

Meeting you and little Steve would certainly be a pleasure and I hope it's not too long until that day is here. Give my regards to Clint's Mother and Dad and thanks again for your encouraging letter.

I remain Sincerely,

Kat

Knowing Clint's character, he would also thank others he considered to be of great importance in helping him through his darker moments, and the one that stood out above many had been the 352nd Flight Surgeon Jim Cope. They had become good friends during Clint's time on the Squadron and Jim was the one person who Clint could call his confidant. He was a man of great integrity, who understood that whilst Clint was still a young man, he was mature and sensitive, and he had been able to relate to that fine doctor. He owed him a great deal.

Did the Group Leader of the 353rd FG thank him? One can only hope he did, for the legendary Colonel Glenn E. Duncan could certainly see that Clint had been an outstanding pilot. At Squadron level, when requests came down the line from those in higher command, it would have probably been 352nd FS commander Lt Col. Bailey who would have allocated Clint for specialist tasks; that implied trust in his ability to carry them out and still make it home. Tasked with met flights, Clint was the 'specialist'. In fact, his somewhat-extended tour was the result of those in command utilizing those skills for the benefit of the Eighth Air Force, and his awards would be testament to those skills. But now there was no longer the stress of early morning calls for briefing, and no possible chance of being shot down by German fighters or flak, or ducking flying bombs or other bits of hardware dropped or thrown up by the enemy.

He had time to reflect—but not too long, as orders came through to inform him that he was not going home quite yet. Although Clint had racked up the 300 hours on operations, some high-up guy had sensibly considered that his experience should be passed on to the rookies coming over from the States. Those fledgling fighter pilots would receive 300 hours of training, with at least one-third of that time on operational fighters, before going on operations—so before being let loose on the enemy, they needed the guiding hands of experienced combat pilots. The fresh-faced young men who thought they could take on the Luftwaffe single-handed needed combat training, and so Clint was ordered to report to the 495th Fighter Training Group, AAF Station 342 at Atcham, near Shrewsbury, in the County of Shropshire, somewhere in the West Midlands of England. He was going to be an instructor, and departed Raydon to return only once during the rest of the war; it would then be half a lifetime before he would see the beautiful, undulating fields of Suffolk again.

However, before Clint took his leave there was one official ceremony that he had to attend, extending his stay at Raydon for a few days. At regular intervals there were medal presentations, and the one on 7 July would involve Clint; it was an award of his first Oak Leaf Cluster to his Distinguished Flying Cross. As these events followed several weeks behind notice of the awards, it is certain that Clint's second DFC Cluster would have followed him to his next posting. On 23 March 1944 he had already received his third Air Medal Cluster, and no one would doubt that he would have earned all of those awards for his service to the United States of America.

Clint finally prepared to say his goodbyes to the colleagues he had fought with for so many months—it was tough, as they were like family. There would be some who were not there (absent, killed, POWs, or tour expired), and he would miss them all. He was scheduled to leave on 7 July 1944, but he didn't enjoy the departure as the message came through, just before he left base, that the Jerries had finally nailed the Colonel on a mission that day. Glenn Duncan was down somewhere in north-west Germany. The Group were shattered, although at that time they were not to know that he would evade capture and eventually make it back to Raydon before the end of hostilities—an amazing story on its own. With that bad news, Clint left with the knowledge that the Group structure would now change. Maybe he was leaving at the right time? Only time would tell.

As his tour came to an end on the 7th, Clint had one last flight, but not in a P-47—it would be in the station hack, the Proctor. He hadn't flown for several days, so maybe it had been to keep his flying fresh or maybe someone was going to drop him off at an air station convenient to his journey north. Whichever, he

The medal ceremony at Raydon, 7 July 1944. Clint is being presented with his first Oak Leaf Cluster to his DFC medal by Brig. Gen. Murray C. Woodbury, Commander of 66th FW. (*National Archives*)

The end of the combat tour. Clint packs up his gear at Raydon, ready for his next assignment at Atcham. (*Sperry*)

left Raydon on that date, and no more flying appeared on his IFR until 17 July 1944. He richly deserved those ten whole days of rest before his next assignment. He had left the Group and, more significantly, had left his mark on the damaged Reich. But one thing was certain—his colleagues and friends in the Squadron would always be remembered. Those lost and those who survived would always belong, with Clint, to the 352nd Fighter Squadron.

Roped in as an Instructor

As Clint entered through the gates and reported to the guardhouse at Atcham, it is difficult to know exactly how he was coping with the realization that he was completing his extended period with the 352nd Fighter Squadron, 353rd Fighter Group. Did he regret leaving? It is almost certain that at some period during his time in England he may have given consideration to return for another tour, but the extension probably settled the decision for him. He would fulfill his required duty, and then head for home to his family. He had earned that right.

From early December 1942, when he had commenced flight training and preparation for combat in the European Theater of Operations, Clint had been a key member of 352nd FS. He had encountered the stress and early difficulties of fighting a dangerous enemy and also escorted bombers without the means to protect them all the way to their targets. Then there were the bombings, strafings, accidents, weather, and enemy guns that took so many of his good friends. He had experienced and been closely involved in many traumatic events. Although his previous flying experience was a major contributing factor, he could see that luck had played no small part in his survival. It is most probable that he would be aware that the odds for that survival were diminishing, and that there were many young and eager pilots waiting to take his place. With his enforced extended operational time, Clint had more than fulfilled his duty to the Air Force. As he later said, 'Tour extension didn't affect me for I had already accepted staying on. Did not want to go home and have to return.' That statement gives us reasonable assurance that he did not expect or seek to have a second tour of combat, as the thought of going home for a break and then returning a month later did not appeal to him. After all, he had a wife and young son at home, and they were certainly influencing his decision to see out his active period of service in England.

A little more time served in a non-combat role would be an acceptable solution. Besides, Clint kept reminding himself that there would be no more early calls, no mission briefings, no buzz on take-off, and no more aggressive flights over Europe. It would be a physical and mental release, shedding the extreme tension of air combat, bombing, and ground strafing, though there was perhaps a hint of reluctance that he would not be requested to carry out any more Met flights. Those, he felt, he was able to control as a solitary pilot, rather than formation responsibilities for others when carrying out Squadron missions. In effect, instructing was a perceived easier assignment—or was it?

Being one of the most experienced pilots in the 352nd FS and the Group, Clint would have been very much aware that some of the conditions in which they were ordered to fly were extremely perilous, not only from the perspective of enemy action, but because of mechanical failure and the weather. During the winter of 1943–44, the weather had been appalling, and it was absolutely certain that if he had been a commercial pilot, in some instances his instructions would have been 'don't fly'. However, the necessity of flying some of those missions in less-than-marginal conditions was determined by those in higher authority, who were pressing to fulfill the very serious policy of attrition of the enemy; it has to be noted that they fully expected to lose pilots on that basis alone.[1]

We have previously alluded to the fact that young pilots trained in the States were not fully prepared for the conditions that prevailed in the ETO. Although controversial, it was recorded by many observers that the young rookies were 'pushed' through the training program whilst they still lacked the ability to capably and confidently fly on instruments. That was the one attribute that gave Clint an advantage over many others when it came to flying those difficult missions. Now, as an instructor, Clint had to teach those young guys vitally important lessons. He had to improve their ability and awareness to cope with all weather conditions, and also to prepare them for combat with the enemy. Eager they may have been, but they would be cannon fodder for the Messerschmitts and Focke-Wulfs without those necessary skills. He had to teach them to stay alive.

With regards to in-flight training, it would be almost unfair to blame the instructors over in the States, as not that many would have had time in the combat zone, and the pressure from high up gave them few options. For that reason, the fresh would-be fighter pilots had to listen and learn from someone who had the experience and had survived. There was no doubt that Clint would have to take the task extremely seriously, for lives were at stake and the cost of replacing a pilot was very high. There were plenty of young hopefuls over the other side of the Atlantic, although the quality required to carry out the task at Squadron level eliminated a great number. The time element alone was not on their side. The Air Force needed fighter pilots immediately as the losses that had been sustained were unacceptable, so the dictate was 'push 'em through as fast as you can'; however, it needed to be as safe as possible, without spoiling their natural aggression to disrupt, damage, and destroy the enemy.

Clint reported for active duty to Colonel Humphrey, the base commander at Atcham. He very quickly had Clint back in the cockpit and checked out in a North American AT-6 Harvard, the regular advanced trainer being flown by nearly all would-be fighter pilots. Being a natural behind the stick was soon evident to the guys checking out fledgling instructors, and ground-school initiation came easy to Clint as he progressed very quickly back onto flying his beloved Thunderbolt.

Nevertheless, instructing was an art; it was not to be rushed. It would not be wise to put a guy fresh from combat in charge of tyros—the chief instructors had to be sure that the new instructor would not pass on bad or uncoordinated habits that had the tendency to kill the unwary. Those habits might save the experienced fighter pilot but not a new guy, fresh into the confusing turmoil of air combat. For that reason, they were not going to let Clint loose until they were sure that he would follow correct procedures when his time came to take responsibility for his students. The trainees didn't see themselves as students, and Clint would be the one to drag them into the real world of combat—not the picture-house glamour, but the uncertain and potentially deadly war in the air. If Clint didn't get it right, by giving them the best of his knowledge, it would be them who would die. Therefore, it was vital that he fitted into the training system by learning his new role.

Clint did have a friend at Atcham, for a fellow Squadron pilot had been ensconced on the course for several weeks. One of the original members of the 352nd FS, Capt. Charles Kipfer, had finished his tour at the end of April, and although one rung up the ladder from Clint, they swiftly re-engaged as Squadron buddies. Yes, he might even get to enjoy his posting!

Clint had seventeen flights before his final check-out with a senior instructor on 9 August, once again in the familiar cockpit of a Harvard. During that period he put in over twenty hours in P-47Cs and also a couple of hours in P-47Ds. He would be teaching and flying both of those types during his tenure at Atcham, and one or two other interesting aircraft besides!

From 6 August, having been cleared for instructing the previous day, Clint flew once, sometimes twice a day. There is virtually no detailed record relating to the instructing period of his new career, but he did carry out regular daily flights with trainees of anything from one hour and fifteen minutes to one hour and forty-five minutes—teaching, cajoling, coaxing, and ultimately, in some cases, blatantly ordering the young pilots to learn fresh habits or risk death. They learned.

Having settled in and established a routine, Clint began to look around for something to stir his rapidly waning combat psyche. He still needed a challenge! Being part of a combat training unit, he was well aware that there were some other ships to fly around the base. The one that caught his eye immediately happened to be a Lockheed P-38 Lightning—the twin-engine, twin-boom 'fork-tail devils' as the enemy called them.[2] Naturally, being a new kid on the block, he waited for the right moment before requesting a flight. He started one jump ahead of the rest because of his previous qualifications on twins, so on 18 August (having obtained his Transition ticket the previous day) his request was granted and he managed a thirty-minute flight to get the feel of that feisty fighter. It had gained quite a reputation since the early days of the USAAF entry into the war, and although it was fast and maneuverable, the Lightning found it tough when

Rumour has it that this slightly concerned picture of Clint is when he hitched a ride in a B-17 of the 100th Bomb Group. (*Sperry*)

Clint took this picture from the right-hand seat! (*Sperry*)

taking on the best of the Luftwaffe. One other rather discomforting disadvantage was that at height it was mighty cold for the pilot, as the so-called cockpit heating system was virtually non-existent. The pilots were therefore none too happy about high-altitude escort missions, but it did the job, and those distinctive twin booms and two engines made it easy for our guys to spot them real quick. It took poor eyesight to knock one of those down with 'friendly fire'.

Clint had fun. He didn't get another opportunity to fly a Lightning for a few more days, but on the 29th he managed to secure a P-38J for a more extended trip back to Raydon. It certainly impressed his old buddies back on the Squadron, as they remembered only too well at the 353rd Reunion in 1983:

Reinhardt: Remember when Clint Sperry went up to Stone after he finished his tour and then Clint brought a P-38 down one day to the Group.

Waggoner: No, I don't remember that.

Reinhardt: Anyway, Clint came in with this '38. Of course, all of us wanted to fly the damn thing … we kept badgering and badgering him so he finally said, 'Well, okay, God damn it, you want to fly it.' … he gave us the throttle settings and all that stuff. I taxied the damn '38 up and I got out [on the perimeter track], ran up the engine to check the mags and make a turn to get out on the runway, and got the nose wheel cocked on that son-of-a-bitch [laughter]. I'd never flown a twin-engine airplane before. What the hell is this?
    That's what they say: 'If it's got motors on it and wings, eventually you'll get it into the air'.

Clint obviously enjoyed meeting up with his buddies again, but in the short time that he had been away from Raydon, things had changed at his old base. He later recalled:

September was a month of many changes for 353. Duncan was on the ground somewhere in Holland and we had a whole team of C.O.'s. I was stationed in Shrewsbury (Atcham) on the west coast training replacement pilots in combat tactics from July 7 through September, getting into trouble flying P-38s and other adventures.

So what became of his first combat P-47 while he had been away? While on operations, there is no doubt that Clint had more than a passing respect for his 'own' Thunderbolt, the olive-drab and well-polished P-47D-2-RA, registration 42-22466, code SX-E, *Mary Jayne*, a 'Razorback'.

After working up at Goxhill, it is probable that Clint first received '466 in early August 1943 with the Group move to Metfield. When Clint joined up with this aircraft, it was soon carrying the name of *Mary Jayne* on the nacelle, and he flew

A P-38 visiting Raydon some time in summer '44. With no discernible unit markings, it is probably the Lightning from Atcham; therefore it could well be the day that Clint visited. (*Cross*)

the ship until the spring of the following year, when it was reputedly the oldest P-47 in the Group. Clint had a real bonding with the plane over the period he was flying it, although records indicate he might have relinquished '466 as early as late April 1944, when he was allocated a brand new Thunderbolt.

However, the story did not end for Clint's war-weary '466. Evidence shows that sometime after he ceased to fly it, '466 was re-coded SX-J (bar), and on 12 August 1944 it was being flown by Lt James Tuttle of the 352nd FS, who was tasked to go Thunder-bombing with the Group SE of Paris.[3] Lt Tuttle later reported:

> Took off and arrived in the target area without incident. Other Squadrons in Group found a convoy of trucks and staff cars and destroyed either most or all of them while we circled as top cover. Then we spotted a camouflaged train and dive bombed it. Following this, my wing man and myself strafed it. On the first pass, I was very low and starting to pull up when it must have exploded. My plane tried to snap roll to the left. Then smoke filled the cockpit so I opened the canopy. Tried to pull up but the engine cut out and the controls were damaged badly. Oil covered the canopy and I saw a field ahead by sticking my head out. Had full trim on elevator and aileron and full rudder and stick. Landed safely after hitting a tree and a telephone pole.

His son, James Tuttle Jr, later enhanced his father's story.

> He bellied in, on fire, and according to my Dad, was unstrapped and on the wing before it stopped in the field [near Nangis]. I could never get him drunk enough to talk more about Paris. Lord knows my brother and I tried. He did relate a humorous anecdote about having to hide in a room pretending to be a lover with his woman (a female underground compatriot) while the Germans

A sad end to a fine P-47. SX-J (bar) (SX-E) lies burnt on a field in France. Fortunately the pilot, Lt Tuttle, escaped before the plane was engulfed by fire. (*Tuttle*)

searched the building. When one young German soldier opened the door and found this naked woman and 'her man' in bed, she raised such a ruckus screaming at the soldier in anger that he turned beet red and left. Soldiers humor of course. I also can imagine the tense anxiety of the situation.

He successfully evaded capture, but for '466 it was the end. Almost completely destroyed by fire, it would never take to the air again—a sad end to an aircraft that carried Clint through many difficult and dangerous months and put another pilot safely on the ground when mortally damaged. Yes, '466 was a fine aircraft.

Having relinquished '466, and because of his seniority, Clint was able to take a brand new P-47D-22 (42-26121) as his regular aircraft. The plane immediately became SX-E for the remaining few weeks of his tour.[4]

By the time of Clint's visit back to Raydon in the P-38, it is quite possible that he may have found out the fate of his first Thunderbolt. Like Col. Duncan, Lt Tuttle was down and on the run, and the old SX-E had been destroyed, but he could not dwell on that as he had a pressing need to get back to his important job as an instructor.

After flying down to Raydon for three hours and fifty-five minutes, he had set a precedent that he could enjoy a few more times during his stay at Atcham. In fact, over the next two days he virtually had the P-38 to himself as he was in the air for a further six hours and forty-five minutes. However, where he went and what he got up to has not been recorded. What was certain is that he was having fun, and as he just inferred, that fun would lead to trouble!

Clint kept his head down and carried on with the task that he was allocated, and although he was able to take a few more short trips in the P-38, it was reasonably obvious that his Operations Officer, Major Miller, was not taking too kindly to the fact that Clint was using the Lightning primarily for fun. So, there were no more long hauls away from Atcham. He was rumbled, but what more could they expect from an experienced fighter pilot?

The desire to get out of the training role for short periods was an indication that Clint was beginning to get the energy and excitement of pure flying back into his system. During those times away from instructing he was also changing from the seasoned and combat-weary fighter pilot to the rather less-disciplined and yet extremely experienced aviator. Rather than have to fly and fight, he now wanted to enjoy the experience. Not having to look constantly over his shoulder for enemy aircraft or flak whistling past him from ground batteries was the release that had lifted him once more from necessity to pleasure. So, what does a fighter pilot do? Naturally, he wanted to push the boundaries again, but he had to wait a little longer, for any infraction might wreck his ultimate aim of getting home.

He behaved himself for a few more days and trained the new boys in the art of survival. There is no doubt that at every opportunity they would be asking Clint and other tour-expired fighter-pilot instructors what combat was really like. Some would embellish and some would tell them how it really was, but one thing was sure—the young bloods soon found out that it was no cake-walk.

The time was approaching when Clint would finish his period as an instructor. He was toiling with the responsibility of trying to get the young fledgling fighter pilots as prepared as possible for their tough times ahead, and then he would head back home to an unknown future. Yes, back to Mary and his son, Steve, who he had not yet seen; that would be the greatest draw for him.

However, it seemed that Clint had not lost his spirit of adventure, and it appeared that the powers that be at Atcham began to realize that you can't take the fighter plane away from the pilot without some form of rebellion. The anticipated celebratory juices were beginning to flow on 17 September (a week before Clint was due to finish), when the following incident occurred. Clint takes up the story:

After completion of [my] tour as instructor of combat tactics for new pilots in Atcham, for diversion on a bad weather day (so no training flight), Major Jim Jones and I decided on a wager for excitement. We bet that we could take-off, circle the field and land without breaking the 25 feet of rope between the two 'Forty-Sevens'. Low ceiling and poor visibility caused me to lose sight of the runway and overshoot in my turn to line up for landing. That meant going round again which meant gear up, flaps up—another attempt for final approach and all that goes with it—gear down, flaps down and roll-out to dead stop. It takes longer to write about it than it did to do it! Rolled to a stop on the runway with rope still intact.

Anyway, we did it only through the fantastic ability of Jim Jones in holding position through some unplanned, and certainly unexpected procedures. It's important to state that there was no radio communication between us. Radio silence was mandatory for training groups to keep the airways open for the guys that might need them.

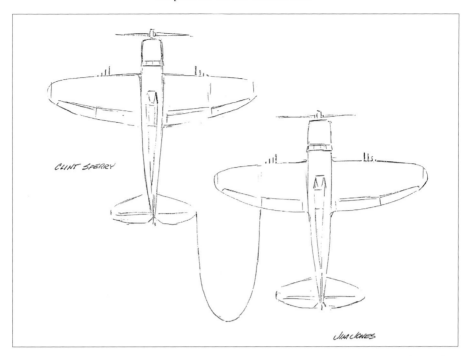

This is the personal sketch by Clint of the two P-47s roped together. A rank spoiler! (*Sperry*)

A jeep also arrived carrying Base Commander Col Humphrey who did not think the feat set a very good example of flight safety. Jim was the guy who really had to fly.

We won the bet but were reprimanded by an impressed CO, who also felt that it was a very dangerous and, in retrospect, a bad example for new pilots. So Jim lost a little rank, as did I, but it was a highlight at Atcham.

As Clint later observed, it was '...just *one* of the 'rank' spoilers'. In fact, rumor had it that when the Colonel told him he was busted, he informed Clint that a large number of guys had money on the stunt, with many being senior officers—and more than half of those were betting against him! That wasn't good for promotion prospects.

Although I was never fined in dollars directly, and actually never disciplined for any episodes that may have deserved a reprimand, it is evident that much must have been entered on my record that restricted or influenced recommendation for additional rank. In observing two years of overseas records ... my rank remained unchanged throughout my operational flight status. Although I was pleased that it had no bearing on my squadron status, I learned much too late that my casual disregard for military politics and protocol was much to

This picture is marked 'Celebrating the bet' on the reverse. Jones and Sperry (second right) receive acknowledgement from Kipfer (right) and Ledner, Shrewsbury (Atcham) 5/12/'44. A further note reads 'Later reprimand from Gen. Woodbury & CO & cut $35 (split).' (*Sperry*)

blame. There was occasional 'social' embarrassment in later years, but I doubt I would have done it any differently a second time. I tired quickly of the normal 'Officers Club' indulgence and spent my free time relaxing with thoughtful and understanding English people. They knew how to treat those who they knew must regularly witness tragedy and face daily risk and did not ask, or expect you to relive your day. I thought of them as family and they accepted me as one of theirs. To these people I am forever grateful.

Sadly I never asked for promotion, and consequently, never got one. Advice: You may not gain rank for a number of reasons, but if you don't ask, chances are good it won't happen.

It is not known the extent of Clint's loss of 'a little rank' for the rope trick; at least he retained his rank of 1st Lieutenant. However, he has made it clear that because of his attitude towards military politics and protocol, and also some of his so-called flying excesses, he was not top of the list for a step up to the next rung. But those thoughts were in the back of his mind; his combat duty had finished, and the time he spent instructing had completed his tour. He really was heading home.

The Later Years

Clint's son, Steve, relates the events that occurred after the end of Clint's tour:

Dad left England. With his departure he was looking toward re-entering a life that was interrupted by his deployment to England a year and a half before. Ahead were my mom and me (who he had yet to meet), his folks, his friends (some of whom were gone, not to return). There was the familiar landscape of his youth and the distinctly American way of life that was familiar but different than Britain....

There was another aspect to his departure from England that was not anticipated. He was leaving behind a life filled with harsh realities of course, but it became apparent to me during our two visits to England together (1994 and 1997) that he was leaving a place and a people that he had fallen in love with during this tumultuous time. He was leaving a life of brilliant color even when it was over a gray and foreboding seascape ... I am sure, though, that my father set foot on a troop ship on 7 November 1944 destined for New York with many conflicting emotions. Anticipation, relief, remorse, anxiety were part of the mix that he and I reckon many or all the veterans aboard were experiencing as they began their journey home.

I'm quite surprised as I look into Dad's first months after returning from England. Though, at one-year-old, my intake of events regarding my father's whereabouts at any given moment were on a rather different plane, I have formed a rough picture over the past 70 years that I thought was reasonably accurate. It wasn't. It appears that after an initial period of union with Mom and me the AAF shipped him out to Michigan for the month of January 1945 where he would ferry P-47s to California.

On 20 February (1945) he was moved to Gabreski Field in Farmingdale (Long Island), NY where he would continue his combat instructing. There is some question about what airplanes were used at Hillsgrove Airport, Rhode Island, but in Farmingdale, home of Republic, mock battles over Long Island were fought in Thunderbolts.

Over the next four months Clint would fly mostly once and sometimes up to three times a day, training aspiring fighter pilots or possibly on an occasional anti-submarine patrol. All told, during that period he flew in excess of 136 hours, passing on his knowledge and experience to fledglings, hoping that in some way he had contributed to their survival and, if they were good and lucky, their ultimate ability as operational fighter pilots.

Steve continues:

> The war in Europe would end (May 7th, 1945) while Dad was based at Gabreski Field and it was time to decide what road to take. He was flying a lot and could remain with the USAAF (soon to be the USAF) and probably get into the next generation fighter or he could head off into the civilian world using either his flying skills or his art. It appears that he opted to take a shot at commercial art. An educated guess (based on a one, going on two-year-old memory) as to the motivation toward this avenue would have to include two major issues. First, flying had been, pretty much, his daily routine for the past two years, which by itself wouldn't be enough to remove airplanes from his life but it might, very temporarily, diminish his interest. Second and surely most importantly, most of his flying hadn't been risk free or family orientated. Enter my mom. Her focus was family and my sister Lee was on her way to making us a family of four.[1] Anyway, the decision was made to first, give up his commission and second, back away from flying. That said, the regular earth-based job in New York City had a short life.

At the end of the course, following four hard months of flying and teaching, he had finally made up his mind. Clint's Individual Flight Record was formally marked 'Closed' on 28 June 1945, and his 'Separation' document shows that he was released from service on 29 August 1945. There is no record that he flew again for the Air Force. The final Wing score credited Clint with five enemy aircraft destroyed or probably destroyed, awarded the Distinguished Flying Cross with two Oak Leaf Clusters, the Air Medal with three Oak Leaf Clusters, and the European, African, and Middle Eastern Theater Campaign Ribbon—and never lost or damaged his aircraft in combat. Unlike many unfortunate souls, Clint had survived the war and more than fulfilled his active duty. Finally, after taking advantage of some accumulated leave, Clint had thought long and hard about the options, and no doubt discussed them with Mary to find the answer.

Steve expands further on their important, life-changing decision:

> Next stop was back to Hillsgrove (late 1945) and East Coast Aviation run by John Griffin, a former Northeast Airlines pilot. East Coast was a Stinson dealer at the time so Clint flew most of that line of which he had a Voyager to do with as he chose.

Clint later recounted that period:

> During 1946 through 1950, I was employed as a Commercial Pilot by East Coast
> Aviation Corp in Rhode Island.... In those early days, one was called upon for
> all sorts of flight related responsibilities, both challenging and opportunistic.
> I became manager of flight operations, employing 7 flight instructors, plus a
> maintenance operation including 15 aircraft technicians and a business staff of
> 4. We operated a flight school for new pilots, instructor ratings and instrument
> ratings. We also acted as broker for aircraft sales of all types, but were a Stinson
> dealership.

However, from time to time there was an interesting assignment:

> Through a sub-contract arrangement with the Navy Department, I was one of 4
> pilots to be assigned to check on Navy fighter pilots safety habits. A Navy pilot,
> a Marine Corps pilot, an Airforce pilot and an X-fighter pilot (me). The pilots
> (spied on) had no clue and did their understanding best to get us drunk at the
> O.C. to find out what we were doing. Of course there were reports of problems
> … but far fewer than actual. They were flying F8Fs.[2] We reported to the Base
> Admiral every morning.

There is no doubt that Clint's name wasn't just drawn out of a tattered hat for
that assignment; someone had obviously favored his experience and aptitude in
both his 'specialist' fighter-pilot role in the USAAF and, later, in commercial flying
circles. Someone in authority had noticed and remembered.

In mid-1950, the United States and their Allies were once again at war in the Far
East. Whether Clint had considered that he might be called back into service is not
known, as he had already re-evaluated his position at East Coast and decided on a
change of direction. Following an East Coast charter flight for the Rodney Hunt
Machine Co., Clint immediately hit it off with Company President Earl Harris. The
two had much in common, and it wasn't long before an offer was made for Clint to
join the company as chief pilot. That they both immensely enjoyed sailing and flying
was no coincidence in the decision, for their association grew over the years into a
strong and abiding friendship. Clint had been working with Earl for about two years
when, as a result of the escalating Korean War, he received a letter from 'Headquarters,
First Air Force, Mitchel Air Force Base, New York'. It informed him that he was to be
appointed as a Reserve Officer in the United States Air Force with the rank of 1st Lt.
Fortunately for Clint and all in the Western world, there was a cessation of fighting
the following year (1953), and an uneasy but mutually suspicious peace remains to this
day. Clint could now concentrate completely on his new flying venture.

In 1966, with four children (Toby and Lisa still living at home) and having been
with Rodney Hunt Machine Co. for sixteen years, Clint decided that it was time to

make a positive move into the full commercial world of advertising. His last four years with Earl weren't in a flying capacity, for sadly his professional flying days were over. Having had the background and experience as advertising director for Earl, he was subsequently interviewed and accepted for a post as an advertising sales executive with McGraw Hill Publishing. He was with them for about ten years, and immersed himself enthusiastically in his new advertising vocation.

Clint made one more career move, in search of the ideal employer that could utilize his undoubted skills. He was offered a senior post at the New England head office of Yankee Publishing, the periodical destined for homeowners, which provided information on travel, food, events, and countless other interesting and informative subjects. It would be a long association, and for the vast majority of his time there, Clint would gain considerable satisfaction from that particular publishing and advertising career. It was sufficient as a vocation to ensure that he stayed there for twenty-three years.

Many Air Force veterans over the years had repressed, forgotten, or sidelined their memories of time served in England. Maybe their sons and daughters had asked the inevitable question, 'Dad, what did you do in the war?' For those who wished to look back, curiosity overcame the reticence. Clint was one of those who needed a gentle push to be involved in that revival. As a result of this interest, he began to talk more often with his close friends in the 352nd FS who had survived the war and were still around. Steve recollects:

Cliff Armstrong may have been Clint's best friend in England. His name would often come up in our conversations and Cliff lived not far from us … Cliff was a farmer and except for his time as a fighter pilot he remained a farmer. Dad had great respect for Cliff's flying ability. One of his favorite stories was of flying with Cliff. Each was flying a '47. Cliff was on Dad's left wing and he rolled his airplane over the top of Dad and slid alongside on Dad's right wing. That is a very nice piece of flying.

However, those kinds of flights didn't always go according to plan. Steve:

On a short flight around the field with Cliff Armstrong flying alongside, Cliff started to strenuously motion that something was amiss. Dad didn't pick up on his meaning before a major part of the engine cowling passed over his head clearing not only his canopy, but the entire tail as well. He landed without further incident. I suspect there were two adrenaline pumped pilots inspecting the damage after they landed. My first thought is preflight, preflight, preflight (easy for me to say), but it could well have been a fatigued piece of aluminum.

Because of the revival of those stirring memories, veteran aviators were being approached by an ever-growing band of enthusiasts; they were hungry to take

Cliff Armstrong relaxing
between missions, probably
in a Suffolk field somewhere
near to Raydon. At least the
sun is shining! (*Sperry*)

in stories of combat and life on operations during the Second World War. In the
early 1990s, the young historian Graham Cross (later Dr) was a prime motivator
of veteran returns by encouraging visits of the wartime airmen of the 353rd
Fighter Group to England. In so doing, he enhanced his knowledge for recording
the Group's history. He was still in his teens when he started to compile the
book that has now become the accomplished and definitive official history of
the Group, 'Jonah's Feet Are Dry'.[3] Clint, however, had yet to meet him, and as
the years drifted away, the pictures that Clint had retained in his memory were
fading. Prompted by Steve's personal wish to find out more, they made that trip
to England in 1994. Steve's recording of the event in his written Prologue shows
just how difficult it had been for Clint to dredge up those events of fifty years
ago. The eventual meeting in the Raydon village pub, The Chequers, together
with members of the Raydon Airfield Preservation Society (RAPS), enabled Clint
and Steve to meet Graham and John, and other key members.

Although Clint and Steve's visit was their first in following Clint's path to war,
there had been several visits previously by veterans of the 353rd Fighter Group
to Metfield and Raydon. Apart from more organized trips, individuals had made
the journey to England with their families and were well-received by village folks
when they visited Raydon.

Led by Graham, further initiatives were stirring in England. RAPS wanted
something significant and lasting to stand as a memory to those based there

Lt Gordon Burlingame's SX-M (a/c 44-14620), *Davy Don Chariot*, together with ground crew. Left to right are: Asst Crew Chief Charles B. Perkins, Capt. Gordon S. Burlingame, Armorer Sgt Joseph S. Mortorana, and Crew Chief S/Sgt Otto J. Stopen. 'Gordo' was one of Clint's closest friends in the Squadron, and visited Raydon during the 1990s. (*National Archives*)

during the war—not just a plaque or a stone, but a formal recognition of the sacrifices made on behalf of their generation. Their ultimate aim was to build a memorial on the airfield. There was also an opportunity to arrange the continuing visits to Raydon by the veterans and their families. That was achieved, and in the company of visiting veterans, the memorial was officially dedicated on 10 June 1995. Clint was not immune to that happening and John had kept him in touch with progress. He had been hoping that he might be able to travel to England for the dedication, but he couldn't make it due to business and family commitments.

Further events followed, and motivated by John, Graham and keen local people, the first official Raydon Air Show took off in a rain-soaked sky in 1997. The special guests for that small inaugural event were Clint and Steve (who even helped erect the marquees!). Clint was wearing a flight jacket with the Slybird patch, but it wasn't his original, as Steve related:

Dad wasn't wearing his original squadron jacket during our visit to Raydon. While a member of our local town fire department he loaned the original to a guy whose house was on fire on a cold winter night and it was never returned.

On that day at Raydon, Clint was representing all the guys from the Group—both past and present. Clint and Steve did them proud, as unfortunately no one else could make it over to England for the event. Although there were aircraft of varying vintage, Spitfires, Corsair, Harvard, and others, two Mustangs had landed in to the delight of the small crowd that had braved the 'typical' English summer weather. However, most important for Clint was the emotional appearance of a P-47. Although it gave a spirited display, because of its weight it had been unable to land for fear of getting bogged down on the still young and very wet grass surface. But it was there; a Thunderbolt had returned!

Following the visit, Clint mailed John:

> On reflection, not during a single interview did anyone ask how many aircraft I shot down—nor how it felt to fly such a lethal aircraft. You can't imagine how grateful I was for that sensitivity among all with whom I conversed. It brought to mind that John Anderson, like my son (and probably all in attendance), accepted these wonderful aircraft as they should be ... not only as flying machines of history, but of beauty, power and excitement, and no reminder was needed of their purpose in war. I hope that my impromptu sentiment was from one who admires them as you and Steve—and from one who was involved with the capabilities for which they were designed.
>
> On Friday Sept 5 following our return home I took the afternoon to peacefully reflect on a most cherished week with friends and new acquaintances in England. As the pictures will show, the air was light and sea very comfortable, but just right for rest and relaxation ... In sequence, I left the mooring under sail, eased slowly

Clint standing outside The Chequers public house when he visited with son, Steve, in 1994. (J. Dudley)

out of Sippican Harbor in Marion to find still very light air in Buzzards Bay. With the wind getting very light, and no power that I wish to use, I barely slipped back to the mooring, stowed and covered the sails and rowed back to the Yacht Club as the early evening air finally gave out. Sailing has many of the same elements as flying. Where one can feel humbled by the vastness of air and water and realize how small we really are. I may be concerned about work before I go, but quickly adjust to the elements that make life a rewarding experience.

Steve continues:

At 79 (1999), Dad was hearing rumbling noises from Yankee that maybe he ought to give some thought to retiring. Maybe travel a little or visit children and grandchildren or ... yes! Spend some time sailing! One of his greatest pleasures. He sold his Rhodes 19 and bought something he could take Ellen (second marriage), Jen and Steph (my half-sisters) out on the Bay with or sail comfortably alone. He loved that and found reason (or no reason) to be at sea sailing his boat.

Although there were further air shows, Clint didn't make it back to England again. He was prepared to travel, but circumstances did not permit. So it was. Clint's last physical link with his wartime service had been severed. His enduring pleasure of sailing would still be available to him, but with his job at risk and concerns about his personal well-being, the future was becoming very uncertain. By the year 2000, Clint was no longer with Yankee, but he still wished to carry on with his sailing. Then, in October of that year, Clint was rushed into a Boston hospital for a serious operation. As the weeks progressed, he slowly began to show signs of recovery. The fighter in Clint was emerging yet again, and the steady progress was maintained. However, sadly the rehabilitation was temporary, for Clint returned once again to hospital. With his family supporting him to the end, he passed away a few days later, on 18 February 2001.

Steve's note to John probably sums up best how it was to lose his father and friend:

Until a few months ago I thought my dad would live indefinitely. I never really thought of him as old except to kid with him. As recent as this past summer we were doing regular things around his house and mine that I might have been doing with my sons ... I miss him John, and certainly I've only begun to accept his passing. I know that picking up the phone to get his input on the weather will remain an automatic response for a long time. And I'll be looking over my shoulder waiting for visits after his sailing afternoons, so we can have a beer and talk about his sailing and my flying. Alas, I find myself talking with him anyway and, though it comes with a longing, I don't have to leave a message or wait for his physical presence...

A Final Reflection

As mentioned in the beginning of this book, John Anderson and I are about the same age (I'm younger!). He was born in England and I in America, and over the course of writing the book we have found, as might be expected, that our views did not always align. Initially I pinned these differences to my desire to describe my dad realistically and modestly and still present a fine and very able character while John chose to present him, and fighter pilots in general, as somewhat larger than life. As the book progressed and our differences didn't really change much, I began to realize that there was a much deeper and ingrained reason that was at play here; one that describes a Brit as much as warm beer, tea and cricket and one that endears them to me. My own early memories of the Second World War were few, fleeting, and far from real. Not until I was in the service myself did I have a remotely real sense of that time, and even then it was sprinkled heavily with romantic notions and images. I remember little or nothing about the healing of my country, although that's what much of the world was doing. I am certain that my parents' generation of Americans required varying degrees of healing, but what I saw and remember was not that. It seemed that in the US the sharp edges had rounded and the harshness had faded before the forties became the fifties. My parents were building, but not rebuilding; their peers were adjusting, but not beginning. The war was over and, unlike London, a trip to New York showed few reminders of its havoc. On the other side, the British people lived with the harsh reality of war for five years. The country was filled with reminders of the war for years after its end, and although John and I haven't discussed his remembered experiences of the forties, their influence is distinctly apparent in memorabilia, old airfields, conversations in pubs, and, maybe more than anything else, an obvious and deserved pride in withstanding and eventually overcoming an incredibly powerful opposing force. I have found these things embedded in the culture of England and John Anderson has shown me emphatically how he and his countrymen and women feel about those who fought against the Axis forces during the Second World War. He is not timid about accolades or superlatives where people like my father are concerned. What I now know to be fact is that these tributes are heartfelt and real, and, as my dad discovered all those years ago, very little is taken for granted and their warriors are held in the highest esteem ... Thanks John for your determination, understanding and patience in educating this American. Dad loved England and I've become rather fond of the place myself.

Steve Sperry

Endnotes

Chapter One

1. The 8th Air Force was designed to carry out the strategic policies laid down by AWPD-42. It was the largest air striking force committed to battle, and carried out more than a thousand separate missions during thirty-four months of hostilities. Ref: *Mighty Eighth War Diary*; Roger Freeman, Jane's.
2. The origins of the name 'Slybird' are unclear, although Fighter Groups did have names that were easily recognized within the Air Force. It was rumored the 'Slybird' art had inputs from several 353rd Fighter Group sources, but it does seem likely that Clint may have been the artist to take ideas and turn them into the final design.

Chapter Two

1. The German word '*blitzkrieg*' means 'lightning war'. The Luftwaffe sent their fighters, bombers, and Stuka dive-bombers to weaken their opposition, then rolled through with ground armor and troops. When first used in Europe, the results were swift and deadly.
2. Born of an American mother (Jennie Jerome), Winston Leonard Spencer Churchill replaced Neville Chamberlain as Prime Minister on 10 May 1940.
3. The generally accepted dates for the Battle of Britain were that it commenced on 10 July 1940 and concluded on 31 October 1940. During that period, 537 RAF pilots were killed and 1,017 aircraft were lost. Ref: *The Battle of Britain—Then and Now*; ed. Winston G. Ramsey, Battle of Britain Prints International Ltd.
4. During the Battle of Britain, the Luftwaffe suffered a total loss of 2,662 airmen killed, including 549 Me109 and Me110 crewmen. This was as a result of 1,882 aircraft destroyed, including 871 Me109 and Me110 fighters,

during that period. Ref: *The Battle of Britain—Then and Now*; ed. Winston G. Ramsey, Battle of Britain Prints International Ltd.

5. Operation 'Sealion' (*Unternemen Seelöwe*) was postponed by Hitler in September 1940. In June 1941 he attacked Russia, which ultimately cancelled any opportunity of invading Britain.

6. The Tripartite Pact was signed by Germany, Italy, and Japan on 27 September 1940.

7. FISCAL YEAR 1942—cost ready for battle. When first produced in 1942, the cost of a P-47 had been around $105,000, the P-51 just under $60,000, and the twin-engine P-38 $120,000. *Army Air Force Statistical Digest—World War II.*

8. During 1943, Nazi Germany produced 18,953 (Axis total 19,584) compared to 101,639 for the Allies. During 1944 the numbers were 33,804 vs 125,718. In 1945 the numbers were 6,987 vs 60,494. In the ETO (non-Mediterranean MTO) during 1944, USAAF lost 1,293 fighter aircraft to enemy fighters, while losing 1,611 due to German flak. *Army Air Force Statistical Digest—World War II.*

9. Held on 14–24 January 1943, the Conference (code name Symbol) was comprised of main players President Roosevelt and Prime Minister Churchill. With them were their senior Generals and also representatives from France. The aim of the Conference was to decide their main strategies and, particularly, how to carry on the offensive against the Germans in France. Although the Russian leader, Stalin, had been invited, he was unable to attend due to pressing needs on his home front.

Chapter Three

1. The Civilian Pilot Training Program (CPTP) had been formed in 1939 to provide aspiring pilots with the opportunity to get full ratings for commercial flying, but also acted as a planned progression into service flying for national defense. After the United States entered into the Second World War in 1941, the training program became known as the War Training Service.

2. In the United States Army Air Force a pilot's Individual Flight Record followed his every flight during service. Basic items were recorded, including name, rank, service number, division of Air Force, station, date, aircraft flown, hours flown both for individual flights and monthly totals, number of landings, type of sortie, combat hours, and instrument time. It was a simple but comprehensive document, certified monthly by the pilot's senior officer.

3. Capt. Leslie Cles was repatriated at the end of the war, but was sadly killed in a flying accident whilst instructing in the United States.

Chapter Four

1. Originally designed with the Allison engine, the P-51 suffered from poor performance at altitude. It was decided that it would be an advantage if the British Rolls Royce Merlin engine could be fitted, offering better performance in height and speed; the legend of the Mustang had begun.

2. In March 1940 the 81,000-ton Cunard liner 'Queen Mary' sailed for Sydney, Australia, to be refitted and repainted as a troopship. She then carried service personnel both ways between America and Britain during the war.

Chapter Five

1. The son of the first private-owner pilot in Imperial Russia, Alexander P. Seversky learned to fly in 1914 as the First World War commenced. In July of 1915 he lost his right leg when his bomber was shot down. He later became a fighter pilot, shooting down thirteen German aircraft. In 1917 he was sent to the USA as part of the Naval Mission, and following the Russian Revolution he stayed in the US to work as a consultant engineer, ranked as a Major, for the Army Air Service. In 1922 the US Government bought the rights of a bombsight that he had designed, and with that money he formed what later became the Seversky Aircraft Corporation. During the 1930s, with Major Seversky himself being the chief designer and test pilot, the company designed and built both civil and military aircraft. It was in the early '30s that he met and became friends with fellow Russian Alexander Kartveli, who eventually became responsible for all designs. By 1939, with the company in financial trouble, Major de Seversky relinquished the presidency of his company and stood aside for William Kellett, a former senior director.

2. Alexander Kartveli was another who found himself without a country when the revolution occurred. He had been sent to France to study military tactics, but when he was unable to return he gained degrees in aeronautical and electrical engineering and worked for several aeronautical companies. In 1927, a chance meeting in Paris with entrepreneur Charles Levine saw him heading for the US to work at the Colombia Aircraft Corporation, then moving on to the Fokker Corporation in New Jersey. However, fate provided a meeting with Major de Seversky where he commenced work as his assistant chief engineer. Their initial design, the SEV-3, was a floatplane aimed at both the civil and military market. It was the plane that began to show several features of the Thunderbolt, and further progressive designs gained the attention of the public and the military as they obtained many

speed records. With the guiding hand of Kartveli, in May 1941 the XP-47B emerged—by this time under the new company name of the Republic Aviation Corporation. The legend of the Thunderbolt was born.

3. P-47 Thunderbolt. The prefix 'P' stands for Pursuit (this was changed after the war, when the 'P' was replaced by 'F' for Fighter); the '47' was the manufacturer's designated number for the project design. *Thunderbolt*; Roger Freeman.

Chapter Six

1. It is fair to say that throughout the war and inter-war years there were many examples of ships being severely under-equipped with lifeboats. Basic lifesaving gear of a life belt or life vest was, to many, totally insufficient when a ship was sinking—whether it was in mid-ocean or within sight of land.

2. In many respects, the British countryside was similar to some parts of America—especially the areas familiar to Clint. But the fields and hills were smaller and very different from the vast arable corn-growing areas, plains, and mountains in the United States. Consequently, the beauty of the landscape was condensed and visually enhanced for the observer.

3. 'Axis Sally' (real name Mildred Gillars) was a German-American who was introduced on the airwaves from Germany to radios throughout the European and Mediterranean regions of conflict—specifically targeted at American forces. Captured in 1946, she was eventually convicted of treason and jailed.

4. Both Grimsby and Hull were main fishing ports on the east coast. The Luftwaffe was fully aware that the ports were providing sustenance to beleaguered Britain, and they suffered regular raids that destroyed valuable resources and deprived the dockyards of labor.

5. Equivalent ranks (approximate) of USAAF, British, and German Air Forces.

USAAF	RAF	LUFTWAFFE
General	Air Chief Marshal	Generaloberst
Lieutenant General	*no equivalent*	Generalleutnant
Major-General	Air Vice-Marshal	Generalmajor
Brigadier-General	Air Commodore	*no equivalent*
Colonel	Group Captain	Oberst
Lieutenant Colonel	Wing Commander	Oberstleutnant
Major	Squadron Leader	Major
Captain	Flight Lieutenant	Hauptmann

First Lieutenant	Flying Officer	Oberleutnant
Second Lieutenant	Pilot Officer	Leutnant
Flight Officer	*no equivalent*	*no equivalent*
Sergeant-Major	*no equivalent*	Hauptfeldwebel
Master Sergeant	Warrant Officer	Stabsfeldwebel
Technical Sergeant	Flight Sergeant	Oberfeldwebel
Staff Sergeant	Sergeant	Feldwebel
no equivalent	*no equivalent*	Unterfeldwebel
Sergeant	Corporal	Unteroffizier
Corporal	Leading Aircraftsman	Obergefreiter
Private First Class	Aircraftsman 1st Class	Gefreiter
no equivalent	Aircraftsman 2nd Class	Flieger

Via *Aircrew Remembrance Society*.

Chapter Seven

1. Plan of Metfield Airfield. *Jonah's Feet Are Dry*; Dr Graham Cross.
2. This was the period designated for combat operations as laid down by Fighter Command for the ETO.
3. The Boeing B-17G was powered by 4 x 1200-hp Wright R-1820-97 air-cooled radial engines, with a wingspan of 103 feet 9 inches and length of 74 feet 9 inches. The Flying Fortress was so-named for its perceived armaments, with .50-inch guns for hitting power. It was crewed by nine or ten airmen and had a maximum speed of 295 mph and cruising speed at around 200 mph at 30,000 feet. With a maximum bomb load of 13,600 lbs, it weighed 72,000 lbs and (depending on bomb load) a radius of between 650–800 miles. *Mighty Eighth War Manual*; Roger Freeman.
4. One of several variations of the Consolidated B-24H was powered by 4 x Pratt & Whitney R-1830-65 air-cooled radial engines, and with a wingspan of 110 feet and length of 67 feet 2 inches, the Liberator was so named for its expected duty. 10 x .50-inch guns protected the aircraft. It was crewed by ten men and had a maximum speed of 290 mph and a cruising speed of 205 mph at 25,000 feet. With a maximum bomb load of 12,800 lbs, it weighed in at 67,800 lbs and (depending on bomb load) had a radius of around 700 miles. *Mighty Eighth War Manual*; Roger Freeman.
5. Designed as a low-level bomber, the Martin B-26 Marauder B-26B-4 was powered by 2 x Pratt & Whitney R-2800-43 air-cooled radial engines, and with a wingspan of 65 feet and a length of 58 feet 3 inches, the Marauder fought as its name implied. It was armed with 2 × .30-inch and 2 × .50-inch machine guns. It carried a crew of six and had a maximum speed of 317 mph

and a cruising speed of 200 mph at 14,500 feet. With a maximum bomb load of 4,000 lbs it weighed in at 34,000 lbs and (depending on bomb load) a radius of up to 800 miles. *Mighty Eighth War Manual*; Roger Freeman.

6. The Ninth Air Force began as a listed air-support command, later becoming the main tactical air force in the European Theater of Operations. Initially commencing operations in the Mediterranean, it transferred to the ETO in 1943 to provide invaluable support for the invasion of Europe.

7. Known by the Allied pilots as the 'Abbeville Kids' (or 'Abbeville Boys'), they were the Me109 (and later Fw190) pilots of *Jagdgeschwader Schlageter* (JG) 26. They were also referred to as the 'Yellow Nose Bastards' as they painted the aircraft nose cone and forward nose yellow—and they were good. Within a short space of time, other units followed suit.

8. The fighters needed longer legs to increase the distance needed to escort the bombers. However, it wasn't until 28 July 1943 that belly tanks were first used for a mission. They couldn't take the fighters all the way to the bombers' distant targets, and they were unreliable—but it was a start.

9. As a result of longer missions into Germany, Eighth Bomber Command desperately needed better weather reporting. Consequently, within each Fighter Group certain pilots with good navigational skills were designated for training.

10. The Messerschmitt 109 is often called the 'Me109', but it can also be known as 'Bf 109'—which is probably the more correct abbreviation. The 'Bf' stands for *Bayerische Flugzeugwerke*, where the aircraft was manufactured. However, the guys facing them would use 'Me', 'Me 109', or even just '109', and therefore the authors have decided to reflect their usage in this book.

11. '*Viermots*' were 'four motors', the '*Dicke Autos*' were 'fat cars'—the 'Big Friends'. The accompanying Allied fighters were called 'Indians' by the Luftwaffe pilots.

12. Longer-range fuel tanks and the P-51 Merlin-engine Mustang were the answers.

Chapter Eight

1. Designated staff in the Control Tower handled communications and recorded significant events in all aircraft movements on the ground and in the air, together with other relevant observations. The CTL had been an important record of events for the 353rd Fighter Group and a valuable reference for this book. The records were originally preserved by the head of flying control, Capt. Henry H. Zielinski. When Eighth Air Force historian Roger Freeman became aware of them he obtained a copy for his records. Thanks to them both, the Control Tower Log survives to this day.

Chapter Nine

1. Fighter Groups considered themselves fortunate to be based on an established RAF airfield. The pre-war facilities were permanent and luxurious in comparison to those built after the conflict started. Most RAF bases even had central heating, whereas a pot stove would be the welcome for any Group moving into a newly prepared (and frequently unfinished) air base.
2. Magneto—a vital part of the electrical circuit of the engine. They generate the spark for combustion. As Clint found out, if one of the two magnetos failed, the considered danger meant it was an offence to run on only one.

Chapter Ten

1. Nissen huts were the low-cost result of providing living and working quarters for airmen in the War years. They were utilitarian, practical, and quick and easy to build—just find a concrete slab, fix the semi-circle frames to the base, and cover them with corrugated iron sheets. Then brick up both ends (leaving a place for a wooden door) and cut a few holes for metal window frames. Finally, and inadequately, put in a pot stove for heat. Some were lined inside, some not, but they were never warm enough in the winter. However, they worked, and there are no records to suggest anyone died of cold in them.
2. When the weather was poor or there were no aircraft available, pilots would have to do time on the Link. Invented in the late '20s by Edwin Link of New York, they were an invaluable training aid for pilots to improve their bad weather and night-flying instrument skills. An instructor passed messages to the 'pilot', and he reacted accordingly, with the mechanism of the Link providing realistic movements—it even looked like a very small aircraft. Blind flying on the Link was part of all pilots' training and operational requirements and, no doubt, saved many lives by its results.

Chapter Eleven

1. The P-47D-15 had an official maximum bomb load up to 2,500 lbs, and could have six to eight .50-in. guns with capacity from 267 rpg to 425 rpg. *Thunderbolt*; Roger Freeman.
2. It just wasn't in a fighter pilot's psyche to talk about death or dying. It was a certain black humor that brought out different ways of saying that a guy didn't make it. 'Buying the farm' alluded to the fact that the wife would

get $10,000 from the free insurance, so she could pay off debts or 'buy the farm'. Many received that payout—none had ever wanted it.

3. In simple terms, whenever an aircraft needed to land rapidly as a result of damage, low fuel, or state of the weather, the nearest base on the English coast was the best. The RAF base at Manston, on the Kent coast, was a regular emergency base, and Woodbridge, near the Suffolk coast, another.

Chapter Twelve

1. The V1 pilotless Flying Bomb (*Vergeltungswaffe 1* or Reprisal weapon) was designed by Fieseler as a means to repay the Allies for the bombing of German cities. It came with many nicknames—Doodlebug, Buzz Bomb, and Diver being examples. Powered by a pulse-jet that sounded like a loud single-stroke motorbike, it travelled at around 350–400 mph, carrying a lethal payload of nearly one ton of Amatol explosive in the nose cone. It was launched from 'ski' ramp sites, many being in the Pas de Calais area, with most aimed at London, and when it reached the city the engine was designed to cut out. However, it was a random and inaccurate weapon, and many areas in the South-East of England and East Anglia would dread the sudden silence when it ran out of fuel. The RAF encountered the first V1s in early May 1944; thousands would follow. It is on record that approximately 10,500 had been launched against England, including those that were air-launched from He111s. Of those, over 4,250 were destroyed by aircraft and flak. Sadly, V1s had accounted for over 6,000 fatalities when the war finally finished.

2. 'Bogies' are unknown aircraft; 'bandits' are identified as enemy aircraft.

3. The earlier 'razor-back' models had good handling characteristics. With the advent of the bubble canopy, it was noted that stability was compromised. It was cured by a small strake leading up to the tail appendage from the top of the rear fuselage. Similar problems occurred when the P-51s changed to bubble canopies.

4. Contrails form at high altitude when hot, humid air from aircraft engine exhausts mixes with air of lower vapor pressure and low temperature. They may form at different heights but, for any high-flying aircraft that wanted to remain unseen, they could be a dead giveaway.

Chapter Thirteen

1. An extremely brave lady who assisted 130 evaders to safety during the occupation of Belgium. At the end of the war, several countries decorated

Anne for her remarkable service. Her daughter subsequently wrote a book about Anne and her family story, the title of which can be found in the Bibliography.

2. Major General James 'Jimmy' Doolittle was a legend in the Air Force. In his early years as an Air Force Reserve, he was an exceptional aviator, setting records and winning the Schneider Trophy in 1925. Following the famous 'Doolittle Raid' on Tokyo, he was promoted to Brigadier General and then Major General when he became commander of the Twelfth Air Force in North Africa, then the Fifteenth in Italy, and finally the Commanding General of the Eighth Air Force. James Doolittle was a very aggressive and valuable asset to American fighting forces.

3. Major Walter C. Beckham hailed from De Funiak Springs, Florida. A charismatic good guy and a very successful fighter pilot. All his victories were in the air and all were fighters. An excellent marksman; at one time he was the highest scorer in the Air Force. When he was shot down on 22 February 1944, he had destroyed eighteen e/a, probably destroyed several, and damaged many. He survived to spend the rest of the war as a POW. He was special.

Chapter Fourteen

1. Research appears to show that the pilot was 2nd Lt Robert Schimmel of the 731st Squadron, 452nd Bomber Group (not Squadron). He appears to have survived his tour in the UK.

2. There were different names for different types of operations carried out by Fighter Command. Those operations were also carried out by the RAF.

A RAMROD was an attack carried out by a few fighters or fighter bombers against a ground target. This could entail both the dropping of bombs and strafing.

A CIRCUS was a small force of bombers escorted by many fighters. The aim was for the bombers, as bait, to draw up enemy fighters into combat. Losses during this type of operation could be quite high on both sides if the enemy co-operated.

A RODEO was a normal fighter sweep over enemy occupied territory.

A RANGER was a fighter sweep intended to intimidate and annoy the enemy into coming up to do battle.

A ROADSTEAD was an attack by bombers on shipping and maritime targets. They were heavily escorted by fighters.

A RHUBARB was a bombing and strafing operation carried out by two or more fighter aircraft.

A ROVER was an armed reconnaissance over enemy territory.

3. Lieutenant General Carl 'Tooey' Spaatz had served at the very end of the First World War as a fighter pilot. He served in many different commands, rising through the ranks until the United States entered into the war, when he was appointed to the temporary rank of Major General in charge of the Eighth Air Force in the ETO. In March of 1943 he was again given a temporary rank of Lieutenant General. After the war he was appointed as commanding General of the Army Air Forces, with the permanent rank of Major General.

4. Dive-bombing and strafing caused a new and lethal problem for the pilots. It was called 'target fixation'—over-intense concentration onto the target, disorientation, distraction, miscalculation, or other dangers. Whatever the cause, the pilot could leave it just too late to pull out of his diving attack and dive straight into the ground.

Chapter Fifteen

1. Although Raydon and Lower Raydon have changed very little in appearance since the war, there have been great changes in culture, community, and social integration. The countryside is very typically Suffolk, with gentle, rolling hills, narrow country lanes, and trees and hedgerows that are alive with wildlife. Serving airmen may well have frequented The Chequers Inn, situated at the west end of The Street. A photograph in Chapter 24 shows Clint outside the Chequers when he visited with son, Steve, in 1994. Sadly, the pub became a private dwelling soon after Clint and Steve's visit.

2. Rather than have the lead aircraft and lead bombardier instructing the bomber force when to toggle their bombs, as with carpet bombing, Pathfinders were employed to obtain greater accuracy on small, difficult, or important targets. They would mark the target with different color flares and the bomber force would bomb on those markers.

3. Although sometimes attacked when they were spotted by chance, targets of opportunity could also be ones that had been identified by intelligence as possible alternatives if the primary target was socked in by weather, or if the attack was considered impractical.

Chapter Sixteen

1. KG200 was the secret Luftwaffe squadron that consisted of Allied planes that had been captured when forced down in enemy territory. They had examples of virtually every single type of plane, and on rare occasions flew them deviously as the example suggested.

2. The young pilots were constantly under pressure. It was therefore considered a most sensible initiative when rest homes were introduced by the Air Force. Usually, large country houses were chosen and all luxuries for those visits by the pilots were laid on. Of course, they soon became tagged as 'flak homes', for it was not always by choice that the pilots arrived at these venues. *Jonah's Feet Are Dry*; Dr Graham Cross.

3. 'Overlord' was the most important and vital operation of the Second World War. The planning had been in progress for many months, and the strategy of all Air Forces was broadly tuned to cumulate on D-Day, 6 June 1944, with the landings on Normandy beaches.

Chapter Seventeen

1. Weather patterns, together with the correct timing of moon periods, were just not suitable to commence in May. Also, the practical supply and military issues were not yet completed. Based on all the information flooding into various headquarters, the date was sensibly postponed until the first week in June 1944. Everything had to come together at the right time.

Chapter Eighteen

1. Part of the overall plan to disrupt the German transportation system, 'Chattanooga' missions were predominantly aimed at supplies and armaments moved by rail. No doubt inspired by Glenn Miller and his Orchestra playing 'Chattanooga Choo Choo'. *Jonah's Feet Are Dry*; Dr Graham Cross.

2. Like Lt Dwight Fry, Lt Jack Terzian was another 353rd Fighter Group pilot who was assisted on his tortuous route home by Anne Brusselmans.

3. Those fledgling fighter pilots would receive 300 hours of training, with at least one-third of that time on operational fighters, before going on operations. So, before being let loose on the enemy they needed the guiding hands of experienced combat pilots.

4. Stalin was an evil dictator. His purges of the military and intellectuals prior to the Russians entering the war gave more than a little indication of his intent. The 'Iron Curtain' would soon be drawn between the Soviet Union and the free West after the war.

Chapter Nineteen

1. 'Operation Fortitude' was an operation of bluff and counterbluff to persuade the Germans that an invasion would occur in the Pas de Calais region of France, designed so that Hitler would concentrate his forces in that region instead of where the planned landings would actually be—Normandy.
2. General Eisenhower was the Supreme Allied Commander of all the forces invading France on 6 June 1944. Prior to that, in 1942 he commanded all forces for the Allied landings in North Africa.
3 'Fortitude' was not the only operation to deceive the Germans. Without all the deceptions, both before and just prior to the invasion, the outcome of 'Overlord' would almost certainly have been extremely doubtful.
4. As a result of the heavy seas, several small landing craft were lost, but the greatest single disaster (apart from those craft sunk by enemy fire) had been the loss of the DD (Duplex Drive) tanks. They were swamped in the rough seas.
5. It was reported that of the 11,590 aircraft available for D-Day operations, 14,674 sorties were flown and 127 aircraft were lost. *D-Day Museum.*

Chapter Twenty

1 If ever there had been a 'day of infamy', then 31 July 1941 would probably be significant as the most evil in history, as it demonstrated the worst and most despicable excesses of the human race. It was on this day that Reinhard Heydrich obtained the final signature of Reichmarschall Herman Goering on a document that sealed the fate of millions of Jews throughout Europe. It became known as 'The Final Solution'.
2 Type 16 missions were those where radar was used to plot Luftwaffe air activity so that the Group could 'home in' to them to gain an advantage, but it was reported that they weren't very successful. *Ref: Jonah's Feet Are Dry*—Dr Graham Cross.

Chapter Twenty-One

1. For the stated length of flight (two landings—total four hours and fifty-five minutes), and because of the configuration of bombs on board, Clint may have had a belly tank, although Lt Reinhardt '...dropped my tanks and bombs...', thus insinuating that they were wing tanks. Tough one to prove.

2. All Squadron records state that Clint was leading Blue Flight. Probably an error based on recall, or a late retrospective entry by the Squadron diarist.

3. Included in those who claimed was Bill Tanner. Expected to return home after the episode on 9 June, he managed to sneak in one more mission and claimed one Fw190 destroyed and one damaged. He then shipped off home for a well-deserved rest, before returning to the ETO until the end of hostilities. *Jonah's Feet Are Dry*; Dr Graham Cross.

4. Brigadier General Murray C. Woodbury headed up the 66th Fighter Wing (Eighth Fighter Command), which consisted of five Fighter Groups—the 353rd (Raydon), 55th (Wormingford), 78th (Duxford) 339th (Fowlmere), and 357th (Leiston).

Chapter Twenty-Two

1. There is no doubt that, for the sake of security, most information of a delicate or potentially dangerous nature was withheld from the Armed Forces and the general public. The overall picture could only be the domain of those in command at the top—and they didn't always know!

Chapter Twenty-Three

1. At the war's end it was estimated that Eighth Air Force fighters had destroyed over 5,000 enemy aircraft in the air and over 4,000 on the ground. It was also estimated they lost over 2,000 aircraft and 1,500 pilots achieving this total (various sources). Taken from 1 January 1944 up to D-Day, and excluding aircraft that crashed returning to base, they lost 1,407 heavy bombers, 100 medium bombers, and 673 fighters. Over 18,000 aircrew were either killed, wounded, evacuated, missing, interned, or captured (*Army Air Forces World War II*).

2. Powered by two Allison V-1710 engines, each of 1,425 hp, the twin-boom Lockheed P-38J Lightning was capable of 414 mph at 25,000 ft. Like the P-47 Thunderbolt it was limited in range and had to rely on external fuel tanks. Fitted with a 20-mm cannon to supplement the four .50-in. machine guns, it packed quite a punch when in combat. *Mighty Eighth War Manual*; Roger Freeman.

3. When Clint gave up 42-22466 it became Harrison Tordoff's first 'Anne' as SX-J (bar). He flew it on twenty-two missions in July and August '44. Tuttle was borrowing it from Tordoff when he crashed. Tuttle's regular aircraft was actually SX-M (42-26661), and when 42-22466 crashed on 12 August it was coded SX-J (bar) not plain SX-J, meaning it was the

second J in the squadron (James Tuttle Jnr, Dr Graham Cross, Ashley Gant).

4. P-47D-22-RE, 42-26121, SX-E, NMF (Natural Metal Finish, and one of the first in the Group)—another 'Razorback'. Following Clint's departure from the 353rd in early July 1944, the aircraft became the regular mount of Capt. Frederick Uttenweiler, who named it *Lady Louise*. She ended her days on 16 September 1944 at RAF Southend, when 2nd Lt Anthony Rosatone had to carry out an emergency landing when returning from an operation to Mannheim/Kaiserslautern. The plane was wrecked and formally declared as salvage on 20 September 1944 (Ashley Gant).

Chapter Twenty-Four

1. Clint's first family with his first wife, Mary Jayne, includes Stephen (born in 1943), Marylee (born in 1945), Toby (born in 1949), and Lisa (born in 1956).
2. Grumman F8F Bearcat. Introduced at the end of the war, it was too late to see combat service.
3. Clint contributed several articles to assist Dr Graham Cross in compiling the history of the 353rd for his book *Jonah's Feet Are Dry*.

Appendix I:
Clinton H. Sperry Mission List, 9 August 1943–1 July 1944

Year	Month	Day	Type	TIA*	Region
1943	August	9th	Fighter Sweep	1:50	Abbeville
		15th	" "	1:50	Knokke/Gravelines
		15th	High-Cover Escort	1:10	Brussels (mission abort)
		17th	" " "	1:50	Regensburg
		27th	Close-Support Escort	2:10	St Omer
		31st	" " "	1:50	Paris
	September	2nd	High-Cover Escort	2:00	Brussels/Evere
		9th	" " "	2:00	Vitry-en-Artois
		22nd	Fighter Sweep	1:50	Dutch Islands
	October	4th	High-Cover Escort	2:50	Frankfurt
		8th	" " "	2:50	Bremen
		9th	" " "	2:35	Danzig/Gdynia
		10th	" " "	2:00	Münster
		18th	" " "	2:25	Düren (mission abort)
		20th	Other Operation	0:35	Düren (aborted)
		22nd	High-Cover Escort	2:00	Cambrai
		24th	" " "	2:25	St Andre
	November	3rd	" " "	1:30	Wilhelmshaven
	December	4th	" " "	2:00	Gilze-Rijen
		11th	" " "	1:15	Emden
		20th	" " "	3:10	Bremen
		22nd	" " "	2:50	Osnabrück
1944	January	4th	High-Cover Escort	3:05	Münster
		14th	" " "	3:00	Pas de Calais
		21st	" " "	3:35	Albert
		25th	Thunder-bombing	1:30	Leeuwarden (aborted)
		30th	High-Cover Escort	3:10	Brunswick

February	6th	"	"	"	3:15	Nancy
	10th	"	"	"	2:25	Brunswick
	11th	"	"	"	3:15	Frankfurt
	13th	"	"	"	3:10	Albert
	20th	"	"	"	2:45	Leipzig
	21st	"	"	"	2:00	Gütersloh
March	6th	Ramrod			3:10	Berlin
	15th	"			3:15	Brunswick
	16th	Ramrod			4:00	Friedrichshafen
	17th	Dive Bombing			2:00	Soesterberg
	18th	Ramrod			2:45	Friedrichshafen
	20th	"			1:50	Frankfurt (mission abort)
April	1st	High-Cover Escort			1:30	Ludwigshafen
	8th	"	"	"	3:30	Oldenburg, Diepholz
	9th	"	"	"	3:00	Gdynia, Marienburg
	10th	HCE or BBBoys			2:15	Brussels or Villaroche
	12th	High-Cover Escort			3:30	Schweinfurt
	13th	"	"	"	3:00	Oberpfaffenhofen, Augsburg
	17th	"	"	"	2:15	Wizernes
	18th	"	"	"	4:15	Berlin
	19th	"	"	"	3:15	Gütersloh, Paderborn
	22nd	"	"	"	3:15	Hamm
	24th	"	"	"	4:10	Landsberg, Erding, Oberpfaffenhofen
	25th	"	"	"	3:10	Metz, Nancy, Essay, Dijon & Longvic
	26th	"	"	"	3:10	Brunswick
	27th	"	"	"	3:20	Pas de Calais
May	7th	High-Cover Escort			3:50	Münster, Osnabrück
	8th	"	"	"	4:15	Berlin
	9th	"	"	"	3:00	Laon/Athies, Laon/Couvron
	11th	"	"	"	2:45	Brussels
	12th	"	"	"	3:35	Brüx, Zwickau
	20th	"	"	"	3:25	Villacoublay, Orly
	21st	Dive Bombing			4:00	Bremen
	22nd	"	"		1:45	Liège
	23rd	High-Cover Escort			2:50	France
	24th	"	"	"	4:15	Berlin
	29th	"	"	"	3:00	Posen, Sorau, Cottbus
	30th	"	"	"	4:45	Halberstadt
	30th	Dive Bombing			3:15	Verberie, Compiègne
	31st	"	"		3:45	Gütersloh

June	2nd	Unknown	2:45	Operational
	4th	High-Cover Escort	3:50	Pas de Calais, St Quentin
	4th	" " "	3:10	St Avord, Romorantin & Bourges
	5th	High-Cover Escort	3:00	Boulogne
	6th	Area Patrol	4:15	Clermont
	7th	Thunder-bombing	3:00	Paris
	7th	" "	3:00	Beauvais/Tille
	8th	" "	4:15	St Brice, Tinténiac
	10th	" "	1:30	Vannes/Guer
	10th	" "	3:00	Rouen, Paris
	11th	" "	4:00	Beauvais
	12th	" "	4:55	Dreux
	13th	" "	4:00	Le Port Boulet
	14th	" "	3:45	Beauvais/Nivilliers
	15th	High-Cover Escort	4:30	Chalonnes
	18th	Thunder-bombing	2:30	Ham
	21st	High-Cover Escort	5:15	Berlin
	21st	" " "	3:25	Pas de Calais
	22nd	" " "	4:00	Paris
	23rd	" " "	4:10	Paris
	24th	" " "	5:15	Bremen
	25th	" " "	7:05*	Paris
		Thunder-bombing		Evreux/Fauville
	27th	" "	4:00	Epernay
	28th	High-Cover Escort	3:15	Juvincourt, Laon
	30th	Thunder-bombing	4:00	Nogent
July	1st	" "	3:30	Compiègne, Noyon, Soissons

*Combined, the total time in the air for for the missions to Paris and Evreux/ Fauville was seven hours and five minutes.

Total: 94 Missions

Note: Some missions marked 'Aborted' have been credited and counted as a mission when they were considered complete by Headquarters. Written evidence supports ninety-four full missions.

Weather and Relay Missions

Year	Month	Day	Type	TIA*	Region
1943	August	16th	Met flight	1:20	Duxford
		27th	" "	3:30	Predannack
		28th	" "	0:20	Ipswich
		31st	" "	0:50	Thorney Island
	September	9th	" "	1:00	CS marked for Bomber Command
	October	20th	" "	0:35	Marked 'Other Operational'
	November	17th	" "	1:00	CS marked for Bomber Command
	November	18th	Met flight	1:00	CS marked for Bomber Command
		30th	" "	2:05	Unknown. Hit barrage balloon
	December	13th	" "	1:50	Marked as 'Other Operational'
1944	April	11th	" "	2:45	Marked as 'Other Operational'
	May	31st	" "	3:45	Possibly for Bomber Command
	June	16th	" "	2:15	Possibly for Bomber Command

Total: 13 Met Flights—Other Operational unconfirmed

*Time In Air

Appendix II:
352nd Fighter Squadron Losses During the Second World War

Date	Name	Status
17-4-43	2nd Lt Morgan J. Barton	KIFA
29-6-43	1st Lt William M. Mathias	KIFA
24-7-43	1st Lt Harry H. McPherson	KIFA
24-7-43	2nd Lt Jack D. Lepird	KIFA
31-8-43	2nd Lt Lester L. Dansky	KIA
6-9-43	F/O Earl M. Perry	KIA
15-9-43	2nd Lt Walter Donovan	KIA
18-9-43	2nd Lt Francis J. Hajosy	KIFA
23-9-43	2nd Lt George S. Dietz	KIA
22-12-43	1st Lt Leroy W. Ista	KIA
11-1-44	1st Lt Victor L. Vogel	KIA
22-2-44	1st Lt Edison G. Stiff	KIA
16-3-44	1st Lt Robert A. Newman	KIA
16-3-44	1st Lt Harry H. Dustin	KIA
8-4-44	1st Lt Gordon L. Willits	KIA
30-5-44	1st Lt Francis L. Edwards	KIA
7-6-44	2nd Lt Luther Avakian	KIA
10-6-44	F/O James R. Hicks	KIA
10-6-44	1st Lt William S. Marchant	KIA
10-6-44	2nd Lt Virgil C. Johnston	KIA
12-6-44	1st Lt Richard Keywan	KIA
1-8-44	F/O Kenneth Ames	KIA
8-8-44	2nd Lt Richard Daines	KIA
18-8-44	F/O John J. Swanezy	KIA
28-9-44	2nd Lt Charles E. Sladek	KIFA
25-11-44	2nd Lt Stephen J. Kritz	KIA
27-11-44	1st Lt James F. Cross	KIA

3-1-45	Major James N. Poindexter	KIA
18-1-45	1st Lt Anthony R. Rosatone	KIA
11-3-45	1st Lt Arthur C. Cundy	KIA
17-4-45	1st Lt James W. Lamb	KIA
3-7-45	1st Lt Edward A. Knickelbein	KIFA
12-7-45	2nd Lt Donald F. Blaicher	KIFA

KIA—Killed In Action   KIFA—Killed In Flying Accident

Approximately 26 per cent of 352nd Fighter Squadron pilots lost their lives between 17 April 1943 and 12 July 1945.

Bibliography

353rd Fighter Group's 1983 Reunion Memoir; University of Illinois, Norris L. Brookens Library

Aircrew Remembrance Society

Army Air Force Statistical Digest—World War II

Army Air Forces World War II

Belgium Rendez-Vous 127 Revisited; Yvonne Daley-Brusselmans. Sunflower University Press, 2001.

Big Week; Glenn Infield, Brassey's (US), 1974.

Dangerous Skies; Peter A. Anderson with John N. Anderson, Raydon Wings, 2007.

D-Day Museum Archives.

Flight Journal P-47 evaluation; Corwin 'Corky' Meyer, Air Age Media.

Jonah's Feet Are Dry; G. E. Cross, Thunderbolt Publishing, G. E. Cross 2001.

Mighty Eighth War Diary; Roger A. Freeman, Janes, Roger A. Freeman 1981.

Mighty Eighth War Manual; Roger A. Freeman, Janes, 1984.

The Battle of Britain—Then and Now; Ed. Winston G. Ramsey, Battle of Britain Prints International Ltd, *After the Battle* Magazine 1980.

The First and the Last; Adolf Galland, Methuen & Co. Ltd., 1955.

The Hub; Roger A. Freeman, Airlife.

The Last Battle; Peter Henn (pseud. Alfons Schertl), William Kimber.

Thunderbolt; Roger A. Freeman, Arms and Armour Press, 1978.

Index

The Republic P-47D Thunderbolt from the Duxford-based The Fighter Collection was arranged by Dr Graham Cross to be presented in the colours of the 350th Fighter Squadron, 353rd Fighter Group. The occasion marked the return of Veterans of the 353rd to Raydon in 1999. (*P. Anderson*)

The North American P51D Mustang owned, restored, and flown by Maurice Hammond. Janie is shown in the colours of Major William Price of the 350th Fighter Squadron, 353rd Fighter Group. The Mustang continues to be a regular visitor to Raydon. (*K. Anderson*)

The unofficial 'Slybird' emblem for the 353rd Fighter Group. (*Pleasance, via Cross*)